Steeples and Stacks

Cambridge Studies in Religion and American Public Life

General Editor

Robin W. Lovin

Books in the Series

Merrill D. Peterson and Robert C. Vaughan   *The Virginia Statute for Religious Freedom*
William R. Hutchison   *Between the Times: The Travail of the Protestant Establishment in America, 1900–1960*

Steeples and Stacks

Religion and Steel Crisis in Youngstown

THOMAS G. FUECHTMANN

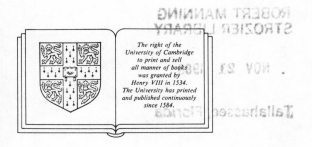

The right of the
University of Cambridge
to print and sell
all manner of books
was granted by
Henry VIII in 1534.
The University has printed
and published continuously
since 1584.

CAMBRIDGE UNIVERSITY PRESS

Cambridge

New York   Port Chester   Melbourne   Sydney

Published by the Press Syndicate of the University of Cambridge
The Pitt Building, Trumpington Street, Cambridge CB2 1RP
32 East 57th Street, New York, NY 10022, USA
10 Stamford Road, Oakleigh, Melbourne 3166, Australia

© Cambridge University Press 1989

First published 1989

Printed in the United States of America

Library of Congress Cataloging-in-Publication Data
Fuechtmann, Thomas G. (Thomas Gerhard), 1938–
Steeples and stacks: religion and steel crisis in Youngstown/
Thomas G. Fuechtmann.
  p. cm. (Cambridge studies in religion and American public life)
ISBN 0–521–33481–0
1. Steel industry and trade – Ohio – Youngstown. 2. Plant shutdowns – Ohio –
Youngstown. 3. Iron and steel workers – Ohio – Youngstown. 4. Ecumenical
Coalition of the Mahoning Valley.
I. Title.
HD9518.Y8F84 1989
338.4'7669142'09 – dc 19

88–29195
CIP

British Library Cataloguing in Publication Data
Fuechtmann, Thomas G.
Steeples and stacks
1. Ohio. Youngstown. Steel industries.
Role of Christian church, history
I. Title
261.8'5

ISBN 0–521–33481–0

Contents

Tables and Figures

Figures

Acknowledgments

The Ecumenical Coalition of the Mahoning Valley is now a memory, along with most of the Valley's steel mills. The effort by clergy and steelworkers to make steel again at Youngstown Sheet and Tube's Campbell Works did not succeed. In place of new steel, there remains but a story.

To all who wrote this story, in their deeds, in their words, in their support of my research, my profound thanks. If they recognize here their own energy or voice or vision, they should know I am deeply grateful for their role in bringing this book to light.

My wife, Maureen, who will forever be "from Youngstown," first suggested this study. She and my sons Tom and John have lived with "Daddy's book" for many of our years as a family. I appreciate, as only they can know, their patience and their encouragement.

This book leaves my desk with a wish and dedication.

The wish is twofold: that the ending of this story might have been different for the steelworkers of Youngstown. And that the telling of this story may help future efforts on behalf of working people and their communities to succeed.

The dedication – fitting, I believe, for a book titled *Steeples and Stacks* – is to a Youngstown steelworker and a Youngstown priest: my father-in-law John J. Lynch, Sr., and Father Edward Stanton.

John Lynch was born in Ireland in 1885 and came to the United States in 1907. Having married in Chicago, he settled his young family in Youngstown in 1917, where he worked in the "Sheet and Tube" until the 1919 steel strike and in other Youngstown steel mills until his retirement in 1956.

John Lynch was a "greenhorn" – as he called himself – for whom the American dream came true. He worked hard and he prospered – his wife and ten children with him. Until his death at ninety-eight years of age, John Lynch loved steel. In and through the fierce heat and back-wrenching labor of tending an open hearth furnace, he felt the pride of an artisan at the forge, drawing out of earth and fire the steel to build up his new land.

There is much of him in these pages, gleaned from long talks across his kitchen table and mine. For his wisdom, his encouragement, his prayers, and his friendship, this book is a memorial.

John Lynch shares this dedication with Edward Stanton, Youngstown's "steel priest." Ed was totally committed to the welfare of steelworkers and their community, with a heart and a gruff compassion as big as his considerable presence. As staff director of the Ecumenical Coalition, Stanton in particular was concerned that the story be told.

He often cited a previous experience that had made a deep impression. As a board member of the National Federation of Priest Councils, he and several fellow priests had met at O'Hare Airport in Chicago for a trip to Missouri, where they were to confront a bishop on a personnel matter. By chance, they met church historian John Tracy Ellis, who had taught them in the seminary. Ellis upbraided them for not thinking to take notes on what Ellis considered a historic occasion in the American Catholic Church.

Years later, Stanton remembered that chance meeting. As a consequence, he never threw away a single piece of paper connected with the Coalition. Moreover, he made it all available, flattering or not, so that the process of evaluation and learning could go on. He felt that, even if the Coalition in Youngstown should fail, some other group down the line might try again, and succeed.

The Coalition was Stanton's last big project. Not long after the attempt to reopen the steel mill came to an end, Stanton contracted cancer. He died on April 1, 1984.

Introduction

At ten o'clock in the morning on Monday, September 19, 1977, vice-presidents of the Youngstown Sheet and Tube Company appeared for hastily arranged appointments at various offices around Youngstown, Ohio. Reporters were summoned to a news conference at company headquarters, where they were handed a brief press release: "Sheet and Tube" was closing its largest steel mill in its home city. It was expected that five thousand jobs would be terminated, with layoffs beginning the following week.

Context

As an old steeltown, Youngstown knew what it meant for the fires in the furnaces to be blown out. Steel families were nourished on the practical wisdom that smoke and soot from the big smokestacks meant food on the table. Clean skies meant hard times: from strike, recession, depression. Most other times, the furnaces had started up again. One thing could be counted on: the consuming appetite of a young nation for steel to build its bridges and skyscrapers, railroads and ships, cars and appliances. But this time was different. Company officials (since a 1969 merger they were based in New Orleans) were saying that the old mill that was once Youngstown's biggest producer and biggest employer was down for good. Tough third-generation steelworkers walked out the plant gate on their last day with tears in their eyes. In a way, they had known it was coming. Problems for the old mill had been mounting for several years. Production facilities were twenty to forty years behind current steel technology;

1

however, workers could see that normal maintenance was being ignored or deferred. Customers increasingly voiced complaints about quality control. Inventory was cut back, adding to the time necessary to fill orders. And then there was the news of other old plants closing, caught in the steel crunch of 1977. The Alan Wood mill in Conshohocken, Pennsylvania, shut down, with 3,000 jobs lost. Bethlehem Steel closed mills in Johnstown, Pennsylvania (4,000 jobs), and Lackawanna, New York (3,850 jobs), and terminated more than 5,000 jobs at other scattered locations.

And yet the Sheet and Tube shutdown was both a surprise and a shock. Union officials had been assured just the week before that the company had no plans to shut down. Workers in the open hearth shop were setting new production records with their antiquated furnaces. Windbreaker jackets with the company logo to be awarded as prizes to the record-breaking shift were still lying in the front office when the shutdown was announced, waiting to be picked up. It was hard to believe that this was happening with Sheet and Tube – the company that used to be the best one to work for, the company that steelmen used to call "the boss" in Youngstown.

The announcement on "Black Monday" carried a note of anxiety about the future of other old mills in Youngstown. With the major portion of Sheet and Tube's Campbell Works down, there was fear that its other mill across town (Brier Hill) would also be closed.[1] And the two U.S. Steel plants had a dubious future, especially with talk of U.S. Steel building a mammoth new automated facility on the Lake Erie shore at Conneaut, Ohio. The wait for the other shoe to fall lasted two years. In November 1979, shutdown dates were announced for the two U.S. Steel plants and for Brier Hill. In less than three years, approximately 10,000 steel jobs were terminated in Youngstown.

The Campbell Works shutdown was but one significant event in the pattern of plant closures that became identified as "the deindustrialization of America." In their book by that title, Bluestone and Harrison (1982: 6) describe the trend: "By *deindustrialization* is meant a widespread, systematic disinvestment in the nation's basic productive capacity." Observers of the American economy in the past decade have differed about the causes of the phenomenon. One type of economic theory sees plant closings as a manifestation of the "creative destruction" that is an inherent part of a vital economy. As technologies change, plants and whole industrial processes become outmoded. For a healthy economy, the capital invested in them must be refocused in "sunrise" industries (computers rather than steel, business services rather than machine tools). Another explanation for "deindustrialization" is that America is undergoing a long-term shift from an industrial to a service-based economy; the closing of manufacturing plants is an inevitable consequence of that secular trend. In these two explanations, plant closings have a positive interpretation; they are simply part of the dynamism of a vital national economy.

There is another, less optimistic view – well articulated by Bluestone and Harrison:

Controversial as it may be, the essential problem with the U.S. economy can be traced to the way capital – in the forms of financial resources and of real plant and equipment – has been diverted from productive investment in our basic national industries into unproductive speculation, mergers and acquisitions, and foreign investment. Left behind are shuttered factories, displaced workers, and a newly emerging group of ghost towns. (Ibid.: 6)

The Campbell Works closing – like many of the steel mill shutdowns that followed it – is an instance of the kind of "deindustrialization" that requires blind faith in the economic theory to see the sun behind very obvious gray clouds.

From the Campbell Works shutdown through the recession of the early 1980s, plant closings and job terminations became such standard bad news that the shutdown story became almost a journalistic literary form. The newspaper account generally included the sudden announcement of shutdown, the sense of shock among employees and others dependent on the plant, the recall of a sense of foreboding about the plant's future, and the personal stories woven in and around the impact of the shutdown on the local community. For instance, the *Chicago Tribune* account (June 24, 1983) of the shutdown announcement for Westinghouse's famed Hawthorne plant in Cicero, Illinois, includes all the elements that have become drearily familiar throughout the industrial heartland.

In Youngstown, though, as the fires in the furnaces went out, the story took a different twist. By the spring of 1978, something was happening. Journalists and television crews, not only from around the country but also from Europe and Japan, began to converge on Youngstown. In national papers like the *New York*

Times and the *Washington Post*, articles appeared about a local movement to restore the Campbell Works to production as a community–worker-owned enterprise. Network television presented the story to the nation on the evening news and the *Today* show. ABC-TV taped a half-hour documentary for a special program.

It became evident that the White House was directly involved in the Youngstown project. Because the project touched so many federal departments, a Youngstown task force was being coordinated in the office of Jack Watson, assistant to President Carter.

Something unusual was indeed happening in Youngstown. The day after Black Monday, Episcopal Bishop John Burt of Cleveland (formerly a pastor in Youngstown) called Catholic Bishop James Malone, head of the Youngstown diocese, to ask if there was anything the churches might do to help. Church people and steelworkers met together to assess the problems in the Youngstown area and explore what to do about the shut-down steel mill. Gerald Dickey, secretary of a steelworkers local, suggested, "Let's buy the damned thing and run it ourselves." The idea caught on. Church leaders formed a "coalition" and hired a staff, with funding assistance from national church offices. The religious coalition established links with a Washington think tank, the National Center for Economic Alternatives, that had been working on the idea of community industrial ownership. The Department of Housing and Urban Development provided a $335,000 research grant to develop the project. By January 1, 1978, the Ecumenical Coalition of the Mahoning Valley was recognized as the lead agent in Youngstown for dealing with the steel shutdown.

The effort to reopen the Campbell Works made Youngstown widely known, not simply as the location of another shutdown, but as a community with a new and different kind of response to economic crisis. A study of the job terminations by Bethlehem Steel in Johnstown, Pennsylvania, in the same year as the Campbell Works shutdown emphasizes the uniqueness of Youngstown:

What is most remarkable in Johnstown is the almost total submission of the steelworkers and their community to the will of Bethlehem Steel. There has been no organized effort to stop the cutback, no plant occupations, no protest demonstrations. Since 1973, when the first cutback announcement was made (later to be rescinded), no one has suggested that Bethlehem Steel has any less than an absolute right to decide the fate of this western Pennsylvania community.

. . . The industrial Northeast, from Maine to Illinois north of the Ohio River and Maryland's southern boundary, lost more than 1.5 million manufacturing jobs from 1967 to 1976. Virtually none of these job losses were challenged. The valiant effort since 1977 by steelworkers and their community to reopen the Campbell steel mills near Youngstown, Ohio, is a rare case, the exception that highlights the rule. (Metzgar 1980: 10)[2]

The present study will both report and analyze the effort by the Ecumenical Coalition of the Mahoning Valley to reopen the Campbell Works. The Youngstown case attracted widespread attention. It is, first of all, an interesting story: the tale of a "town that refused to die." But more than that, Youngstown became the testing ground for some new ideas to deal with the kind of local community crisis occasioned by deindustrialization. First, the community response to the Youngstown steel crisis was seen as a new development in the interaction of religion and public affairs in American life. Second, Youngstown was seen as the testing ground for a different model of local community action in the face of deindustrialization and economic crisis. On both counts, Youngstown provides an important learning experience. In the 1980s, the churches in America have become more, rather than less, involved in public affairs. And though there are signs of economic revival in some parts of the industrial heartland, local community economic crisis has not disappeared from the land. Even though the project of the religious coalition in Youngstown did not succeed, the group's efforts may have provided a basis for people in other local communities to understand their own situation a little better.

Focus

This book focuses on the Ecumenical Coalition of the Mahoning Valley from its origin in September 1977 to the end of its Campbell Works project in April 1979. It is a "tentative theoretical case study." The study is theoretical in the sense that it employs elements of theory from several disciplines in order to explain the Coalition. But the starting point remains the case itself. The study is tentative in at least two ways. Any attempt to explain a particular happening or situation is always open to new insights; in that sense, this account of the case stands open to correction. Moreover, even twelve years after the initial shutdown, it would be hard to say – without going far beyond the case itself – what it has meant for later developments in the relationship between religion and public life, in attempts at employee ownership of industry, or in local community economic planning.

The Coalition has already been the subject of considerable printer's ink. While the Campbell Works project was under way, it was reported not only in the Youngstown *Vindicator*, but also in such national papers as the *New York Times*, the *Washington Post*, and the *Wall Street Journal*. It was written up in *Newsweek* and *Business Week* as well as in such liberal journals of opinion as *The Progressive* and *Mother Jones*. The religious press gave considerable attention to the Coalition in such periodicals as the *National Catholic Reporter* and the Presbyterian *A.D.*

Two books on the Youngstown steel crisis have appeared. The first is by Staughton Lynd, the attorney for the Coalition: *The Fight Against Shutdowns: Youngstown's Steel Mill Closings.* Lynd, who was a historian at Yale before becoming a lawyer, has written a participant-observer's history of the steelworkers' fight against successive shutdowns in Youngstown – at the Campbell Works, at Brier Hill, and at the two U.S. Steel mills. Lynd admits that "there is no such thing as 'the history' of what happened in Youngstown" and that each major participant would tell the story differently. Lynd himself (1982) has "deliberately placed rank-and-file steelworkers in the center of the narrative" (11). This choice of viewpoint fits the story of the fight against the Brier Hill and U.S. Steel shutdowns better than the first closing at the Campbell Works. Regarding the attempt to reopen the Campbell Works, one of the central questions is why steelworkers were so *un*involved in the whole process. In short, surprisingly little of the Coalition story is related in Lynd's book.

Some of the most extensive scholarly research on the Youngstown steel crisis has been conducted at the Center for Urban Studies of Youngstown State University. Terry F. Buss and F. Stevens Redburn have published *Shutdown at Youngstown: Public Policy for Mass Unemployment*, a volume based primarily on their comparative panel survey of steel- and autoworkers. During the period of the Coalition effort, Buss and Redburn were most active in studying and shaping the delivery of human services in the Youngstown area – the topic that is the principal focus of their book. They provide only a cursory account of the work of the Ecumenical Coalition. "A full post mortem of the failure of the Coalition must await more information on government and industry motives and internal decision-making" (Buss and Red-burn, 1983: 25).

The present study is intended as something more than a "post mortem" – an autopsy to determine the cause of death. It is true that the effort to set up a community–worker-owned steelmaking corporation at Campbell did not succeed. But the final chapter of the story is still being written. Because the Coalition dealt with such fundamental issues involving business and workers, church and community, the Coalition effort has functioned as a kind of seminal event with wide ramifications in industry, labor, church, and government policy circles. James Smith, economist and assistant to the president of the United Steelworkers of America, has said:

We have a conflict going on in which conglomerate business is saying to each community: make yourself attractive, compete with all other communities, so that you can see how big a return you can provide for us on our very simplistic financial books. And communities are going to have to choose between accepting that dictum, or they are going to have to develop some alternative responses.

I look on the effort of the preachers in Youngstown as the first big-scale attempt to develop an alternative response. I certainly don't think it will be the last. (Personal communication)

As Staughton Lynd has documented, the fight against shutdowns in Youngstown itself did not end with the demise of the Ecumenical Coalition of the Mahoning Valley. It would be impossible – or at least beyond the scope of this study – to identify all the instances of plant closing or local economic crisis in which the experience in Youngstown has helped to shape new possibilities for other communities.

The purpose here will be to articulate what has been learned from the Youngstown experience. That will demand coming to terms with the Coalition story – its origin, its operation, and its manner of coping with the problems created by the Sheet and Tube shutdown. In the real world of local communities and particular organizations, one can discover a wide range of factors that impinge on the explanation of how and why things happened the way they did. The microlevel analysis here attempts to weigh the importance of both systemic factors, such as the long-term difficulties of the American steel industry, and idiosyncratic factors, such as the difference of personalities within the Coalition staff.

Just as Staughton Lynd has warned that there is no absolute "history" of the Youngstown shutdowns, so too there is no single and unequivocal analysis of the Ecumenical Coalition of the Mahoning Valley. In all fairness, this author should identify his own viewpoint on the Youngstown events.

My acquaintance with Youngstown dates to 1971, the year of my marriage to Maureen Lynch, then a lifelong resident of the city. Through Maureen's father, John Lynch, Sr., and her brother Lawrence, both Youngstown steelworkers, I came to know and appreciate steelworkers and their way of life. When the Sheet and Tube shutdown came, and when the unlikely group of clergy emerged as the lead agent negotiating with government and corporation to set up a new community-oriented industrial enterprise, my instincts as a trained political scientist and theologian locked in on this new happening. During a year's leave from Loyola University of Chicago, I studied the Coalition and become something of a participant-observer myself.

In my view, the Ecumenical Coalition of the Mahoning Valley developed out of a linkup between the group of local religious leaders on the one hand and dissident steelworkers and the tradition of liberal economic criticism on the other hand.

In Youngstown, steelworker dissident activity was centered in Local 1462, led by Ed Mann, president, John Barbero, vice-president, and Gerald Dickey, secretary. Attorney for Local 1462 was Staughton Lynd, who came to Youngstown after completing his law degree at the University of Chicago. Lynd in turn provided a contact with Gar Alperovitz , a former Harvard economist who had set up a liberal Washington think tank, the Exploratory Project on Economic Alternatives. Lynd and Alperovitz (1973) had coauthored a slim volume proposing a new direction for the socialist movement in America. They saw the starting point for their program in "local communities, the subunits of which are sufficiently small so that individuals can, in fact, learn cooperative relationships in practice" (Alperovitz, 1974: 214). In the late 1970s, the Exploratory Project was developing the theme of community–worker ownership as an alternative to the economic dislocation of urban plant closings. When the Campbell Works shutdown was announced, Alperovitz had an idea waiting for a place to happen.

The particular policy and program eventually adopted by the Youngstown Coalition were strongly influenced by Alperovitz.

But the fact that there came into existence a serious, sustained political response to the Sheet and Tube shutdown can be attributed largely to local religious leaders. It was their decision to step to the front and assume responsibility for organizing a challenge to the corporation and developing a proposal for putting people back to work that made Youngstown different from other steeltowns.

This author's focus on Youngstown, then, differs somewhat from that of Staughton Lynd. In the Campbell Works case, the religious leadership was not simply an incidental footnote, but was crucial for what happened in Youngstown. The title of this book reflects what this observer saw in Youngstown. Church steeples and steel mill smokestacks not only dominated the physical landscape of the city. They also – particularly for the period under discussion – represented the institutions that dominated the mindscape.

The title has still another echo. In two landmark books, Protestant pastors and theologians studied the relationship between the churches and the industrial community of Gastonia, North Carolina. *Millhands and Preachers*, by Liston Pope (1942), and *Spindles and Spires*, by John R. Earle, Dean D. Knudsen, and Donald W. Shriver, Jr. (1976), have become classics in their field. The title of my own study, on the relationship of interfaith community to industrial organization in Youngstown, is intended as a gesture of respect and admiration.

CHAPTER I

Steeltown

In 1980, a statuary group depicting two steelworkers tending an open hearth furnace was placed in a prominent position on Youngstown's Federal Plaza – the heart of the downtown business district. The sculpture had been commissioned by the city and executed by a local artist. At the same time, the Youngstown office of the Ohio Historical Society was negotiating with U.S. Steel for the acquisition of an aging blast furnace from one of its newly shut-down steel mills. The blast furnace would be used as the centerpiece of a museum on steelmaking in the Mahoning Valley. By 1980, steel in Youngstown could no longer be taken for granted. Statues and museums were needed as reminders of the historic role of steelmaking in the development of the Youngstown area.

Steel Industry: Local Origins

Ironmaking in the Mahoning Valley began not long after the arrival of the first European settlers. The historian Kenneth Warren (1973) notes:

In 1804 and 1806 the first blast furnaces in Ohio were built in Poland Township and at Struthers near Youngstown. They supplied simple castings and hardware to local farmers and tradesmen, but from quite an early date iron was sent from this area to foundries and rolling mills in Pittsburgh. (55)

In that period, local entrepreneurs began to exploit the iron ore found in the rocky hills along the river banks, smelting it in stone

10

furnaces that were given names, just like sailing ships. (Often the furnaces were named after the wife or daughter of the owner.)[1] Occasionally a farmer would discover that the iron ore on his property was more valuable than his produce, gather stones to build a blast furnace on the back forty, and set himself up as a mini-industrialist. These early stone blast furnaces were fueled by charcoal made from the ample timber in the area.

By 1840, however, bituminous coal from Brier Hill, just north of Youngstown, began to be employed for ironmaking; it developed that the coal was of sufficient quality that it did not have to be coked before use in the blast furnace. The Civil War brought an expansion of the ironmaking industry in Youngstown: "The *Youngstown Telegram* observed in 1863 that the town would soon have seven blast furnaces, three rolling mills, a steelworks, and two machine shops and foundries" (Warren 1973: 56).

At the turn of the century, these small local enterprises (some of them little more than "mom and pop" iron or steel shops) had grown or consolidated with others to form thriving concerns. Economies of scale were dictating the construction of ever larger steelmaking facilities, integrating the different stages of the steelmaking process into a single large plant. At the same time, agglomeration economies led to the founding of businesses to service and supply the mills with railroad transportation and mill machinery. By 1900, iron- and steelmaking was so well established in the Youngstown area that the industry was thriving, despite the exhaustion of the local deposits of iron ore and coal. By the twentieth century, Youngstown steel was being made with iron ore shipped across the Great Lakes and coal transported from southwestern Pennsylvania and West Virginia. Despite the comparative transportation disadvantage, growth in the steel industry was generating a boom-town expansion.

Steeltown, 1900–1950

In 1900 – the same year as the consolidation of U.S. Steel – Youngstown resident James Campbell founded the Youngstown Iron, Sheet and Tube Company on three hundred acres of river land just east of the city of Youngstown. Campbell's career was typical of an industrial elite of Youngstown in the period when the steel industry was beginning to boom on the banks of the

Mahoning River. Campbell, who had previously founded the Youngstown Ice Company and then worked as manager for a local ironmaking company, became concerned about the pattern of company mergers in the iron and steel business in the Youngstown area. He persuaded three other Youngstown executives to join in the founding of a locally owned company as a way of stabilizing the industrial future of the area. The new company was such an immediate success that, only one month after incorporation, its initial capitalization was raised from $600,000 to $1,000,000; two years later, capitalization was $4 million. Campbell at first served as vice-president and general manager, becoming president of the company in 1905.

Under Campbell's management, Youngstown Sheet and Tube ("Iron" was eventually dropped from the name) was a success. In 1923, Campbell's company acquired the Brier Hill Iron and Steel Company, developed by the Tod family on the west side of Youngstown, within the city itself. The company also acquired steel-production facilities in the Chicago area. By the time Campbell retired as president in 1929, Youngstown Sheet and Tube was one of the four largest steel companies in America. Campbell's executive capability was recognized nationally and even internationally. He served as director of the American Iron and Steel Institute, and during World War I he was placed in charge of allocating all steel tubular products in the United States – a service for which he was knighted by the French government.

Campbell naturally had a strong impact on the Youngstown area, particularly on the manufacturing suburb of Youngstown that eventually named itself after him. The new Sheet and Tube plant was built in an unincorporated portion of Coitsville Township about two miles downriver from the city of Youngstown. The area adjacent to the new mill became a boom town of its own, attracting thousands of workers. By 1908, the area around the mill had developed sufficiently to become incorporated as the village of East Youngstown.

Living and working conditions in and around the mill were difficult. Dr. William H. Hudnut, who became pastor of Youngstown's First Presbyterian Church in 1899, recorded his impressions on a tour he made of a local steel plant in the company of its superintendent:

"We were standing above the great ore pit where far below some 'hunkies,' as they are called, were working who had recently emigrated from Europe," Dr. Hudnut recalled. The minister raised a question concerning the welfare of the men who were toiling in the pit beneath him, to which the superintendent replied, "We work them out, and then get in a new batch." The superintendent had expressed what Dr. Hudnut called "a characteristic attitude toward labor. The ingot was reckoned of more worth than the individual. Those men in the pits were just numbers." (Aley 1975: 158)

In 1916, the conditions described by Pastor Hudnut brought on a major industrial riot in East Youngstown. Workers from the Sheet and Tube went on strike, asking for a raise from $19\frac{1}{2}$ to 25 cents per hour. After the arrest (and subsequent release) of a striking worker, strike leaders harassed the mill guards on the Wilson Avenue bridge leading into the mill. A shot was fired, and the nervous guards returned a volley of their own. The riot was on. Saloons were looted, and fires set. In the several days of mass violence that followed, much of the village was burned to the ground. Order was restored only when one thousand army troops armed with machine guns occupied the village and the steel mill property.

The 1916 riot attracted nation-wide attention, giving the village of East Youngstown an opprobrious reputation. The village, however, set about rebuilding its physical facilities as well as mending the social fabric. The key to the reconstruction effort was a new interest on the part of the steel company in the living situation of its workers. Four months after the riot, Sheet and Tube directors allocated $250,000 for the construction of housing for the workers. Company apartments, which rented for as little as $15 per month, were popular and had a long waiting list. For its time, the company housing was revolutionary in providing equally modern and pleasant "low-rise" facilities for both black and white workers. These moves evidently paid off; in the 1919 strike, there was no violence in East Youngstown.

Village and steel company together prospered in the 1920s. James Campbell's Buckeye Land Company provided extensive residential development, building a number of homes in the $5,000 to $8,000 range. On January 1, 1922, the village of East Youngstown became a city. But community leaders were still bothered by the association of their city's name with the "unrest" of 1916. After several years of discussion, they decided to name the city after James Campbell. On January 26, 1926, East Youngstown officially became the City of Campbell (Galida 1976).

Relations between the steel company and the city of Campbell continued to be on good footing. Taxes on the steel mill property, as well as taxes on the income earned in the plant, provided a prosperous revenue for the city of Campbell and its school district. According to Mayor Rocco Mico, lifetime resident of Campbell and mayor of the city from 1966 to 1975 and again from 1978, the friendly yet businesslike feeling between company and town was typified in the joint annual meeting of the Sheet and Tube board of directors with the Campbell City Council (a custom that was discontinued when Sheet and Tube was acquired by Lykes in 1969).

The city of Campbell was named after the company founder, but the steel company itself was named after the city of Youngstown. And it was with the city of Youngstown that James Campbell had an even closer association. Campbell was a resident of Youngstown, and it was there that both his business and his social life were centered. Sheet and Tube headquarters were located downtown in eight floors of the Stambaugh Building, and the company's Brier Hill mill was in Youngstown on the city's west side. In addition to heading Sheet and Tube, Campbell was a director of two local banks and president of the Youngstown Ice Company, the Buckeye Land Company, the Youngstown Steel Car Company, and four mining companies.

In March 1930, James Campbell surprised and shocked the city of Youngstown. Shortly after he had retired as president of the steel company but while he was still chairman of the board, Campbell proposed a merger between Youngstown Sheet and Tube and Bethlehem Steel. The merger was opposed, however, by a group of local stockholders, led by Myron Wick. The local group was backed by Cyrus Eaton, the organizer of Republic Steel, who himself owned 20% of Sheet and Tube stock. Eaton wanted to prevent a merger that would strengthen Bethlehem Steel as the nation's second largest steelmaker – a position Eaton coveted for Republic. Opponents of the merger brought suit in federal court, which resulted in "the most famous trial ever conducted in Mahoning County, and at that time one of the most noted and lengthy civil trials in United States history." (Aley 1975: 492). The coalition of local stockholders with Cryus Eaton were successful in blocking the merger. For the time being, Sheet and Tube was to remain a Youngstown company. Forced to depend on the company's own resources, Campbell drew up

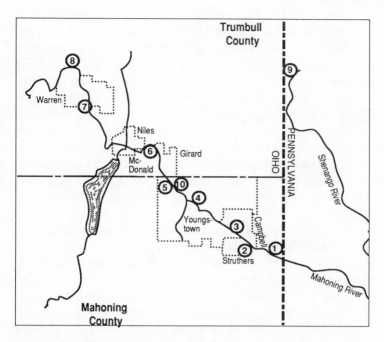

Figure 1.1. Mahoning Valley steel mills. 1, Youngstown Sheet and Tube Struthers rolling mill; 2, Youngstown Sheet and Tube steel pickling; 3, Youngstown Sheet and Tube Campbell Works; 4, Republic Steel; 5, U.S. Steel Ohio Works; 6, U.S. Steel McDonald mill; 7, Republic Steel Warren plant; 8, Copperweld Steel Company; 9, Sharon Steel; 10, Youngstown Sheet and Tube Brier Hill Works. *Source*: Western Reserve Economic Development Agency.

plans for a new 79-inch hot-strip mill (then the largest in the industry) that would consolidate the company's position in the industry for the next two decades.

The personal career of James Campbell and the rise of his steel company are typical of the development of Youngstown as an archetypal "steeltown" in the decade from 1900 to 1950.

The urban geography of the area was dominated by the steel mills. The mills were located on the banks of the Mahoning River for access to water and waste disposal. By midcentury, virtually the entire river valley, from Warren on the west to the Pennsylvania line on the east, was an almost solid strip of steel facilities (Figure 1.1). Some mills (Sheet and Tube's Brier Hill Works and mills acquired by U.S. Steel) were located in the city of Youngstown proper. Others became the centers of manufacturing suburbs along the river valley (McDonald – U.S. Steel; Campbell and Struthers – Sheet and Tube; Lowellville – Sharon Steel-Hoop). Youngstown was the urban center, with its business and commercial district located just north of the river, between the Brier Hill mill to the west and the Republic mill to the east. The wealthy residential district, including the palatial homes of the "iron barons" along Wick Avenue and adjoining streets, bordered the central business district on the north. Housing for the workers was located away from the center, within walking distance of the plant gates. As times improved, many workers were able to realize their dream of owning property; block after block of sturdy frame houses lined the streets stretching up the hills above the river valley.

The local economy, like the landscape, was dominated by the steel mills. Not only was steel the largest single employer; it was the largest purchaser of materials and services from local business. A number of steel-related industries sprang up to service the mills with raw materials, transportation, and milling equipment. Steel was also the supplier for steel fabricating companies and for metal furniture and equipment manufacturers (steel kitchen cabinets from Youngstown Kitchens, steel office furniture from General Fireproofing, railroad car doors from Youngstown Steel Door, and machine parts from Commercial Shearing). Retail and service sectors were naturally dependent on steel company payrolls to provide cash for food and clothing, cars and gasoline, hardware, housing, and haircuts. Virtually the entire local economy depended on steel.

Furthermore, the steel industry in Youngstown was, if not dominated by, at least strongly influenced by Youngstown Sheet and Tube in the whole area of community relations. Older steelmen in Youngstown remember Sheet and Tube as the "boss" in local steel. Sheet and Tube was the largest producer and the largest employer in the Youngstown district. The company was a leader in steel technology. For a time, it had the largest hot-strip rolling mill in the industry. Its seamless steel pipe was in demand worldwide for use in oil-well drilling. As the last locally owned and operated steel mill (shortly after the war, Republic moved its headquarters to Cleveland), Youngstown Sheet and Tube became uniquely identified with the prosperity of Youngstown. Not only was the company important for the economy, it was a symbol – a kind of flagship for the city, advertising the "Youngstown" name to the world. The company's choral ensemble, the Sheet and Tube Men's Chorus – the best in the area – provided entertainment at many civic functions.

The demographic pattern of Youngstown was also dominated by the steel industry. At the top socioeconomic level, the elite of Youngstown was constituted largely by the "iron barons" (Ingham 1978). At the turn of the century, this was a relatively well defined group of seventy industrialists, most of them from families who had long been established in the city. In ancestral origins, they were predominantly English (46%) or Scotch-Irish (16%), with others of Scottish, Welsh, German, or Irish (only 3%) descent. Until 1918, the great majority (84%) lived in large residences (some could properly be termed mansions) in the Wick Avenue residential district. The group was entirely Protestant, 60% being Presbyterian. The Presbyterians' church – First Presbyterian – retained its reputation as the "management" church into the 1970s.

Virtually all of the iron and steel elite belonged to the Youngstown Club, founded in 1902 by four steelmen with four other prominent citizens. Located at first in the Dollar Bank Building, the club moved in 1926 to the top three floors of the Union Bank Building. The lunch tables of the Youngstown Club provided a setting both for the steel business of the nation and for the civic business of Youngstown (ibid.: 63–9, 197–210).

Farther down the socioeconomic pyramid, a large proportion of the population consisted of steelworkers and their families. The population of Youngstown surged in the first two decades of the twentieth century, as workers poured in to fill the jobs in the new steel mills (Table 1.1). Like other manufacturing cities in the Northeast and Midwest, Youngstown became a city of immigrants. Many of the newcomers arrived from the Catholic countries of Europe: Italy, Czechoslovakia, Poland, Hungary, and Ireland.

For the new residents of Youngstown, the religious culture and religious organizational structures became strongly identified with and supported ethnic identity. The newcomers typically clustered in the same neighborhoods, close to relatives or acquaintances. Their religious needs were provided by parish churches that sometimes formally, and more often de facto, were ethnic parishes. In the churches, sermons were given and confessions heard in European languages. Parochial schools pro-

Table 1.1. *Population of Youngstown, 1900–1980*

Year	Population	Percent change
1900	44,885	—
1910	79,066	+76
1920	132,358	+67
1930	170,002	+28
1940	167,720	−1
1950	168,330	0
1960	166,689	−1
1970	139,788	−16
1980	115,436	−18

Source: U.S. Census Bureau.

vided informal (and sometimes formal) lessons in ethnic heritage along with the 3 Rs and the catechism. Parish bazaars and church weddings preserved ethnic social and food customs.

In the first half of the twentieth century, Youngstown and its manufacturing suburbs enjoyed a phenomenal growth, culminating in the war decade of the 1940s. The war effort and the reconstruction that followed strained the Youngstown mills to capacity. Steel employment in that period also reached a high point. It is estimated that during the war Youngstown-area mills employed sixty-five thousand workers directly in iron- and steel-making. It is also estimated that the city of Youngstown itself reached its population high point in 1943. The fifty years of growth had cast the Youngstown area in the mold of an archetypal "steeltown." The area's steel heritage provided both its resources and its liabilities for coping with the future.

Steeltown, 1950–1977

From 1900 to 1950, the dominant trend in Youngstown was growth. By the 1950s, however, the city of Youngstown and to a varying extent its manufacturing suburbs were moving into a period of no growth, and eventually of population decline. In this new era, the economy of Youngstown continued to be dominated by the steel mills. But the mills in and around Youngstown were old, many of them (like the Campbell Works) dating from the turn of the century. Some facilities in those mills could practically qualify as industrial antiques – for example, the 1908 vintage steam engine with a 22-foot flywheel that still served as power source in one U.S. Steel facility until it was closed in 1979. Although some portions of the mills had, of course, been modernized, by and large the obsolescence of their production facilities made the old mills in Mahoning County particularly susceptible to the ills that befell the American steel industry in the 1970s (see Chapter 2).

The dominant note for the Youngstown area in the third quarter of the twentieth century was transition. Youngstown did not suddenly cease to be a steeltown. But changes began setting in that, with increasing speed in the 1970s, affected the economy, the urban geography, the social demography, and the politics of the area.

Economy

Well into the 1970s, steel remained an important foundation element in the Youngstown economy. But three important shifts in the economic structure of the metropolitan area were discernible by the 1970s. First, newer industrial development began to move west and north to Youngstown, with Trumbull County emerging as the manufacturing center for the Youngstown–Warren Metropolitan Statistical Area. In 1975, Trumbull County had almost 45,000 employees in the manufacturing sector, compared with 35,000 in Mahoning County. Second, automotive manufacturing emerged as the second largest industry, with General Motors the largest single employer in the metropolitan area. (In 1966, General Motors built an auto assembly plant at Lordstown, west of Youngstown, adding an adjacent Fisher Body plant in 1969.) General Motors had a third plant in Warren, Packard Electric, manufacturing automotive electrical components. Third, the employment pattern in the Youngstown–Warren metropolitan area marked a clear shift away from manufacturing and into the wholesale and retail trade, service, and government sectors. This trend, typical of metropolitan areas in the Great Lakes region, was expected to continue. Table 1.2, comparing the composition of the labor force in the Youngstown–Warren metropolitan area in 1967 and 1976 (the ten years before the Campbell Works shutdown) demonstrates the shift in the role of manufacturing employment. In that period, the total number of jobs in

Table 1.2 *Nonagricultural wage and salary employment in Youngstown–Warren metropolitan area, 1967 and 1976 (in thousands)*

Industry	1967 Average	1976 Average	Percent change, 1967–76
Total	181.2	203.5	+12.3
Manufacturing	86.1	80.6	−6.4
Durable goods	79.0	74.5	−5.7
Primary metal	43.8	41.0	−6.4
Blast furnace and basic steel	32.4	26.0	−19.4
Transportation equipment	10.3	9.8	−4.8
Nondurable goods	7.1	6.1	−14.1
Nonmanufacturing	95.1	122.9	+29.2
Wholesale and retail trade	32.3	43.3	+34.4
Services	24.0	32.7	+36.3
Government	17.7	24.0	+35.6

Source: Ohio Bureau of Employment Services, Division of Research and Statistics.

the metropolitan area increased by 21,300. But the number of manufacturing jobs declined by 5,500, from 47.5 to 39.6% of the labor force in 1976.

Despite the relative decline in the manufacturing sector, however, manufacturing employment in the mid-1970s still provided the major input into the local economy in terms of employee income (Figure 1.2). A comparison of the average weekly paycheck in steel with that in other sectors (Figure 1.3) shows that it took, on the average, 2.5 jobs at K-Mart to replace the income of a single steel job.

The trend in employment patterns, then, is important at both the aggregate and individual household levels. For the economy as a whole, an increase in total number of jobs did not necessarily mean an increase in total employee earnings. For the individual household, a change from manufacturing (particularly steel) to other employment could involve a drastic cut in household disposable income.

In spite of the declining trend in manufacturing employment in the economy as a whole, and the loss of 6,400 jobs in basic

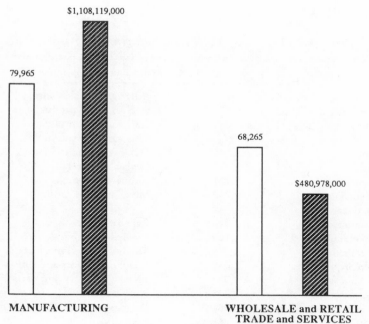

Figure 1.2. Youngstown–Warren metropolitan area: employment and payroll, 1975. Shaded bars: payroll; open bars: number of employees. *Source*: U.S. Department of Commerce, County Business Patterns, 1975. Cited in Franz-Goldman (1978), p. 75.

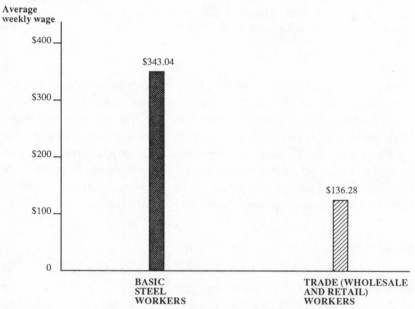

Figure 1.3. Average weekly wages in Youngstown–Warren metropolitan area, 1977. *Source*: Ohio Bureau of Employment Services, Department of Research and Statistics. Cited in Franz-Goldman (1978), pp. 49, 51.

Table 1.3. *Principal Mahoning Valley manufacturing firms*

Company	Employment	Product description
General Motors	17,474	Autos and trucks; wiring
Youngstown Sheet and Tube	12,174	Steel and steel products
Republic Steel	11,658	Steel and steel products
U.S. Steel	—	Steel and steel products
Wean United	3,545	Metalworking machinery
Copperweld Steel	2,900	High-alloy steel
General Electric	2,431	Electric lamp bulbs
General Fireproofing	2,250	Metal office furniture
General American Transportation	2,146	Railroad and tank cars
American Welding	1,109	Welded assemblies
Reactive Metals, Inc.	1,082	Titanium; metal products
Youngstown Steel Door	1,080	Freight car doors and sides
Commercial Shearing	1,023	Metal machinery and parts
North American Rockwell	1,008	Auto bumpers
Aeroquip (Republic Rubber)	966	Rubber products, hoses
N.R.M. Corporation	868	Foundry
Grinnel Corporation	793	Industrial pipe
Pittsburgh Steel	767	Steel coatings
E. W. Bliss Co.	735	Rolling mill equipment

Source: Aley (1975), 532. Reprinted with permission of the Youngstown Historical Society. Information supplied by the Youngstown Chamber of Commerce.

steel in particular from 1967 to 1976, basic steel and steel-related manufacturing continued to be the dominant force in the Youngstown–Warren area economy. A list of the principal Mahoning Valley manufacturing firms shows that most of the area's largest employers (a) were engaged in the production of steel, (b) involved in the manufacture of steel-related products or services, or (c) depended on a labor supply skilled in primary metal production or metals fabricating (Table 1.3).

Social Demography

In Youngstown's boom period, industrial and civic leadership in the city was to a large extent the prerogative of iron barons such as James Campbell. The postwar period, however, saw virtually a total exodus of the old iron and steel elite from the city. The process had begun well before the war, as families began to move out of the Wick Avenue neighborhood in the 1920s. Some moved to north Youngstown, but others abandoned the city entirely:

The suburbs by 1938 had not yet become truly attractive living areas for the iron and steel elite in Youngstown. It is apparent that most of those who longed to escape the city went to suburban areas in other cities – either to Cleveland or to the east coast. (Ingham 1978: 202)

In the 1950s, the descendants of the iron barons had "virtually forsaken Youngstown." "The exodus was so complete that by 1968, only 16 percent of the original thirty-seven iron and steel families remained in the area" (ibid.: 203).

The exodus of the iron and steel elite largely predated the expansion at the urban rim that would be characteristic of Youngstown – along with many other American cities – in the postwar period. Before the war, the suburbs of Youngstown were largely manufacturing centers on the Mahoning River (e.g., Campbell, Struthers, Lowellville, McDonald). By the 1960s, however, Youngstown began to experience the new suburbanization that became characteristic of other northern cities. Residential developments outside the city in Boardman and Austintown and Liberty Township attracted middle- and upper-middle-income householders from the city. New shopping malls built by DeBartolo and Cafaro (Youngstown-area construction men who became two of the nation's largest mall developers) attracted commercial investment away from the downtown business district.

The new suburbanization coincided with the rising affluence of steelworkers. Through the power of their national union, steelworkers became a kind of elite within the labor movement. In Youngstown, the average weekly steelworker paycheck in 1977 amounted to $343.04. By comparison, the average weekly manufacturing wage for the nation in that year was $226.75. Steelworkers who were making well over $20,000 per year no longer had to live in bungalows near the plant gates. They could afford ranch houses in the suburbs and cars to drive to work.

Suburbanization tended to scatter steelworkers' places of residence over a wider geographical area around the urban rim. At the same time, the core of the city of Youngstown became increasingly occupied by black residents. Blacks had come into Youngstown earlier than they had in some other Northern cities.

During the 1919 steel strike, the steel companies brought in several thousand blacks from the South to act as strikebreakers. Steel employment did provide an avenue for upward economic mobility, but, except for company housing, their residential location had been limited largely to the old ethnic neighborhoods of inner-city Youngstown, the largest concentration of blacks in the Youngstown–Warren metropolitan area.

Despite the suburban migration out of Youngstown, the area as a whole gave the outside observer an overwhelming impression of community stability. This was particularly the case with communities like Campbell and Struthers, surrounding the Campbell Works. The ethnic heritage remained strong. Figures from the 1970 census show that 22% of individuals in the metropolitan area were foreign-born, of foreign parentage, or of mixed parentage, compared with only 9% for the state of Ohio as a whole. In Campbell, 45.6% and in Struthers 33.7% were of foreign stock. Campbell is strongly Czechoslovakian (12%), with significant groups of Italians (7%) and Poles (5%). Struthers is strongly Italian (11%) and Czechoslovakian (7%). The census data almost certainly provide a minimal estimate of persons whose social and cultural patterns were actually affected by ethnic identity.

Religious structures, particularly in the Catholic Church, still served to reinforce ethnic cultural patterns. Although the bishop tried to move away from designating certain parishes as officially "Slovak" or "Polish" or "Italian," the social reality remains. An extensive system of ethnic social clubs also helped ethnic heritage to flourish. The Saxon Club, the Italian-American clubs, and a variety of others provide lodges with excellent and inexpensive food and drinks, as well as places for social conviviality. In more recent years, sharp distinctions based on ethnic lineage have tended to blur. (It is possible, for example, to belong simultaneously to the Saxon Club, an Italian-American club, a Serbian club, and the Ancient Order of Hibernians.) Blacks seemed to be the only group clearly excluded from crossing ethnic lines.

Family and home were central values. The extended family pattern was very much in evidence, with three or four generations of a family often living within a short walking distance of one another. Homeownership was a first principle of providing for one's family. In Campbell, almost 75% and in Struthers almost 80% of the residents owned the houses (there were few apartments) in which they lived.

The result of these social patterns was considerable community stability. A survey of workers laid off at Sheet and Tube in 1977 indicated that the average steelworker had lived in the community for 28.9 years. Fifty-seven percent of the respondents said they had been lifelong residents of the communities where they presently lived. Of the steelworkers surveyed, one-third said they had paid off at least 75% of the mortgage on their homes (Franz-Goldman 1978: 202).

Politics and Community Leadership

Generalizations about the structure and pattern of community leadership in Youngstown are necessarily somewhat tentative. There are few historical or other studies on which to base a political analysis. Howard Aley's (1975) celebrative bicentennial volume and Ingham's (1978) documentation of the iron and steel elite are the principal published resources. The author's own participant-observation in the 1970s and interviews with key informants contributed some information. Given these qualifications, the following general pattern suggests itself.

Before World War II, the community power structure was essentially elitist, with the iron barons largely dominating civic as well as economic and social life. By the postwar period, however, this group had almost totally disappeared from Youngstown. Their exodus left a political vacuum. At one level, community leadership was taken over by the major industrial corporations that remained in the Mahoning Valley. At a second level, labor union and ethnic politics dominated the local scene. Curiously absent in community leadership was a strong role for the local business community.

Major corporations. The steel mills founded by the iron barons were still present, but they were no longer under the ownership and/or management of a local elite. Instead, Youngstown's major industries increasingly came to be controlled by out-of-town corporations. Republic Steel, once a Youngstown-based company, moved its headquarters to Cleveland, and, of course, Youngstown Sheet and Tube came under the control of the New Orleans–based Lykes Corporation. U.S. Steel, General Motors, General Electric, Rockwell, Aeroquip – all were headquartered outside the Youngstown area.

The major corporations did not often intervene directly in the local political sector. Their participation in community decision making at the local level was more informal. Youngstown in this respect resembled the "Bigtown" studied by Pellegrin and Coates, though it differed in being Northern (rather than Southern) and contracting (rather than rapidly growing). Pellegrin and Coates's (1956) description of decision dynamics in a city controlled by absentee corporations seems to fit Youngstown:

In the relative power vacuum which exists in Bigtown, community projects are usually doomed if they lack the approval of the industrial, absentee-owned corporations. There is no single crowd or clique of representatives of them, but their top executives communicate with one another informally and arrive at agreement on matters of policy. The executives of each corporation are then informed of the decision, making it possible for given community projects to be supported or vetoed through united action. Corporation support probably assures the success of a proposed project, while disapproval spells doom for it. Thus absentee-owned corporations are a decisive force in the power structure of Bigtown; they constitute a balance of power among the competing interest groups of the community. (67)

In terms of power in the local community, the major absentee-owned corporations do possess a great degree of control over the political economic agenda of local communities. The decision to invest or withhold capital can be crucial for the development plans of a local community. The decision to start or stop production can determine whether a municipality will grow or decline, the level of its revenues, and the shape of its budget.

One Youngstown issue in which the corporations had a significant interest was the proposal of Henry Ford II in the 1950s to build a major Ford auto assembly plant on a site just north of Youngstown that was being used to scrap old railroad cars. The major corporations, acting in coalition with local industrialists, were evidently able to obstruct the project long enough that Mr. Ford became impatient and abandoned the idea of locating in Youngstown. The proposal was effectively vetoed because it would have introduced unwanted competition in the Youngstown-area labor market, thereby driving up the cost of labor.[2]

The older iron baron elite also had such power. But they were largely in and of the local community. The new elitism of the absentee-owned corporation was aptly symbolized by the way the decision was made to close the Campbell Works: Members of the corporate board met on a Sunday afternoon at the Pittsburgh airport, with most of the board members flying in from New Orleans and New York, Boston, and Chicago, and returning home right after the meeting.

Within the parameters staked out by the major corporations, regarding issues in which the corporations had little interest, local groups did have some measure of political influence.

Labor. One major factor in the Youngstown power structure is organized labor. Youngstown has traditionally been a blue-collar town, with high levels of union membership. The United Steel-workers of America (USWA), organized in 1937, emerged as a power on the local scene after the war. With some fifty thousand members in its Youngstown District 26 in the 1960s and 1970s, the steelworkers union became a major power in the local community. According to Youngstown resident John Lynch, a state appellate judge with a lifetime of experience in Ohio politics, the election of the United Steelworkers district director was second in importance only to the mayoral election. In 1970, the steel-workers union was able to put its man in Congress; Representa-tive Charles Carney went from the district staff of the USWA to Washington. Although Carney was defeated in 1978 by Republi-can Lyle Williams, the power of the steelworker vote produced the anomaly of a Republican politician filing a suit in federal district court against U.S. Steel, seeking to delay the shutdown of the corporation's Youngstown facilities.

Local business. In the 1970s, owners of local business in Youngs-town did not present a well-organized front within the commun-ity. On the whole, the local business community typically fell into the role of reacting to initiatives taken elsewhere.

Youngstown was the home of two wealthy real estate devel-opers, Edward DeBartolo and Anthony Cafaro. DeBartolo, re-portedly worth more than $500 million, controlled a shopping mall empire around the country and professional sports teams (including the San Francisco NFL franchise). Neither of these men, however, took a prominent role in local politics. Nor did the owners of prominent local companies such as Commercial Shearing, Standard Slag, or Lyden Oil.

Youngstown's retail community – typically a backbone of the local business establishment – was hard hit by the development of suburban shopping malls, which brought in the major national retail chains (Sears, Penney's). Downtown retail business in the 1970s was suffering a long-term decline.

In the late 1970s, it was owners of service-type businesses that emerged as leaders in the Youngstown Chamber of Commerce – for example, Jack Meerman (owner of a travel agency) and Forest Beckett (owner of a private aviation company).

The business community did succeed in establishing strong links with the Youngstown mayor's office in the administrations of both Republican Jack Hunter (1970–7) and Philip Richley (1978–9). However, the business elite had little or no influence with the Youngstown City Council.

Parties and political office. As one might expect from the social demography of the Youngstown area, Mahoning County was a typical post–New Deal Democratic stronghold. Organized labor, particularly the steelworkers union, was strong in Youngstown, with the local unions providing support for the Democratic Party. In addition, the Catholic ethnics traditionally found their political home in the Democratic Party, forcing Youngstown politicians to reckon seriously in terms of the Italian, Slovak, and Irish voting blocs. When the party was careful to slate candidates for political office with due regard for ethnic balance on the ticket, the ethnic blocs provided reliable support for the Democratic Party. Finally, the city of Youngstown developed a large concentration of black voters, who in the postwar period likewise traditionally supported the Democratic Party.

The principal electoral office for the area was the 19th District congressional seat. The congressman provided the principal link between the Mahoning Valley and Washington, a link that grew in importance as local governments in the 1970s found an increasing portion of their funds coming from federal grants. Likewise, the congressman provided the area's principal line to the national political party, bringing in national political leaders and possibly assistance and funds from the party's national committee to help local campaigns. In 1977, that congressional post had long been controlled by Mahoning County Democrats; the incumbent was Charles Carney, the Mahoning County Democrat formerly connected with the United Steelworkers Youngstown district.

After the congressman, the second-ranking elected official was the mayor of Youngstown. Normally, the Democratic Party was able to control the mayor's office. In 1970, however, an incident of labor violence just days before the mayoral election was instrumental in putting Republican candidate Jack Hunter into office. In a demonstration related to the effort to organize truck drivers who haul steel, shots were exchanged and a man was killed. It developed that the Youngstown police knew the demonstrators were armed and deliberately stayed away from the scene. This revelation shortly before election day hurt the effort of incumbent Democratic Mayor Anthony Flask, and he was turned out of office. Hunter proved to be a popular and able mayor, winning three more two-year terms. But only in his first term did he enjoy a Republican majority in the City Countil. In 1978, on Hunter's retirement, the Democrats were able to elect their candidate with ease. In 1980, in spite of Ronald Reagan's popularity, the Republicans were unable to put forward a serious mayoral candidate.

Democratic strength in the Mahoning Valley was asserted in the context of strong two-party competition in the state of Ohio as a whole. In the 1976 presidential election, the strong vote for Jimmy Carter in Mahoning County pushed otherwise divided Ohio into the Democratic column. At the state level, politics in 1977 was controlled by Governor James Rhodes. Both the governor and the National Republican Committee were anxious to increase Republican strength in the Mahoning Valley.

The Politics of Local Economic Development

The Mahoning Valley has the kind of internal differences of political jurisdiction that are often characteristic of a metropolitan area. The metropolitan area includes two counties, Mahoning and Trumbull (see Figure 1.1), the urban centers of Youngstown and Warren, both manufacturing and residential suburbs, and unincorporated townships. In the postwar period, development favored Trumbull over Mahoning County.

By the 1970s, the metropolitan area was experiencing significant differences in its internal economic development. Industrial expansion was taking place in Trumbull rather than in Mahoning County. With the General Motors plants and Packard Electric, the manufacturing center of the area has shifted to Trumbull County. At the same time, the steel industry in Mahoning County was on the decline. Sharon Steel-Hoop shut down at Lowellville, putting an end to the growth of that manufacturing suburb. Hundreds of steel jobs were phased out at Republic Steel's facility on the east side of Youngstown, adjacent to the Sheet and Tube. In the race for capital investment and jobs, Trumbull County was clearly winning and some municipalities in Mahoning County were clearly losing.

The economic development of the Youngstown area must be situated within a national context. Through the 1950s and 1960s, the role of the federal government in local urban development expanded greatly. Programs initiated during the Kennedy and Johnson administrations expanded the federal share of state and local expenditures nation-wide to more than 25% in 1977, compared with just over 10% in 1950.

With so much federal money being allocated to local projects, the Nixon administration's Office of Management and Budget in 1969 issued Circular A-95, calling for the coordination of intergovernmental planning for federal development programs. "Clearing houses" were to be established at the state, metropolitan, or regional level to coordinate and filter grant proposals from local governments. The A-95 review procedure brought about the institution of "councils of governments" to accomplish this task.

In response to the need for metropolitan-level coordination of development proposals involving federal funds, a Council of Governments was formed including municipalities from Mahoning and Trumbull Counties. However, political differences within the council, as well as differences in approach to local economic development, led to a dissolution of this body. Two economic development agencies emerged from the breakup: the Eastgate Development and Transportation Agency (EDATA) and the Western Reserve Economic Development Agency (WREDA). Each agency had its own political connections and its own economic development "turf."

EDATA was located in Mahoning County. Its director, William Fergus, was politically connected with Charles Carney, the Democratic congressman. EDATA retained the A-95 review authority for planning and research contracted by the Environmental Protection Agency (EPA). EDATA's strength lay in its capacity for studying and planning urban and industrial infrastructure: transportation, sewers, utilities, and so on. Through its Democratic political connections, EDATA was able to set up a special funding arrangement with Mahoning County. Most of its work was done on a contract basis, which meant that the agency was often short of operating funds in the grant preparation phase or when contracted payments were slow in moving through the pipeline. EDATA was permitted to set up a line directly into Mahoning County funds to meet operating expenses, eventually accumulating arrears of almost half a million dollars.

WREDA, with William Sullivan as president, went to Trumbull County. Sullivan, who had once run for mayor of Warren on the Republican ticket, was a popular speaker at Chamber of Commerce and Rotary luncheons. He was perceived as a potential Republican candidate for political office, perhaps for the congressional seat. Where EDATA was connected with the federal EPA, WREDA took most of the contracting from the Economic Development Administration (EDA) of the Commerce Department. WREDA would be responsible for the overall Economic Development Plan and for maintaining an industrial index of the Mahoning Valley. WREDA's political connections were with Ohio Senator Taft, which gave the agency both protection from the Democratic congressman and sufficient clout (particularly in a Republbican administration) to bypass EDA's regional office in Chicago and deal directly with Washington. Like EDATA, WREDA had financial problems. But without similar access to public funds, WREDA had to borrow from banks to meet its payroll. Sullivan also arranged for annual subventions from the four major steel producers in the Valley.

Sullivan believed that Mahoning Valley's economic future was linked with the steel industry; consequently, he made stabilizing the industry in the Valley a primary goal of WREDA, with the ultimate objective of ensuring industrial growth and continued employment. Sullivan, an Episcopalian, sought to associate Father Edward Stanton in these efforts (the two had become friends while Stanton was serving as assistant pastor at a parish in Warren). A year after its founding, Stanton became treasurer of WREDA.[3]

WREDA's first major task was thrust upon it by events in Washington. The EPA decided to act on its mandate to enforce pure-water standards by cleaning up the Mahoning River. Strict enforcement of the EPA standards would have created very serious difficulties for the old Mahoning River steel plants. Because of the jerry-built nature of these old facilities, with multiple outflows into the river, routing effluents through newly constructed treatment facilities sufficient to meet EPA standards would have been extraordinarily expensive. The Local steel people were afraid that strict enforcement of the EPA standards would mean that steel companies would find it financially advantageous to shut down their old mills in the Mahoning Valley rather than comply with federal regulations. In the Mahoning Valley, steel industry executives and the steelworkers union came together in agreeing that "Washington" was the enemy threatening the local steel industry.

In this context, WREDA took up the cause of local steel. Sullivan persuaded the four largest companies to furnish his agency with sufficient data on their internal operations to calculate the real costs of compliance by the companies, as well as the direct and indirect costs to the Valley's economy if the plants were forced to shut down. The study, covering 85% of steel production in the Youngstown–Warren metropolitan area, formed the basis of the industry's case with the EPA (Ernst and Ernst Management Consulting Services 1973). The union also supported WREDA's effort, and steelworkers anxious about their jobs demonstrated outside the hearing room. The evidence of severe community impact was sufficient that Russell Train, director of the EPA, granted a "stay of execution" to the Youngstown mills, giving them a longer time to comply with EPA standards.

WREDA next began a series of studies financed by the EDA on revitalizing basic steel in Youngstown. A corollary finding of the pollution study pointed out that part of the industry's problem in the Mahoning Valley was its inland location. WREDA initiated a study of the Valley's rail connections for transporting ore from the Great Lakes. It was discovered that the problem was not the physical facilities, but the administration of the railroads, which called for five different switches of locomotives and train crews on the sixty-five-mile trip down from Lake Erie, limiting the trains to a net speed of one mile per hour (Klauder and Associates 1976). Another study proposed the idea of a unit train that would eliminate this problem (Beetle 1978). The unit-train report revealed a still further difficulty: There were too many delivery points for this unit train to cover. Why not revitalize the Valley's antiquated ironmaking capacity by centralizing it in a single giant blast furnace capacity financed by a joint venture involving several steel companies? The single blast furnace, in which several companies would have an interest, could supply hot

metal more cheaply and efficiently for the whole valley, stabilizing the industry and holding most steel jobs in place (Hogan
1978).

Working closely with the steel companies, WREDA was gradually developing a grand design for revitalizing steel in the
Mahoning Valley. It quickly lost its position, however. First, the
agency lost its political backing in the 1976 election. The EDA
began hearing from the Democratic congressman, for whom Sullivan represented a Republican threat. The political facts of life
were spelled out for WREDA by the EDA regional director
in Chicago: There would be few EDA contracts in WREDA's
future. Second, with the Sheet and Tube shutdown in 1977,
WREDA began to lose its industrial backing. The steel closures
came too quickly for WREDA's alternative plans to be considered seriously.

In addition to EDATA and WREDA, a third office involved in
economic development was the Youngstown Area Growth
Foundation, since 1976 associated with the Youngstown Chamber of Commerce. The Foundation was essentially a one-man
operation conducted by Laird Eckmann, who functioned as a
public relations ambassador of Youngstown, promoting the city
in trips around the country. Though his office did not really enter
into more technical aspects of planning and development, he
claimed credit for assisting in a number of industrial site choices
in the Youngstown area. Eckmann's approach to area development can be taken as fairly representative of the ambivalent view
of the Chamber of Commerce toward the steel industry. The steel
shutdowns – though harmful to area business in the short run –
would ease pressure on wages and provide an attractive labor pool
for smaller manufacturing business. Eckmann was later to remark
that the Sheet and Tube shutdown was "the best thing that could
have happened to the Youngstown economy."

CHAPTER II

The Industry

The United States was the dominant steelmaker for the world in the period from 1900 through World War II – the boom period for Youngstown. Immediately after the war, the United States was responsible for more than half the total world steel production. But as steel industries in Japan and Europe were rebuilt and expanded, that position naturally changed. Although it was to be expected that the American share of total world production would drop, it was not expected that the United States would become a net steel importer. By the 1970s, America was the one major industrial economy that did not meet its own steel requirements. The relative decline in American steel between the late 1940s and the late 1970s is an integral part of the Youngstown story.[1]

Crisis for American Steel

The year 1959 marks a date when things changed for American steel. During an industry-wide strike lasting 116 days, steel consumers relied on the newly built steel mills of Japan and Europe to maintain their inventories. For the first time since the turn of the century, the United States imported more steel than it exported. The situation was not deemed critical at the time, but it developed that steel contract negotiations every three years brought a significant increase in steel imports, principally as hedge buying against a strike. Partly to stem this trend the United Steelworkers adopted an Experimental Negotiating Agreement with the industry in 1973, ensuring that contract negotiations would be settled without a strike. Nevertheless, imports remained at a fairly high level and even increased. In 1977–8, imported steel captured 18% of the American market, with 80% of that coming from Japan and Europe.

The penetration of the American market by Japanese and European steel is related to at least three key factors: technological superiority of more modern plants, lower labor costs, and government–industry relationships affecting trade.

The two decades of the 1950s and 1960s saw a virtual explosion in the demand for steel. As the world economy finally emerged from the devastation of the war in the mid-1950s, steel was needed for the booming auto and appliance industries, for oil production, and for construction. In responding to this demand, the Europeans and Japanese were in the position of having to build their steel industries from the ground up and consequently were able to profit from the "advantages of backwardness." The new Japanese and European plants were able to exploit the latest steel-production technology sooner than the American steel mills.[2]

For one thing, they were able to build significantly larger blast furnaces (for reducing iron ore to molten iron; see Figure 2.1). A blast furnace producing 6,000 to 8,000 tons of iron per day can be operated with the same manpower as a 1,000-ton furnace, producing six to eight times the metal at the same labor cost. For another thing, the plants coming on stream in the 1960s could employ the new oxygen furnace for the second stage of the steelmaking process. The basic oxygen process (BOP) was a significant improvement over the older open hearth process – used in the American mills built in the 1950s. Where an open hearth required approximately seven hours to produce a "heat" (200+ tons) of steel, the BOP furnace could do it in less than forty-five minutes, and with better quality control. Also, electric arc furnaces were coming into use for melting scrap steel.

The relative backwardness of the American steel industry in adopting the oxygen steelmaking technology is illustrated in Figure 2.2. By 1978, six Western European countries and Japan had implemented the oxygen process more extensively than American steelmakers. A comparison between the United States and Japan on the conversion to modern steelmaking is particularly pertinent. In 1968, for instance, more than 50% of steel in the United States was still produced in outdated open hearths; at that point,

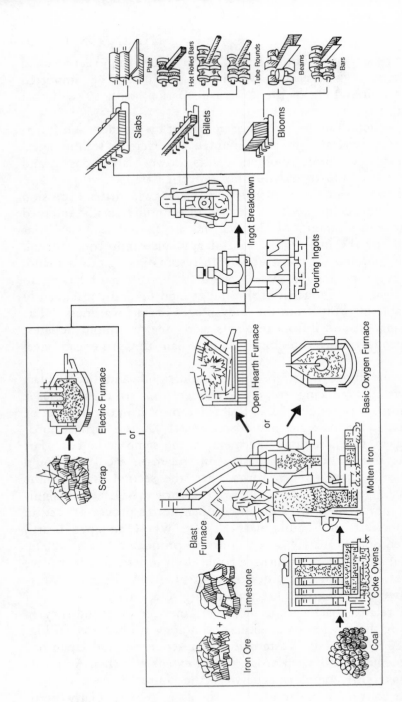

Figure 2.1. The making of steel.

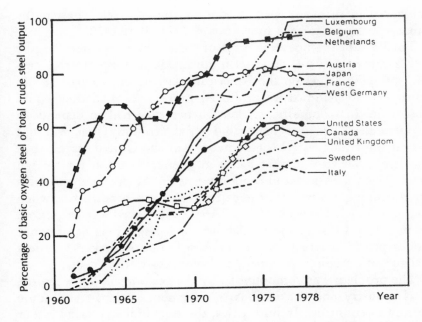

Figure 2.2. The diffusion of oxygen steelmaking in twelve countries, 1961–1978.
Source: DuBois (1983).

more than 90% of Japanese steel was being produced in modern oxygen or electric furnaces (Bari 1977).

In the 1970s, also, the Japanese steel industry was far ahead of the American industry in installing the continuous caster, which produces semifinished shapes directly from liquid steel. By eliminating the steps in the traditional "ingot" route (pouring liquid steel into molds, stripping the mold from the solidified ingot, reheating the ingot to an even temperature, then pouring it into semifinished shapes), the continuous caster can realize significant savings in steel yield, labor, and energy. In 1978, 45% of Japanese steel was continuously cast, as opposed to only 15% in the United States (American Iron and Steel Institute 1980: 35).

Both the Japanese and Europeans were able to produce steel more cheaply because of lower labor costs. Through the 1960s, wage scales in Japan and Europe were considerably lower than in the United States, though in the 1970s the wage factor showed less disparity. However, the investment in modern technology also contributed to lower net labor costs. Japanese productivity –

measured in man-hours to produce a ton of steel – bested the American figure for the first time in 1973 (Bari 1977).

Finally, the competitive pressure on American steel in the 1970s came from the short-term advantage to foreign producers of "dumping" steel on the American market. Both Japanese and European steel industries produced more steel than they could absorb in their domestic markets; hence they had to depend on export sales. The one major industrial economy that was not producing enough steel for its needs was the United States; thus the American steel market had a magnetic attraction for foreign steel. When the American economy was on the upswing and mills were running at capacity, the extra steel was a benefit. But when the notoriously cyclical steel industry experienced a slack period, as it did in 1975–6, the availability of foreign steel at discount prices placed severe pressure on American steelmakers. Orders slacked off, earnings dropped, and workers were laid off.

The problem was compounded by the relationship between the steel industry and the national government in Japan and some European countries. In both cases, the steel industry faced rather higher fixed costs than in the United States, which made it more economical to produce steel and sell it cheaply – even below the cost of production – than simply to shut down the mills during slack periods. In Europe, the fixed cost was in the form of high unemployment benefits that had to be paid to laid-off workers, often amounting to 90% of full wages. In the European case, where significant portions of the mills were government owned and operated, an attractive short-term strategy for slack periods was to keep the mills running and realize whatever earnings could be gained from selling steel at a discount in the United States, rather than to cut back production and still pay high guaranteed wage costs. In Japan, mills were privately owned but were heavily leveraged by government-backed loans. For Japanese steel, the high fixed cost was interest on borrowings, which had to be paid regardless of whether the mills were running at capacity. Again the short-term "dumping" strategy was a way of providing some earnings to offset these charges.

In the steel downturn of 1977, imported steel was being offered at $100 per ton below the U.S. list price (Hogan 1983: 128). Such trade practices were forbidden by the Anti-Dumping Act of 1921 and the Trade Act of 1974. But whether through oversight in the change from the Ford to Carter administrations, or through an interest in holding down domestic steel prices, the U.S. government failed to enforce the laws on the books, a failure that was documented by the General Accounting Office (Comptroller General of the United States 1979). The need for a more aggressive control of foreign steel dumping was admitted by the Carter administration in establishing the Trigger Price Mechanism at the end of 1977. The steel industry charged:

The combination of lost sales and depressed revenues that resulted from dumping on the scale experienced since the 1973–74 boom has had a devastating impact on the American steel industry. In 1977 in particular, profits virtually disappeared, as a quarter of the industry's productive capacity was idled and most producers experienced large operating losses. (American Iron and Steel Institute 1980: 12)

In Youngstown and other steeltowns, billboards in 1977 proclaimed, "Foreign steel, it's a job-robbing deal."

The volume of imports sold at discounted prices had a twofold negative impact on the American steel industry. First, in terms of volume, imports depressed steel earnings by displacing domestic production. The proportion of capacity actually being utilized is critical for the steel industry. It is estimated that the industry's break-even point in 1977 was 80 to 83% and that at least an 85% operating rate was necessary to ensure sufficient steel earnings (Hogan 1977: 16). Second, in terms of pricing structure, the lower import prices forced American producers to hold prices at a level too low for generating sufficient profits to modernize outdated facilities.

Pressure from abroad was not the American steel industry's only problem in the late 1970s. Three other factors closer to home were critical. First, production costs rose as the costs of raw materials and particularly energy increased. These increased domestic costs were not matched by compensating rises in steel prices. Second, because of both the profit squeeze due to steel pricing and depreciation schedules based on original cost of machinery rather than its replacement value, capital for modernization was being generated at much too slow a rate to finance needed modernization of industrial plants:

The impact of insufficient modernization has fallen most heavily on plants in traditional steelmaking areas, particularly in instances where multi-plant companies have tended to channel their scarce capital resources into other locations affording greater investment potential. The result has been a vicious circle of obsolescence in which less modern plants, such as those in the Youngstown area, have been allocated the least modernization capital. (Hogan 1977: 19)

Finally, the American steel industry had to meet increasingly stringent requirements for air and water pollution control. Annual expenditures for pollution control exceeded $100 million beginning in 1968. In 1977, the industry-wide outlay for this purpose was $750 million, representing about half of the anticipated cash flow for that year (ibid.: 22). Again the blow fell most heavily on older plants. For one thing, capital investment for pollution control increased physical plant expenses without increasing productivity. For another, retrofitting pollution controls on older facilities was disproportionately costly, since much of the equipment would not stay in use long enough to justify the investment. It was more economically feasible, then, to shut down older plants and spend the pollution control dollars on new steel mill facilities.

In 1977, all these factors added up to a crisis for American steel. In August of that year, an Argus Research Report concluded that the steel companies were initiating a new strategy to deal with the crisis of the 1970s – de facto liquidation. The report predicted that the steel industry would get rid of as much as 20% of its existing capacity within five years (Bari 1977).

The crisis in the American steel industry created two questions for public policy. The first concerned the steel industry itself as a national resource: What impact would the decline in basic steel have on the American economy as a whole? More than one steel expert in the late 1970s was predicting a capacity shortfall in the 1980s for "the most important engineering material in American society."[3] One consequence would be that the United States would be forced to pay very high prices for steel in world markets (Comptroller General of the United States, 1981: 2–8). A second consequence would be that "such a degree of steel import dependence would raise economic and national security problems for the United States not unlike those now encountered with petroleum" (Office of Technology Assessment 1980: 16).

The second policy question concerned local communities: What effect would the pattern of capital investment (or disinvestment) decisions in the steel industry have on particular local economies? The American Iron and Steel Institute (1980) pre dicted that, without significant federal assistance, the industry would phase out another ninety thousand jobs (40). Furthermore, any modernization of American steel's capital plant was increasingly being focused on "greenfield" rather than "brownfield" strategies. Those who backed the "greenfield" strategy wanted to build new plants in open space because of space restrictions in older sites, the cost of retrofitting pollution control devices in older plants, and the need for deep-water transportation economies. A case in point was the proposal by U.S. Steel to build a new multibillion-dollar steel plant on Lake Erie at Conneaut, Ohio (at the Pennsylvania border). Critics of the greenfield strategy argued that it would create tremendous costs – first, in social and economic dislocation and abandoned urban infrastructure for communities in Ohio and Pennsylvania where older plants would close, and second in constructing new urban infrastructure in the Conneaut area. In contrast, the "brownfield" strategy called for the modernization of existing steel plant locations to make use of existing pools of skilled steel labor and urban infrastructure.[4]

The gathering steel crisis that emerged into public concern with the steel shutdowns of 1977 forced two different, but strongly related questions into the policy arena. What, if anything, should government do about the future of the steel industry? And did the national government have any role to play in the future of American steeltowns?

Crisis for Youngstown Sheet and Tube

A large part of the story behind the Youngstown steel crisis of 1977 is illustrated by the situation of the American steel industry in general. But in addition, factors specific to individual companies were an important part of the Youngstown steel crisis. In particular, firm-specific factors are crucial for understanding why the largest mill in Youngstown – Sheet and Tube – failed to modernize and so keep up with the competition.

Around 1959–60, Youngstown Sheet and Tube began developing a long-range strategy for modernization. Company executives opted for a two-stage game plan. Rather than reinvest directly in the Youngstown plants at Campbell and Brier Hill, the company decided to make a major move into the Chicago steel market. Chicago was emerging as the largest steel market in the nation, surpassing Pittsburgh. Youngstown executives decided that the best guarantee for the future was to establish a position in the Chicago market and then use the profits from Chicago sales to modernize the Youngstown mills. In the late 1960s, the company invested a half-billion dollars in developing a modern steel facility at Indiana Harbor on Lake Michigan (just east of Chicago near Gary). The Indiana Harbor plant included what was then the largest blast furnace in the country, new hot-strip and cold-strip mills, and finally, in 1970, new oxygen furnaces to replace the open hearths.

Unfortunately, two things happened on the way to the second half of the game plan. First, the facility never made any money. The new production machinery developed a series of bugs that were hard to iron out. Not enough business volume materialized in the first years to allow the company to run the new facility at sufficient capacity to generate a profit. In its haste to bring the facility on line, the company compromised its position with the labor unions and accepted what proved to be excess manning for the facility. And the labor force of eight thousand was plagued by disagreement among ethnic factions that made for constant labor problems. As a consequence, the new Chicago-area facility failed to create the capital to reinvest in Youngstown.[5]

Second, the company experienced a jolting restructuring because of a corporate merger with the Lykes Corporation of New Orleans. The corporate merger, accomplished in 1969, proved to be of utmost significance both for the company and for the city of Youngstown. It was important in two respects. First, it saddled the company with almost $350 million in new debts. And, second, it transferred effective control of the company out of Youngstown.

The Lykes Corporation was an aggressive, family-owned business with interests in shipbuilding and the ocean-carrying trade. With the Vietnam War in progress, Lykes was making money carrying war materiel across the Pacific. In accord with the popular merger strategy of the 1960s, Lykes was looking around for a way to expand and diversify its assets through the corporate takeover route. Lykes officials settled on Youngstown Sheet and Tube as a potential target.

In some respects, a merger between Lykes and Sheet and Tube seemed a highly unlikely venture. The steel company was much larger, with assets of $806 million, compared with Lykes's assets of $137 million. Lykes's management had little knowledge of or experience with the steel industry. Proposals for merger advanced by Lykes's officials were rejected by the Youngstown company, largely because it feared that the merged company would be a case of the "tail wagging the dog" – with Lykes assuming a dominant position both in management and in the capital structure.

Yet the steel company represented a potentially profitable target for Lykes. For one thing, it had an annual cash flow of $100 million. For another, Sheet and Tube stock was selling low enough to make a takeover attractive, presenting the chance to acquire a billion-dollar company for something like 30 cents on the dollar. Moreover, Sheet and Tube stockholdings were widely dispersed, giving Lykes with its concentrated holdings a significant advantage. Lykes was able to press that advantage to a successful merger in late January 1969, within a month of the first proposal. In order to accomplish the takeover, Lykes went into debt significantly. The smaller New Orleans company first borrowed $150 million in bank loans to purchase a minority stock interest in Sheet and Tube. Then Lykes issued about $191 million in debentures (with a new issue of preferred stock) to finance the takeover itself. The net result was that the newly merged company began life with almost $350 million in new debts.

The merger, since it involved the seventh largest American steel producer, was investigated by the Anti-Trust Division of the Department of Justice. The report of the investigation, written by midlevel official George Schueller, pointed out that the merger did not bode well for the steel company. Schueller pointed out three major reservations about the proposed merger. First, the new corporate structure would be dominated by Lykes officers, and the capital structure would militate against steel interests:

The combined voting rights of Lykes shareholders will outnumber those of Youngstown shareholders; moreover, Youngstown stock is widely held, while Lykes stock is owned mostly by the Lykes family and its in-laws. Thus it cannot be doubted that Youngstown is slated to become an appendage of Lykes – even though this is a case of the tail wagging the dog – and steel making interests will not be paramount in the new company's product. (Schueller 1969: 39)

Second, the borrowings and the bond and preferred stock issues to finance the merger would drastically increase the debt structure of the new company, from 18 to 32%. The increased debt service and dividend obligations "are bound to reduce, substantially, the funds which Youngstown has available for investments" (ibid.: 40). Third, the company's cash flow (reduced by the new debt) might well be diverted to purposes other than modernizing Youngstown, as indicated in a public statement by the new president of the merged company. Schueller concluded:

In sum, after providing for interests on long-term debts and debentures, and for preferred dividends of LYC (the merged company), the yearly funds available for modernizing Youngstown will decrease; and the new top management, without tradition in steel making and not committed to the old management's "Facilities Plan" and "Opportunities Survey," is much less likely to modernize Youngstown along the lines planned by the old management and found necessary by the industry experts to keep Youngstown competitive." (Ibid.)

Schueller argued that the Department of Justice should oppose the merger: "Given the state of concentration in the steel industry, the threatened decline of Youngstown as a competitive steel producer would play into the hands of the bigget members of that industry – to the substantial detriment of competition" (ibid.) Schueller's advice, of course, did not prevail. Attorney General John Mitchell did approve the proposed merger. There is question whether he had legal authority to prevent it, since existing antitrust legislation was directed at preventing concentration within a single industry rather than at conglomerate acquisitions of firms in different industries.

Schueller's analysis in any case proved remarkably prophetic. First, Lykes people did shortly take over the company. Fred Tod, Jr., whose family had founded the Brier Hill steel mill, resigned from the board of directors in protest at the merger and sold off his family shareholdings in the company. In a press release, Tod voiced his objection to the management of the merged company as newcomers to the steel business, unknown in Youngstown. Tod was criticized for his move. Among the critics was Sheet and Tube president Robert E. Williams. But in April 1970 – only one year after the merger – Williams found himself in the same position; he resigned as president and director of Lykes-Youngstown. Williams went on record in attributing his resignation to "the increasing role Lykes was taking in operating Sheet and Tube" (Youngstown *Vindicator*, June 21, 1978).

Second, the widespread view in Youngstown that Lykes milked Sheet and Tube (other verbs were also heard) is largely substanti-

Table 2.1. *Steel company averages, 1972–1976 (per ton of steel shipped)*

	Earnings	Dividends	Reinvested profits
Youngstown Sheet and Tube	$10.53	$8.26	$ 2.27
Industry average[a]	15.45	5.83	9.62
U.S. Steel	18.92	5.64	13.28

[a] American Iron and Steel Institute average.
Source: James W. Smith (1978).

ated by two independent analyses of company financial records. Steelworkers union official and economist James Smith developed figures from the company's annual reports for 1972–6 indicating that Sheet and Tube's earnings fell below the industry average. Yet in the same years, Lykes took dividends out of Sheet and Tube that were considerably higher than the industry average (see Table 2.1; figures for U.S. Steel Corporation are included for comparison).

A different financial analysis conducted by the firm of Philadelphia steel consultant George Beetle found that in the first years after the takeover, Lykes took out dividends in excess of income (Table 2.2). At the same time that Lykes was taking money out of Sheet and Tube, it was investing elsewhere. In 1969, Lykes acquired the Coastal Plains Life Insurance Company and placed orders for three large, automated cargo ships costing $113 million. In 1971, Lykes bought out W. R. Grace's half of their jointly owned South American Steamship Company and in 1973 purchased Ramseyer and Miller, Inc.

Lykes's financial timing proved particularly bad for Sheet and Tube's position in the steel industry, for 1970–2 were precisely the years when the company should have continued its modernization program, turning attention from Indiana Harbor to Youngstown. Youngstown Sheet and Tube executives have claimed that the company's basic problem in the early 1970s was that Indiana Harbor never generated a profit to finance Youngstown's modernization. That may be true. But Lykes's investment strategies in those years certainly compounded the problem.

When the steel boom finally did come in 1973–4, Sheet and

Table 2.2. *Youngstown Sheet and Tube: dividends as percentage of net income*

Corporate owner	Year	Dividend as % of net income
Youngstown Sheet and Tube	1967	48.3
	1968	42.0
Lykes	1969	94.3
	1970	127.1
	1971	183.1
	1972	157.1
	1973	37.0
	1974	70.5
	1975	48.9

Source: Western Reserve Economic Development Agency.

Tube did make money, but not as much as it would have with better production facilities. In fact, the extra steel business proved to be a problem. *Forbes* magazine commented on September 15, 1973:

Steel mills across the United States are running at 100% and industry's profits were up a handsome 40 per cent in the first half. At the Chicago and Youngstown, Ohio, plants of Lykes-Youngstown Corporation, operations have been at 100 per cent of capacity, but the company finished the second quarter with an operating deficit of nearly $2 million before extraordinary credits. . . . How can a company do so badly in so strong an economy?

The answer was that machinery "kept breaking down at such a rate that it's legitimate to ask if more than steel equipment problems aren't bugging Lykes-Youngstown" (ibid.). Lykes was not able to handle all the orders it received and had to shift business to other companies. The result was that the "additional sales, instead of being highly profitable, brought in nearly as much added costs."[6]

The company's failure to profit from the steel boom is related to the lack of investment in production facilities. After-the-fact analysis of company finances substantiates what the workers on the shop floor knew firsthand: Equipment was being allowed to run down; there was not even basic maintenance, much less any

Table 2.3. *Steel company reinvested profits (per ton of steel shipped)*

Year	Youngstown Sheet and Tube	American Iron and Steel Institute average	U.S. Steel
1972	$(−4.22)	$ 4.06	$ 3.38
1973	3.50	7.44	8.67
1974	6.45	16.45	20.04
1975	7.21	11.72	23.31
1976	(−1.71)	7.81	12.18

Source: James W. Smith (1978).

modernization of the plant. Figures in the United Steelworkers' brief to the Justice Department show that, at the same time that Lykes was extracting relatively higher than average dividends from the company, its reinvestment in maintenance and modernization was woefully inadequate. The figures on reinvested profits show that Youngstown Sheet and Tube was well below the industry average in the years 1972–6 (see Table 2.3; it should be noted that these figures are for the entire company, including both Chicago and Youngstown districts). These figures justify the charges made by Warren Freed, a former Sheet and Tube official and president of another local company, before the U.S. Senate Subcommittee on Anti-Trust and Monopoly. Freed testified that Youngstown Sheet and Tube was a "healthy, productive company at the time of the takeover, while major construction funds to keep the plant up to date were refused by Lykes afterwards." Freed further stated "It took only seven years for some steamboat captains from New Orleans that didn't know a damned thing about running a steel company to wash down the tubes what it took seventy years to build" (Youngstown *Vindicator*, March 24, 1979).

Even with their obsolete facilities, though, the Youngstown district operations were not doing too badly. Jennings Lambeth, company president, made the surprising statement at the news conference to announce the Campbell Works shutdown that the Youngstown operations had actually been more profitable than the newer facilities at Indiana Harbor. "Comparative profit figures for the Youngstown and Chicago districts show the Chicago district lost money in three out of four recent fiscal years when Youngstown mills were showing a profit." (This comment made at the end of the press conference was evidently not intended for the record, but was caught by a reporter whose tape recorder happened to be still running.)[7] One production line – the manufacture of seamless pipe used widely in oil drilling – continued strong as oil exploration expanded after 1973, evidently accounting for the overall profitability of the Youngstown district. As late as 1977, Standard and Poor Corporation, a leading stock market analyst firm, observed of Lykes's steel operation: "Efforts to modernize and expand steel facilities could bring improved long-range earnings, growth, and stability" (*Standard NYSE Reports*, June 22, 1977).

But according to John Stone, vice-president for operations, the problems at Campbell Works were mounting steadily. Labor costs for running the small blast furnaces, as well as for the slow open hearth furnaces, made Youngstown steel comparatively expensive in a highly competitive market period. Furthermore, steel from the open hearths could not meet the demands for precise metallurgical qualities demanded by customers. The 79-inch hot-strip mill that had revitalized the company in 1935 lacked the power and the capacity to produce the size of coils and the accuracy of gauge required by the auto industry (among others). As costs mounted, the company could no longer afford to carry the amount of inventory that permitted a quick response to steel orders. These problems began to affect the bottom line of Sheet and Tube's financial statement. An independent study after the mill closing (based on Sheet and Tube figures) revealed the losses on operations other than seamless pipe (Table 2.4).

What to do about this situation was the agenda for a special meeting of the Lykes board of directors in Pittsburgh on Sunday, September 18, 1977. A study dealing with the mounting losses had been initiated at the highest levels of the company (even some vice-presidents were unaware of it). At the same time, negotiations were under way with the banks that were Sheet and Tube's major creditors. But the banks refused to extend further credit, and the directors could see no solution other than to close down the unprofitable portions of the company's operations at the Campbell Works. This decision was announced by Jennings Lambeth, Sheet and Tube president, the following morning in Youngstown. The company would begin immediately to shut down most of

Table 2.4. *Estimates of net income for closed portions
of Youngstown Sheet and Tube Campbell Works*

Year	Income ($000)
1974	10,737
1975	−58,444
1976	−82,938
1977 (6 months)	−88,390

Source: Beetle (1977), 31.

the Campbell Works, retaining only the seamless pipe mill in operation. Layoffs would begin the following Friday. It was expected that total terminations in the Youngstown district (including salaried employees and union workers) would reach five thousand.

From the company's point of view, three major factors were involved in the decision to shut down the Campbell Works. The first was that the company was experiencing a devastating profit squeeze from two directions. On the one hand, despite the best efforts of its experienced steelworkers, the labor costs associated with running the Campbell were high. On the other hand, competitive pressures from foreign steelmakers intensified as the industry went into a slump in 1975. The existing profit squeeze was exacerbated by competition with foreign steel. In the cutthroat steel market of 1976–7, both European and Japanese producers were underselling American companies in the U.S. market. Precisely at the time when its low productivity was squeezing profits, Sheet and Tube was forced to discount its prices as much as 25% to meet foreign competition (Beetle 1977: 19). At this rate, the company was losing money (except for the pipe division) on virtually every ton of product shipped.

The second major factor was the cost of unavoidable capital expenditures the company was facing. It has been estimated that the company needed to spend $270 million on its plant just to stay in business, that is, to maintain production at its existing (unprofitable) level. Again the squeeze came from two directions at once.

Steel plants are not only expensive to build the first time;

portions of the plant become "used up" in the steelmaking process and must be regularly rebuilt. Blast furnaces, for example,
have a "campaign life" of approximately seven years, after which
they must be relined with new fire brick, a process that in 1977
cost $15 million per furnace. To reline the blast furnaces (and
introduce other needed improvements while the furnaces were
down) would total approximately $100 million. The coke plant
also needed a $67 million rebuilding job, just to keep going.
These costs were for nondeferrable maintenance.

At the same time, the Campbell Works was under pressure
from the Environmental Protection Agency to meet air and water
pollution control standards. The pressure had been eased somewhat in 1975 by the "Train decision" – an administrative ruling
by EPA director Russell Train granting the Mahoning Valley steel
plants extra time for complying with EPA standards. However, a
lawsuit was filed against the EPA by the Sierra Club in federal
district court, asking that the original timetable be reinstated.
(The Sierra Club argued that EPA standards were a matter of
statute and could not be vacated by administrative discretion.) On
Friday, September 16 – two days before the fateful meeting of the
Lykes board – the federal district court in Pittsburgh found in
favor of the Sierra Club and vacated the Train decision. This
action meant that the price tag for keeping the Campbell Works
running was increased by $103 million. (Jennings Lambeth stated
that the federal court decision had no impact on the board's
decision of September 18. By the time of the actual meeting, the
closing decision was evidently a foregone conclusion.)

The price for relining the blast furnaces, rebuilding the coke
plant, and retrofitting pollution control equipment came to $270
million. And these costs would serve only to maintain productive
capacity at existing levels. Modernization of the plant (to replace
the open hearth furnaces with oxygen furnaces and modify the
rolling mills) would require still millions more. Jennings Lambeth
estimated that it would take $550 million to keep the plant in
operation.

The third factor in the closing decision was that the company's
banks were unwilling to extend credit in these amounts. At the
time, Youngstown Sheet and Tube's debt structure was approaching 40% of its capital value. Traditionally, this has been seen as a
kind of limit in American steel financing, which generally oper-
ates in the range of 35% debt, 65% equity. As losses with the

Table 2.5. *Loans to Japanese steel industry*

Bank	1975 ($000,000)	1977 ($000,000)	Percent increase ($000,000)
Citibank	58.94	230.44	391
Chase Manhattan	59.19	204.53	346
Chemical Bank	15.10	82.55	541

Source: Kelly (1978), 5.

existing plant mounted up, the banks simply drew the line and refused to provide capital for the needed modernization.

As we have seen, the Lykes Corporation must bear a heavy responsibility for its failure to improve the Youngstown facilities. But the banking system also shares that responsibility. Sheet and Tube's being cut off by its banks would perhaps not be so noteworthy were it not for the fact that the very same banks that were refusing loans in Youngstown were increasing their loans to Japanese steel. And the Japanese, in turn, are noteworthy for financing their steel industry at a typical ratio of 85% debt, 15% equity. The largest steel company in the world, Nippon Steel, was operating in the late 1970s at about 90% debt level.

The role of bank "redlining" in the Youngstown shutdown has been investigated by the Ohio Public Interest Campaign (OPIC). The three principal banks providing credit to Lykes in 1968, before the takeover, were Chemical Bank, Chase Manhattan, and Citibank. All three drastically reduced their lending to Lykes after 1975. By 1977, Chemical's outstanding loan to Lykes was probably about $7.3 million, Citibank's under $5 million, Chase Manhattan's even less. Yet at the same time as these banks were cutting off credit to Lykes, they were significantly expanding their loans to Japanese steel companies (Table 2.5). The OPIC report argues that these banks share part of the responsibility for the Youngstown shutdown: "When these banks initially helped Lykes take over Youngstown they assumed responsibility for the future of the new conglomerate, yet their subsequent curtailment of credit to Lykes represents a very real abandonment of this responsibility" (Kelly and Schutes 1978: 3).

The information provided by OPIC is consistent with another study of American bank lending to Japanese steel. Shapiro and

Volk (1979: 15) found that, for the same period (1975–7), American bank lending to the six largest Japanese steel firms increased from $270 million to $1,033.5 million. The conclusion is obvious: American banks were helping to finance the Japanese steel development that was at least partially responsible for steel plant closings in Youngstown.

One further element in the paradox is that they were very possibly doing it with the Youngstown workers' own savings. A significant portion of potential capital for reinvestment in Northern industry belongs to the workers themselves in the form of pension funds. In 1978, private, state, and local pension funds amounted to more than $400 billion, with federal pension funds accounting for another $100 billion. Approximately half of the $400 billion in nonfederal pension funds represents the deferred savings of union workers and public employees of the sixteen states in the Northeast–Midwest industrial corridor. Normally, workers have little or no control over pension fund investments. Pension fund management is heavily concentrated in major banks; in 1975, one hundred banks controlled $145.6 billion in pension capital. Although about half of the total nonfederal pension funds were invested in the stocks of major corporations, that pool of investment capital was often directed away from unionized Northern industries and strained local economies:

The irony of it all is that much of the private sector which is now severing its bonds with organized labor and the Graybelt states belongs to the very power blocs it is deserting. For years, the unions and the northern industrial states have been literally chasing after their own funds in what amounts to one of the most macabre Catch 22's in contemporary economic history. The fact is, union moneys are being used to destroy union jobs and state moneys are being used to undermine state economies. This is a contradiction of such monumental proportions that it would be almost amusing were it not for the cruel results. (Rifkin and Barber 1978: 80)

It is possible, without stretching the imagination too far, to construct the following scenario: Youngstown workers' pension funds are placed under the control of major banks. The banks consider Youngstown a poor or less profitable investment, and use the funds instead to finance developments in the Sunbelt or overseas. In effect, Youngstown workers' pensions (a form of savings) are being used to finance the Japanese competition that is putting Youngstown workers out of a job. The actual control of

Youngstown steelworkers' pension funds has not, to my knowledge, been investigated. This paradigm did, however, play a role in the thinking of the members of the Ecumenical Coalition.

From the vantage point of history, it is clear that the financial strategy of the Lykes Corporation contributed to the shutdown of the Campbell Works. We do not know for sure that Youngstown Sheet and Tube could have ridden out the steel crisis of the late 1970s, without the Lykes merger and given a different set of management and investment decisions. What is certain, though, is that the merger scenario worked exactly as Department of Justice analyst George Schueller said it would, that the Lykes takeover would be to the detriment of the Youngstown company.

CHAPTER III

Shutdown

In late summer 1977, everyone knew that the steel industry in Youngstown was having troubles. Over the past ten years, no less than 6,600 basic steel jobs in the Mahoning Valley had been phased out, dropping from 32,000 in 1967 to 25,400 in 1977. In the first half-year, the largest steel producer in the valley, Sheet and Tube, had posted substantial losses. Concerned about the situation, United Steelworkers district director Frank Leseganich and local president Bill Sferra talked to company officials about the situation, but were assured that Sheet and Tube had no plans to shut down any Youngstown facilities.

At a luncheon meeting of Youngstown's Downtown Kiwanis Club on Friday September 16, William Sullivan, having just returned from Washington, where he testified on economic conditions in the Mahoning Valley, "gave a realistic picture of the industrial outlook here but an encouraging one" (Youngstown *Vindicator*, September 19, 1977). The Valley had not yet lost a major steel producer. Republic Steel had announced a $160 million capital investment. U.S. Steel had agreed to comply with environmental restrictions on its Youngstown-area plants. Sullivan thought that Sheet and Tube losses in the second half of the year would not be as heavy as they had been in the first half. Meanwhile, down at the open hearth shop in the Campbell Works, some of the old furnaces had been fitted with oxygen lances to improve their efficiency. One of the turns (as shifts are called in the steel industry) had set new tonnage records that week. In Youngstown there was guarded optimism about the future, as people took off for the weekend and Lykes directors prepared to converge on Pittsburgh for their Sunday meeting.

The shutdown announcement on Monday morning, September 19, clearly came as a surprise. A short list of public officials and community and union representatives were contacted early Monday morning; they were asked to come to a briefing at Sheet and Tube headquarters by company president Jennings Lambeth. By 10:00 a.m., the shutdown announcement was given to the media.

The company would be shutting down the major part of its operations at the Campbell Works, beginning with the blooming mill at 7:00 a.m. the following Friday. The blast furnaces, open hearths, and rolling mills would be shut down by the end of December. The company would concentrate its production at its Indiana Harbor facility, with company headquarters being transferred to downtown Chicago. At the Campbell Works, only the coke oven and seamless tube mill, manufacturing pipe for oil drilling, would remain in production. Brier Hill would likewise remain operating to provide the rounds for the seamless mill at Campbell. In all, about five thousand of the company's currently almost nine thousand jobs in Youngstown would be eliminated. The company said in a prepared statement that "this action is taken with great reluctance recognizing the impact of this decision on our many loyal employees, their families and the communities who have had a deep involvement in the Campbell Works operations since the founding of the company" (Youngstown *Vindicator*, September 20, 1977).

Community and workers were caught in stunned surprise – perhaps more at the manner of the announcement than at the news itself. "It was like Pearl Harbor," said veteran steelworker George Chornock, 62; "we heard only last Friday that there was no chance that this plant would be shut down." Len Balluck, a member of the record-breaking turn at the open hearth only the week before, was coldly furious at being "thrown on the garbage heap." He refused to go to the company office to pick up his prize – a windbreaker with the company logo.

Youngstown mayor Jack Hunter called the shutdown "the worst possible news that your elected public officials, straining to meet the challenge of major problems, could have received." George Reiss, business editor of the Youngstown *Vindicator*, warned that

the decision will not only wipe out the jobs of about 5,000 Youngstown area employees, many with up to 30 to 40 years of service, but will

indirectly end or affect many thousands of other northern Ohio jobs
– those of railroaders, truckers, scrapyard workers or miners, Lake
Erie dockworkers, retail workers, bank employees, professional men,
teachers, and numerous public employees. (Youngstown *Vindicator*,
September 20, 1977)

The *Vindicator* editorialized, "Youngstown Sheet and Tube
Corp.'s announcement Monday was the worst single blow ever
suffered by the economy of the Mahoning Valley" (ibid.). The
editorial went on to voice the sense of shock that was based on
the symbolic identification between community and company:
"Sheet and Tube and Youngstown have been so closely linked
since the company was born – its advertising offers "Youngstown
Steel" – that the public perceived no hint that the measure to
'strengthen and streamline' the company would mean such drastic
actions here" (ibid.).

The Sheet and Tube mill had been for three generations of
workers the reliable guarantor of their household economy. "The
older, the first generation would often look over the top of the
hill to see whether there was smoke coming out of the stacks – to
him that meant prosperity, employment, it meant food on the
table," stated Sam Myers, a Campbell resident and veteran steel
worker (Youngstown *Vindicator*, February 28, 1978). The mill
provided not only an economic livelihood, but the structure of a
meaningful life for generations of fathers and sons who believed
in what they were doing, who found a kind of mystique in taking
coal and ore from the earth and forging it into the stuff for
machines and buildings and bridges. In the old days, it was tough
and dirty labor, but there was an aesthetic satisfaction in being at
the "front end" of the process that turned out the substance of
cities and civilization. For hundreds of teenagers graduating from
Campbell Memorial High School, becoming an adult meant following one's father over the plant bridge across Wilson Avenue
and the railroad tracks into the tangle of steel pictured in the film
The Deerhunter. One steelworker in his 50s recalled on the day
he left the Campbell Works for the last time: "I was seventeen
when I followed my father (he's dead now, God rest his soul) for
the first time to work in the mill. I remember I was so scared
from the fire and the heat that I nearly ran away. But I stayed."
The mill was not only a part of the local economy; it was part of
the local myth that held together work and family, craft and
aesthetics, fellowship and tradition. The realization that the mill

would be gone constituted a kind of psychological earthquake; it was as if a landmark for community and personal identity had suddenly disappeared.

Shutdown as Local Disaster

An economist might point out that the steel companies had been withdrawing capital and jobs from Youngstown for at least the past decade and that the Campbell Works shutdown was simply an acceleration of that process. But for the people directly affected, such an economic analysis would have been too abstract to describe what happened in experiential terms. Gerald Dickey has said, "That is a day in the Mahoning Valley that the people will never forget. They remember it the way people remember the attack on Pearl Harbor, or the day and the moment that John Kennedy was shot." It felt to steelworkers at the Campbell mill as if their livelihood and way of life had been wiped out by the news of that Monday morning, just as surely as if a flood or tornado had roared through the Mahoning Valley. In fact, this kind of economic disaster might well be worse. Buildings flattened by a flood could be rebuilt, but a mill abandoned by its company was more likely to represent a permanent loss, both to individual workers and to the community as a whole.

From both personal experience and community memory, people in Youngstown knew what the stress of unemployment could mean. Many workers would have a hard time finding new jobs in Youngstown; they might have to move, even split up their families for a while. Women might become the principal wage earners, leaving their husbands home to care for the children. Friendships centered around the plant and union hall would dissolve. Unemployment would bring self-doubt and depression; some would drink too heavily. Marriages and families, under the combined economic and emotional stress, would suffer; some marriages would break up.

What people in Youngstown knew from experience is largely confirmed by formal research (though there is little evidence that the research literature contributed to Youngstown's perception of the problem). A growing body of research has looked at the effects of economic dislocation in general, and plant shutdowns in particular, on both individual workers and the communities where they live.

Table 3.1. *Incidence of pathology related to increased unemployment*

Measure of social trauma	Incidence of pathology related to 1% increase in unemployment[a]
Total mortality	36,887
Cardiovascular	20,240
Cirrhosis of liver	495
Suicide	920
Homicide	648
State mental hospital, first admissions	4,227
State prison admissions	3,340

[a] Based on 1970 population, with the 1% change in unemployment rate sustained over a 6-year period.
Source: Brenner (1976), 88.

Studies at the macrolevel, first of all, point out the human costs of economic dislocation. Ever since Durkheim's classic study of suicide, social scientists have focused on the relationship between general economic conditions and social pathology. In the 1970s, research for the Joint Economic Committee of the U.S. Congress by Professor Harvey Brenner at Johns Hopkins University pointed out the impact of unemployment on American society as a whole. For the years studied (1940–73), high unemployment was associated with increased mortality and a higher incidence of mental illness, and criminality (Table 3.1).

By 1977, the year of the Campbell Works shutdown, already a good deal was known about the effects of a major plant shutdown on individual workers. A summary of this research states: "Buried in the statistics on employment are the instances where the job leaves the employee rather than the employee leaving the job or being laid off temporarily. When jobs leave employees . . . the social and personal costs can be devastatingly high" (Mick 1975: 203). A reading of the plant-closing literature reveals consistent patterns in the experience of workers whose jobs quit them.

Unemployment. Workers who lost their jobs in a plant shutdown often experienced lengthy unemployment. A study of plant closings in five cities found high rates of unemployment among the laid-off workers one year after the shutdown: "65 percent in East St. Louis, 34 percent in Columbus, 31 percent in Fargo, 53 percent in Oklahoma City, 22 percent in Peoria" (Wilcock and Franke 1968: 66). In another study of workers laid off at the old Packard plant in Detroit, only 45% were employed 27 months after the shutdown (Aiken, Ferman, and Sheppard 1968: 48). Age, skill level, educational level, and race are factors that affect the probability of reemployment. In the five-city survey, "combinations of advanced age, low level of education, and lack of skill were common. Any one of these characteristics reduced greatly the chance of finding new work; in combination, they produced bleak job prospects and in many cases an 'unwanted worker'" (Wilcock and Franke 1968: 66).

A study of the Wickwire steel plant closing in Buffalo in 1963 confirmed these findings. Older workers and the less educated were more likely to be downwardly mobile, to accept any job available, even in a different occupational category. The same study also found major differences in reemployment patterns between white-collar and blue-collar workers, especially when combined with age and/or other factors: Thus "only 2 percent of the blue-collar respondents 50 and over had found new employment at the time of the study" (Foltman 1968: 107).

Mobility. Blue-collar workers showed a strong attachment to the communities where they lived and often would not consider moving away. This was based both on personal attachment to extended families and the ethnic characteristics of particular communities, and on an economic calculus of interests. When U.S. Steel closed a mill in Ellwood City, Pennsylvania, in the 1940s, workers were offered jobs in Gary, Indiana. Their negative reaction is typical:

I definitely do not intend to go. It takes five years to establish yourself in a new community. I have, let's say about ten years to get going. By the time I have moved along, built up some seniority and all that, it would be time for me to retire. I'm not changing my mind.

We have almost finished paying for our home, and of course we don't like the idea of moving. (Walker 1950: 169, 171)

The preference of blue-collar workers for remaining in their present communities, in spite of economic hardship, is a consistent theme in the literature.[1]

Health. Like any significant stress, unemployment can have an effect on both physical and mental health. Medical research on workers in a plant-closing situation found an increased tendency toward cardiovascular and gastrointestinal disorders (Cobb and Kasl 1977). Other research on the psychological effects of sudden unemployment noted in workers a tendency to define the world as unintelligible, hostile, unpredictable, and unsatisfying, leading to social withdrawal and a lessened ability to cope with their situation (Aiken et al. 1968: 86). Some research even noted higher suicide levels (Cobb and Kasl 1977).

Decline in social contacts. Job termination was associated with the destruction of integrated, closely knit patterns of life both inside and outside the plant (Aiken et al. 1968). Friendships formed on the job dissolved, particularly in urban areas (Ferman and Aiken 1964; Slote 1969; Cobb and Kasl 1977). This withdrawal in turn decreased the chances for finding another job, since blue-collar workers generally depended on an extensive network of relatives and friends in the job-hunting process (Aiken et al. 1968).

By 1977, research in sociology, psychology, and physiology had pieced together a fairly detailed picture of the way an economic disaster could be expected to affect individual workers. Less detailed knowledge was generally available on the impact of such an economic event on the community. One reason may be that events such as a sudden, major plant closing often fade into a picture of generalized urban decline (Rust 1975). Another reason may be that urban economics was a relatively new field and simply had not yet developed the case study evidence.

The best information about the impact of a major shutdown on the community can be derived from theories of economic growth and from procedures for measuring the contribution of different kinds of business to a local economy. One theory is economic base analysis. A key distinction in this theory is the difference between an "export" industry (producing goods or services for consumption outside the community) and the "local" economy (the complex of grocery stores, auto dealers, service stations – the panoply of commercial and service establishments that supply the needs of the local community). New jobs in an export industry (such as steel or meat packing) will create a given number of jobs in the local economy. Different technical approaches can be used to calculate empirically the "economic base multiplier" for each urban economy. One frequently used rule of thumb is that, on the average, there are two jobs in the local economy for every one in the export basic economy (e.g., W. F. Smith 1975).

Estimating the impact of a shutdown on the city's export industry makes use of the same methods. Following the rule of thumb, every job subtracted from the economic base will eventually – without some intervention – cause the loss of two more jobs in the local retail and service economy.

In some circumstances, a major plant shutdown can cause the same level of stress for a local community as a natural disaster. There are two important differences, however.

The first difference is the timing of the impact. Research on communities struck by natural disasters found that the impact was felt primarily in the short term. After the initial impact was a "decaying effect" – the persistence of the damage beyond the first moment of destruction. "Delayed effects" – in which the patterns of normal life were still disrupted – lasted into the second and third months. By the end of the year, however, the communities studied had essentially returned to normal.

In a plant closing, by contrast, there is no immediately visible damage to inspect or dig out from or repair. There is no rush of injured victims to hospital emergency rooms. The streets and houses look the same as they did the day before. In their retail purchases, laid-off workers may be able to maintain almost the same living standard for the 26 or 52 weeks during which they receive unemployment benefits.

Only after some time, perhaps a year or more, does the severity of the shutdown begin to be felt. Retail shops and service businesses may close. The value of housing stock may decline. Younger people, the better educated, and more skilled workers move out of town to find work, leaving the community with an aging, less educated, and lower skilled population. Income levels and tax revenues decline, at the very time that costs for community services and welfare may be on the increase. Over time, the consequences of a plant closing can approach disaster proportions.

The second difference between a natural disaster and a plant closing concerns the prospects for repairing the damage. Research on natural disasters found that

many disaster agency administrators, some local officials, and even some disaster scholars say (usually in private for fear of having their statements misconstrued) that apart from the deaths and injuries, a disaster may be the best thing that can happen to a community, particularly in economic terms. (Friesema and Lineberry 1979: 14)

The idea that a natural disaster – whatever its horrors in the short term – can be a form of instant urban renewal is based on the assumption that new capital will come into the community to replace the physical property lost in the disaster. This new capital typically will come from insurance and government disaster recovery programs. The advantage to the community is that it can start up again with a new and more modern physical plant, giving the community something of a competitive edge over its status before the disaster: "To observe a significant economic change in an area, we would expect that a significant portion of the capital stock would have to be destroyed. Otherwise consumers and producers are still operating with the basic framework they did before the disaster" (ibid.: 177). Where the community's capital stock remained unaffected by the disaster, there would be little economic change.

The difference with a major plant closing in a community's export sector is that it strikes at the basic economic foundation of the community. The ripple effect of a plant closing spreads out more slowly than floodwater. But it does not recede as quickly.

Severity of the Sheet and Tube Shutdown

Research on the way communities respond to natural disasters reveals two concepts that are helpful for understanding what happened in Youngstown.

First is the *severity* of the impact. Severity is the measurement of the actual damage inflicted by the disaster, as counted by the number of deaths and injuries and estimates of property damage. Severity is distinguished from the force of the physical event itself (e.g., the wind velocity of a hurricane or the Richter scale ranking of an earthquake). The severity of a natural disaster depends not only on its physical force, but on the circumstances of the community where it strikes. For example, the Galveston hurricane of 1900 caused six thousand fatalities, but the hurricane of 1961 left only six persons dead. The difference was due not to any striking difference in the force of the hurricane, but to the construction of a sea wall and the development of an early warning system.

Second is the quality of *social response* to the event. A physical event becomes a disaster when it exceeds the normal crisis-management capabilities of a community. What might be only a minor crisis for one community could be a full-blown disaster somewhere else, depending on the community's organizational and institutional capacity (Wenger 1978).[2]

In the Mahoning Valley, the tremors of the shutdown announcement reached deep into the economic foundations of the community. But the severity of the jolt was not dramatically visible. There were no victims under the rubble that Monday afternoon, no blood, no sirens. There was no need for emergency crews providing food, clothing, and shelter. The layoffs began only days and weeks later. The shock consisted not of physical injury or damage, but of the anticipation of what lay ahead.

For the workers, there was no real problem in the short term regarding the physical necessities of life. When they picked up their last paychecks and gathered their gear from their lockers, they became eligible for an elaborate range of unemployment benefits. Workers, first of all, received compensation from the state unemployment insurance program, ranging in Ohio from $106 to $161 per week, depending on the number of dependents. This amount was augmented by "supplementary unemployment benefits" (SUB), a program negotiated by the United Steelworkers in 1956, so that workers laid off in the downturns of the highly cyclical steel industry would not have to depend solely on state unemployment compensation. SUB payments added an average of $70 per week to the benefits package. Finally, Sheet and Tube workers were also eligible for a trade readjustment allowance (TRA), under a program created by the Federal Trade Adjustment Act of 1974. Funded by tariffs and fines paid by foreign companies convicted of "dumping," TRA was intended to help workers who had been laid off and were seeking new jobs because of import competition. TRA guaranteed workers 70% of their weekly pay (up to $208 maximum) for a full year, tax free. In addition, TRA provided expense money for travel outside the area to seek a new job (80% of expenses to $500). In the combination of benefits, Sheet and Tube workers were able to collect up to 90% of their average pay for a full year after being laid off.

Instead of going on layoff status, workers also had the option of accepting a severance payment of $750, thereby cutting ties with the company entirely. Very few took this option. Another option for workers in their 40s and older was early retirement. In the steel industry contract negotiated earlier in 1977, the United Steelworkers had arranged a special employment security provision for employees with 20 or more years of service, called the "Rule of 65" plan. Basically, the company was obligated to provide the 20-year employee "suitable long term employment" or provide retirement under the Rule of 65. The 20-year employee was eligible if "(1) his age plus service equaled 65 or more, (2) he was off work because of a shutdown, extended layoff or disability, and (3) his company failed to offer him 'suitable long term employment' within the two years following his last day worked" (United Steelworkers of America n.d.). With the two-year provision, an employee could "creep" toward retirement eligibility. Thus a 41-year-old worker with 20 years of service (total, 61) would be eligible for retirement if he were not offered "suitable long term employment" within two years of layoff or disability (age 43 + 22 years of service). Rule of 65 retirement included the regular pension plus a $300 monthly supplement payable until the employee became eligible for Social Security. The $300 monthly supplement was reduced if the employee earned more than $4,500 a year in other employment.

One problem was that the Rule of 65 program was due to go into effect on January 1, 1978. According to the company timetable, the terminations would take effect by December. Thus the status of the workers affected, as laid off (and therefore eligible for the plan) or terminated (and therefore ineligible), was a crucial point. There was even some suspicion that the company had deliberately timed the shutdown to take place before the Rule of 65 program went into effect. The union argued that, since the company was continuing to operate the Brier Hill Works and portions of the Campbell Works in Youngstown, the workers should be considered laid off. The union viewpoint ultimately prevailed.

Union officials were proud of the benefits and retirement options they had negotiated. But when they called special meetings at the local halls to explain the unemployment compensation package and retirement opportunities to their members, they met with a surprise. Instead of the gratitude they expected, they ran into a chorus of voices asking what they were doing to get the jobs back. From steelworkers themselves the insistent refrain was "I don't want no relief." To Mahoning Valley steelworkers, "welfare" was a dirty word. Steelworkers had always lived with the reality of temporary layoffs, but long-term unemployment was a situation for which they were unprepared, both psychologically and economically.

Substantial though the benefits were, they were obviously a temporary, stopgap measure. They would cover groceries and housing and almost the same standard of living for a year. But the benefits would run out, and most steelworkers would not be able to count on any further assistance. Ohio regulations prohibited general welfare from going to anyone with $12,000 equity in a home, or who owned a car worth more than $1,000, or who had savings of $300, or who possessed any stocks or bonds. Furthermore, health insurance ran out at the end of six months (for workers with two to ten years of service) or one year (for workers with more than ten years of service), often at a time of life for workers and their families when health concerns were becoming increasingly prevalent and costly.

As workers looked down the road during the first layoffs in September, it was difficult to imagine how their situation could be anything but worse a year hence. If they were eligible, they might elect early retirement. But this would lock them into an income level well below the regular pay scale, and one that could hardly be expected to keep up with inflation. For workers in their 40s and 50s who were not eligible for retirement, the likelihood of finding an equal-paying job was slim. For younger workers, the possibilities were somewhat better. Yet 20% of the basic steel jobs in Youngstown had just disappeared. There was a strong likelihood of further steel shutdowns in Youngstown, throwing even more steelworkers into the local labor market. The steel industry nation-wide was in a retrenchment phase offering little possibility for steel employment elsewhere in the country. In a local economy so strongly dependent on steel, employment possibilities in nonsteel areas would be limited and would very likely pay far less than steel wages. The unemployment benefits brought breathing time, but they only postponed the real problem: finding jobs in the Youngstown economy.

Immediate, "back of the envelope" estimates of the severity of the Campbell Works shutdown were that, in addition to the 5,000 projected steel layoffs, another $2 \times 5,000 = 10,000$ jobs would be lost to the area economy. In the context of average annual employment, these figures represented almost 20% of the jobs in basic steel and more than 7% of the total employment in the metropolitan area.

Early estimates of this sort proved to be very rough, having about the same precision as early damage estimates from a natural disaster. Part of the problem in forming accurate estimates of the severity of the shutdown lay in pinning down the number of jobs actually terminated. Precise figures were hard to come by. The layoffs, first of all, were spread over a three-month period, from late September to December; they did not all happen at once. Also, some workers were placed on layoff status, called back to work (possibly at a lower-paying job) for a time, before finally being terminated. There was never any single list available outside the company (and possibly not even within it) of all the workers actually affected. Consequently, researchers are left with estimates by the company, and principally by union officials and the Ohio Bureau of Employment Services. Approximately a year after the shutdown announcement, the consensus was that terminations of unionized employees never reached the 5,000 estimate, but totaled only about 4,200 production and maintenance workers. In the winter of 1978, union officials estimated that, of that number, about 2,200 were still unemployed, 1,500 had accepted retirement, and the rest had found other work or relocated out of the area.

At the time of the shutdown, some precise data were available on the role of the steel industry as a whole in the local economy from the 1973 study conducted by the Western Reserve Economic Development Agency in the context of pollution regulation. WREDA investigated eight steel plants on the Mahoning River belonging to four companies: Youngstown Sheet and Tube, U.S. Steel, Republic Steel, and Copperweld, representing 85% of the steel production in the Youngstown–Warren metropolitan area. The study looked at the direct impact on the local economy of steel company employee payrolls, the interindustry effect of local purchases and 'sales by the steel companies, and the secondary impact of purchases of goods and services by steel company employees. The study also estimated the tax revenues to local governments from the steel companies. The investigators concluded that the four major steel companies were responsible for between 19 and 27% of all jobs in Mahoning and Trumbull Counties and for 20.5 to 27.8% of local tax revenues (Ernst and Ernst Management Consulting Services 1973: Vol. 2, V-15).

Table 3.2. *Campbell and Struthers: revenues from incomes earned at Campbell Works*

Company	Total city income tax	Total from Sheet and Tube	Percentage of total from Sheet and Tube
Campbell	$1,608,744	$1,241,496	77.2
Struthers	841,173	319,069	37.9

Source: Western Reserve Economic Development Agency.

After the Campbell Works shutdown was announced, several agencies became involved in a general effort to pin down the effects of the estimated 5,000-job cutback at Sheet and Tube. The Battelle Institute of Columbus, Ohio, studied the direct impact on the Ohio economy for the Ohio Energy and Resource Development Agency. Battelle's input–output simulation estimated that total state output would decrease by $427.7 million. Total job losses, statewide, were estimated at 11,199. This information became known and was circulated in Youngstown through Battelle's connection with the Mahoning Valley Economic Development Committee, formed by Congressman Charles Carney in response to the shutdown announcement (see Chapter IV).

Local public officials were quick to voice the problems that the shutdown would cause for municipalities depending on Sheet and Tube for a significant portion of their tax base. WREDA found that Campbell and Struthers, which collected city income tax on paychecks earned at the mill, would be particularly hard hit. In 1977, these two municipalities derived a significant portion of their income tax revenues from incomes earned at Sheet and Tube (Table 3.2). In Campbell, more than half of the salary and operating costs of providing basic police and fire protection services were provided for via Sheet and Tube income taxes.

A detailed study of the economic and demographic impact of the shutdown on the Youngstown area was done for the Ecumenical Coalition by Christine Franz-Goldman (1978), under contract with the Coalition's consultants, the National Center for Economic Alternatives. Her estimate of the socioeconomic costs of the shutdown is based on the conservative figure of 4,100 jobs terminated. In addition to demographic and other aggregate data, she employed a 360-case survey of laid-off Sheet and Tube workers. The overall purpose of the study was to estimate costs of the shutdown to the local economy, on the one hand, and to governmental units, on the other hand, and to determine how such costs would be affected by a reopening of the Campbell Works. Hence the time period for estimating the costs was September 1977 (the shutdown) to December 1980 (when a reopening was to take place).

The annual payroll of the 4,100 laid-off workers was $72.98 million. Because part of that personal income was replaced with TRA and other unemployment benefits, not all of that amount was immediately lost to the local economy. For the 27-month period, the net payroll loss to the local economy was calculated at $52.8–70.5 million. This, in turn, meant a loss of retail sales of $40.4–54 million (based on the average of approximately 76% of income being spent in the retail marketplace in northern Ohio). Secondary job loss and the consequent loss of further retail sales increased these totals still further. Estimates of the total direct and indirect impact on the metropolitan economy for the 27-month period are as follows (ibid.: 104):

Loss of earnings $86.9–134 million
Loss of retail sales   66.5–102.6 million

The study also provides a detailed accounting of tax losses, from the local to federal level, and of program costs to various levels of government. Tax losses for the 27-month period would run $26.8–32 million. Program costs, including $32.6 million for TRA, would total $34.2–37.9 million. The total expense to federal, state, and local governments for the shutdown would be $61–70 million (ibid.: 192).

This accounting of costs of the Campbell Works shutdown differs in two important ways from the accounting of the costs of a natural disaster. First, these losses of income and sales and taxes, as well as some of the program costs, represent continuing costs to the local community. They are not the one-time expenses associated with the loss of business and reconstruction after a hurricane. Without the replacement of the economic base, the cost of an economic disaster continues indefinitely. Second, a plant closing is far less likely to function as "instant urban renewal." A natural disaster brings new capital *into* a commuity from insurance and government grants and loans. A plant closing, in contrast, represents the flight of capital *from* a local community, frequently with no immediate prospects for replacement of the lost investment.

In the days and weeks shortly after it was announced, the Campbell Works shutdown looked and felt like a disaster both to workers and to the immediate community. But the impact was masked by its timing. In a natural disaster, the typical pattern shows recovery in swing within six months to a year after the event. In the case of the Campbell Works shutdown, the impact was more drawn out. The full effect would not be felt until a year or so after the shutdown.

CHAPTER IV

Coping with Crisis: Community Response to the Shutdown

On Tuesday, the day after Jennings Lambeth announced that the Campbell Works would be shutting down, many people got up and went to work the same as they had the day before. But for hundreds of workers, that normal pattern of life would be broken by the end of the week. For thousands, their lives as steelworkers would be ending within two or three months.

As steelworkers and community leaders tried to figure out the severity of the plant closing for themselves and their community, a pattern of response began to take shape. Once again, the study of natural disasters is helpful for understanding the community response to the Campbell Works shutdown.

Disaster Response

There are two key questions in assessing the response of a local community to a crisis event. First, to what extent are the community's traditional institutions capable of managing the crisis? And second, to what extent is external assistance needed to cope with the crisis, and what access does the community have to that assistance? According to Wenger (1978: 26), "Research on natural disasters has found that similar types of events, producing similar levels of physical disruption, can produce a disaster or crisis condition in one social context and have no such effect in a different social setting." In other words, the quality of *response* is what defines a "disaster." The critical factor is the crisis-management capability of the community. The disaster event typically creates new needs in a community. If those needs can be met adequately through normal institutional channels, the crisis event does not constitute a disaster, but rather a community emergency. If, however, the crisis exceeds the management capacity of the traditional structure of community organizations – both public and private – then a new organization to deal with the crisis is likely to emerge.

In addition to the intracommunity organizational aspect, another important factor in the response to disaster is *external assistance*. A local community struck by natural disaster can generally depend on quick responses from a variety of public and private agencies. The Red Cross and other volunteer agencies provide disaster relief. Army National Guard units may be mobilized for rescue and/or security operations. Health and medical agencies may have to be supplemented. Special work crews from the utility companies work to restore power and communications. Insurance companies bring in specially trained agents and mobile offices to facilitate insurance settlements. In a severe disaster, the governor of the state helicopters to the scene, declares an emergency, and puts in a request to the U.S. president for federal disaster assistance.

In Youngstown, external assistance came essentially in the form of temporary income support and social service programs. Welcome as these may have been, they did not replace the jobs that were lost. It was clear that to replace the jobs lost at the Campbell Works, new money – a great deal of it – would have to come from outside the community.

Both of these factors in a natural disaster help to explain the emergence of the Ecumenical Coalition in response to the Campbell Works shutdown. First, the religious coalition was an emergency organization that appeared on the scene because traditional institutions failed (or at least were perceived as failing) to meet the needs of the community. And second, the program developed by the religious coalition – to reopen the Campbell Works under community–worker ownership – was a program directed at gaining the greatest amount of external assistance (in the form of industrial investment capital) in the shortest time.

Traditional Institutions

In the local economic crisis created by the mill shutdown, steelworkers and the community in general looked to three kinds of

Table 4.1. *Youngstown steel crisis: organizations and programs*

Network	Organization	Linkage	Strategy	Program
Local churches leadership	Ecumenical Coalition (12/77)	HUD, NCEA	Reopening	Campbell Works reopening, community–worker ownership
Local business (Chamber of Commerce), mayor	MVEDC (1/79)	EDA, Commerce Department	Diversification	1. Airplane factory 2. National steel demonstration center
Campbell, Struthers, Lowellville leadership	CASTLO (Summer '78)	Ohio Governor Rhodes	Diversification	Industrial park
Steelworkers	Steelworkers United for Employment (SUE, 3/79)	Ecumenical Coalition	Reopening Retention	Reopen Campbell Works Keep Brier Hill operating
Steelworkers union leadership	Union locals and District 26	Steelworkers union headquarters, Pittsburgh	Early: Negotiate benefits Late: Reopening	Reopen Campbell Works
Steel management	WREDA Early (9/77) Late (6/79)	Ecumenical Coalition J & L Steel	Reopening Diversification	Reopen Campbell Works Redevelopment (Facilities Development Team)

institutions for leadership: organized labor, the local business community, and the government. In each case, the effectiveness of these institutions in conceiving and spearheading a credible response was largely neutralized, due to a combination of systemic factors and some sheer coincidence. (Organizational responses to the shutdown from different sectors in the Youngstown community are summarized in Table 4.1.)

Organized Labor

Traditionally, the United Steelworkers had been the largest and strongest union in the Mahoning Valley. It might be expected that this union would play a significant role in challenging the sudden termination of thousands of its members.

When District Director Frank Leseganich and the presidents of the steelworker locals emerged from the meeting with Jennings Lambeth on Monday morning, they immediately launched a massive petition drive throughout the Youngstown area. Initially, steelworkers in the Mahoning Valley accepted the industry argument that the Campbell Works shutdown was largely the fault of foreign steel imports. The industry blamed the loss of steel jobs on the federal government for permitting the "dumping" of imported steel on the American market. Billboards and posters around Youngstown proclaimed, "Foreign steel – it's a job-robbing deal." In one union meeting after the shutdown, a steelworker in his mid-40s spoke out with strong feeling against "the God-damn dirty Japs who killed my father in World War II, and now are taking food from my kids' table."

Steelworkers in Youngstown were tempted to view the Campbell Works shutdown as yet another round in Youngstown's struggle against the government in Washington to keep the steel mills running. In 1973–4, the Environmental Protection Agency threatened to shut down the mills. In that instance, steelworkers organized and demonstrated in support of the steel companies against the federal government. Since street demonstrations had been effective in that instance, workers would adopt the same strategy now. But this time they would carry the demonstration to Washington itself.

By Tuesday morning after the announcement, steelworkers and their families were busy collecting signatures on a petition to be presented to President Carter, calling on him to restrict steel imports. In three days (Tuesday to Thursday) steelworkers collected a reported 110,000 signatures. Early Friday morning four busloads of steelworkers left for Washington. The buses were chartered by the steelworkers local union at the Brier Hill plant of Youngstown Sheet and Tube Co.

In Washington, the steelworkers went directly to the White House, where they asked to see the president and deliver their petition in person. They did not have an appointment and could not be squeezed into the president's schedule. The guard refused to deliver the petition for them, so they marched up the Hill to the Capitol, where they left the petition with Ohio Senators Glenn and Metzenbaum. While they were in Washington, the steelworker contingent was able to meet with Lloyd McBride, president of the international union, who happened to be in the city that day on business. McBride gave the impression of being cool and noncommittal; he was remembered as saying only, "Well, I guess you fellows in Youngstown have a problem." His critics would later point out that it took McBride eight months to make the sixty-five mile trip from Pittsburgh to Youngstown for any show of sympathy and concern for the plight of his unemployed union members.

The incidental meeting with McBride points up an initial divergence of viewpoints between rank-and-file steelworkers and the union hierarchy in Pittsburgh. Officials at USWA headquarters were convinced that the function of a union was limited to bargaining for wages, benefits, and working conditions. In this respect, union officials could argue that they had done their job very well indeed, having just negotiated the new early retirement program for workers left unemployed after twenty years of service. However, when local union leaders in Youngstown called a meeting to explain the benefit provisions to their unemployed members, instead of being applauded for their efforts, they found a hostile crowd of workers demanding to know what the union was doing to get their jobs back.

The answer was: little or nothing. Not only did their concept of the union's collective-bargaining role dictate a passive and reactive posture, but also union officials were caught between competing interests in the union itself. Campbell steelworkers wanted their jobs back. But a company reassessment of the shutdown at Campbell might only lead to job cutbacks elsewhere. The tendency of union officials was to hold on to what was left and not rock the boat. To this end, District Director Leseganich called together the presidents of the six union locals affected by the shutdown to coordinate any Youngstown efforts through his office.

Recent politics within the USWA was also part of the background of the low profile adopted by the union hierarchy toward the situation in Youngstown. The international steelworkers union had held its presidential election just five months before the Sheet and Tube shutdown. Although District Director Leseganich had backed McBride, other Youngstown union officials had supported the campaign of Ed Sadlowski, leader of an insurgent faction based in East Chicago. In the union election of April 29, 1977, the Youngstown district gave Sadlowski 58.6% of its vote. Only Sadlowski's home district, East Chicago, gave him a higher margin (United Steelworkers of America 1977).[1] Opposition to McBride was especially strong in the Brier Hill local, where Ed Mann was president. Attorney for the Brier Hill union was Staughton Lynd – socialist, antiwar activist, and now labor lawyer. Lynd was known, and strongly disliked, in Pittsburgh headquarters for his previous efforts on behalf of Sadlowski and steelworker insurgents in East Chicago.[2] A consistent position of the Youngstown rank and file was that they wanted jobs, not benefits. When it appeared that union officials would represent their interests in receiving what they considered akin to "welfare," but not in recovering their jobs, steelworkers began to look elsewhere. Lower-level union officials (the vice-presidents, secretaries, treasurers, and grievance committeemen) from the local unions began getting together to discuss the situation. Staughton Lynd became a part of these often informal meetings, as did members of the Youngstown clergy. In these discussions in particular, it became clear that the workers' initial reaction to the shutdown – blaming Washington – was only partially justified. And it was in one of these meetings that Gerald Dickey, secretary of the Brier Hill local, first voiced the suggestion "Let's buy the damn mill and run it ourselves."

Only a year and half after the closing did there appear a distinctly worker-based response. By that time, most of the laid-off workers had exhausted their SUB payments and unemployment benefits. By that time also, it appeared that further steel closings at Brier Hill and the two U.S. Steel mills were a real possibility. Only then did two former Sheet and Tube workers,

Len Balluck and John McNichol, begin an organizing effort aimed directly at the unemployed workers. They asked for and received a small subsidy from the religious coalition for office space and supplies. The first public meeting, March 12, 1979, held in the basement of Central Christian Church, attracted a turnout of 250. Within several weeks they had put together a mailing list of more than 400 names. Balluck was offered financial support from the steelworkers union headquarters in Pittsburgh, but the organizers declined, preferring to hold a posture independent of the union. It is significant that the only mass organizing effort by steelworkers themselves was to take place outside the union structure.

The initial labor response, then, unfolded at three different levels. (a) Rank-and-file steelworkers at first stormed into action blaming the federal government, but within weeks they began to realize that this was a superficial reading of their problem. They then largely retreated into inactivity while collecting their unemployment benefits. (b) Top union officials appeared to talk only about unemployment benefits and to dampen the feeling that anything dramatic should be done to get steel jobs back. (c) Some lower-level officials in the locals began meeting with members of the clergy and Staughton Lynd, exploring alternatives to simply giving up.

Business Community

In the Youngstown Chamber of Commerce, one strong opinion prevalent for years was that "steel in the Valley is dead." The Campbell Works shutdown only served to confirm the conventional wisdom. Interviews with Youngstown-area business people revealed a kind of love–hate relationship with the industry. On the one hand, local merchants were naturally happy to profit from the local commerce that the steel payroll engendered. On the other hand, there was strong resentment of the town's historical dependence on the industry. Consequently, there was a strong current of opinion within the Youngstown Chamber of Commerce that the economic future of the area lay in diversification. Attracting nonsteel industry to the area became a formal program of the Chamber of Commerce in 1976, when it adopted the previously independent Youngstown Area Growth Foundation as its economic development effort.

Many local business people felt that one major cause of the Sheet and Tube shutdown was excessive wage demands by the steel union. At the time of the shutdown, wages in the steel industry averaged 65% above the national level for manufacturing. Although there was sympathy for individual fellow citizens who would be affected by the shutdown, there was also a strong feeling that the union was getting what it deserved and that a weakened labor position would only improve the business climate in the Valley in the long run.

Smaller local manufacturers in particular were not happy about having to compete with steel industry wage scales. They objected to the efforts of the dominant steel union to organize and impose steel-level wage scales in smaller fabricating shops. It was widely believed in Youngstown management circles that the steelworkers union was responsible for ruining one chance for industrial diversification: A promising aluminum industry left the area because it would lose its competitive position in the nation if forced to pay steel-level wages in Youngstown.

The basic steel industry itself in the Youngstown area could hardly be expected to regret the loss of a competitor. Other steel companies would benefit from the Campbell Works shutdown in at least two ways. First, they would be able to pick up Sheet and Tube's share of the local steel market. And second, they could profit from the suddenly increased pool of skilled steel labor. Not only could they hire the better workers from Campbell, but the fact that there were so many people looking for steel jobs would give the operating companies extra leverage in dealing with their own work force. The other steel companies, then, were certainly not opposed to a Campbell Works shutdown, however sympathetic the managers and workers of these other firms might be at a private and personal level toward the people laid off at Campbell.

The business and industrial leadership by and large saw the shutdown as a favorable event, at least in the long run. They could hardly be expected to play a demonstrative role in opposing the shutdown.

Government

Since business and labor leaders, for the most part, chose not to mount any visible, programmatic response to the shutdown, the affected workers – and the community in general – looked to public officials for leadership. In the political sector, three factors militated against the development of a clearly articulated, coherent response to the action by Lykes–Sheet and Tube: the absence of metropolitan-level administrative coordination, the lame-duck situation of the Youngstown mayor, and the impact of partisan political rivalries.

Campbell and Struthers, and to a lesser extent Lowellville, were the municipalities most directly affected by the Campbell Works shutdown. The administration of these small manufacturing suburbs consisted essentially of a part-time mayor and a city auditor or finance official; they did not have the planning facilities to develop large-scale proposals for economic redevelopment. At the same time, they were suspicious of allowing "their" problem to be appropriated by the larger city of Youngstown.

At the beginning of the crisis, the city of Youngstown was inhibited from assuming leadership, first of all, by the lack of clear administrative jurisdiction. The Campbell Works property itself was located not in Youngstown, but in Campbell and Struthers; the offices of the company headquarters slated to be closed were likewise located outside the city in Boardman Township. Furthermore, the city of Youngstown was involved in a change of administration. After four terms in office, the incumbent Republican mayor Jack Hunter was retiring from politics. In September, the electoral campaign for mayor was already in progress, with the election scheduled for the first Tuesday in November. The uncertainty in the Youngstown political situation only contributed to the lack of clarity about the city's role. This factor would become particularly important in the event that redevelopment plans should call for federal government funding. Under the terms of the federal Community Development Act, only the city of Youngstown was eligible to apply for an Urban Development Action Grant from the Department of Housing and Urban Development.

The division between the two metropolitan-area planning agencies, EDATA and WREDA, also acted as an inhibiting factor in the development of clear planning leadership. WREDA, which had taken the lead in the steel pollution controversy, was hampered by its Republication identification. William Sullivan, the president of WREDA, had been closely connected with Ohio Senator Taft, whose Senate seat passed to Democrat Howard

Metzenbaum in the 1976 election. With two Democratic Senators and a Democratic administration in Washington, Sullivan was no longer able to bypass the 19th District congressman to deal directly with the EDA in Washington. Political influence over federal funds coming into the Mahoning Valley passed to Democratic Congressman Charles Carney, who saw in Sullivan a potential political rival for the congressional seat. WREDA in 1977 was still attempting to do development planning, particularly around the steel industry. But Sullivan had already been warned by the EDA district director in Chicago that WREDA would be doing less contract work for the federal government.

The days immediately after Black Monday saw a flurry of political activity. Public officials obviously could not ignore a blow of this magnitude to the local economy, as well as the local tax base. Their responses, though, typically manifested a double concern – to address the problem itself and at the same time to consolidate the political base and further the public appeal of their respective political parties.

Democratic Congressman Charles Carney, of the Ohio 19th District, was familiar with the steel industry and its problems. He had grown up in Campbell, graduating from Campbell Memorial High School. Carney came into politics after serving as a union local president and then as district director of the United Rubber Workers Union. While serving for twenty years as an Ohio State senator, he was also a staff representative for the United Steelworkers of America. Carney was elected to Congress in 1970, after the death of the long-time Youngstown-area Congressman Michael J. Kirwan.

In Washington, Carney had organized the Congressional Steel Caucus. Aware of the problems confronting the steel industry in the mid-1970s, he called together steel industry managers and union leaders, asking them to come up with concrete legislative proposals that the members of the Steel Caucus could support in Congress. This initiative produced no results, however. According to Carney, steel labor and management never did present the Caucus with mutually acceptable proposals.

With the announcement of the Campbell Works shutdown, Carney quickly stepped in to try to coordinate the public sector response in the Youngstown area. He called a meeting in the Youngstown City Hall for Friday, September 23. Invited to the meeting were the mayor and several city officials from Youngstown. To represent the steelworkers union, Carney also invited his former employer, Jim Griffin, former director of USWA District 26. Whether by accident or by design, the list of invitees did not include city officials from Campbell, Struthers, or Lowellville, or the incumbent USWA district director, Frank Leseganich, who had defeated Griffin for the director's post in 1969.

The Carney-initiated meeting was to have several important consequences. The central thrust of the meeting was to set up still another economic development agency in the Youngstown metropolitan area: the Mahoning Valley Economic Development Committee (later Commission); it became known as "medvec" through a transposition of the acronym MVEDC. Although it was at first chaired by the Republican mayor of Youngstown, the effort was strongly linked to the Democratic Party. (After the November election, Hunter was replaced by the new Democratic mayor of Youngstown, Philip Richley.) MVEDC also became closely linked to the Youngstown Chamber of Commerce: Laird Eckmann, director of the Chamber's Youngstown Area Growth Foundation, became MVEDC's interim executive director. MVEDC was intended to have two major functions. It would be a coordinating agency for economic development efforts in the Youngstown metropolitan area. And, through Congressman Carney's office, it was intended to provide Youngstown's principal link to federal funds in Washington. An initial EDA grant to fund MVEDC and to pay for a new economic study of the Mahoning Valley was arranged through the new acting director of EDA's Chicago regional office, Edward Jeep.

The meeting called by Congressman Carney was equally important because of the people who were *not* invited. First, the meeting did not include William Sullivan, president of WREDA, although Sullivan – through his agency's work on the pollution case – was perhaps the best-informed local resource on Mahoning Valley steel. Sullivan was identified as a Trumbull County Republican; he was therefore an outsider from the viewpoint of Youngstown Democrats. His economic development agency was in some ways a competitor of EDATA, the agency with links to Congressman Carney and the Youngstown Democratic Party. Furthermore, Sullivan was seen as a potential political challenger for the 19th District congressional seat.

With the inauguration of the new Democratic administration in

1977, Congressman Carney began putting pressure on the EDA to limit research and planning contracts with WREDA. MVEDC was evidently intended to supplant WREDA as the local contact agency for the EDA. This move not only had severe financial consequences for WREDA; it also affected the shape of economic development strategy. Sullivan and WREDA had been closely identified with the retention of the steel industry in the Mahoning Valley. Eliminating Sullivan from MVEDC left that agency more receptive to the diversification strategy favored in Youngstown business circles.

Second, Carney had invited his former employer and political backer Jim Griffin instead of the incumbent union district director, Frank Leseganich. This alienated Leseganich. And it left MVEDC without strong connections to the local steelworker organizations.

Third, municipal officials of Campbell, Struthers, and Lowell-ville were incensed at being excluded from such a meeting and resented what they saw as Youngstown politicans' attempt to take over "their" problem. They saw MVEDC as an attempt both to control the thrust of local economic development efforts in favor of the city of Youngstown and to direct the flow of federal funds to Youngstown – all at the expense of the manufacturing suburbs.

The Republican response to the Youngstown-area steel crisis was initiated by Ohio Governor James Rhodes. On the day after Black Monday, Rhodes visited Campbell and Struthers on a "fact-finding" mission. He promised aid from state discretionary funds to the communities whose tax base would be severely affected by the shutdown. (For the 1979 fiscal year, the city of Campbell did receive $639,000 in Ohio state funds to pay for police and fire services.) The governor quickly developed a reputation among the suburban mayors for being present, for being unafraid of making commitments, and for delivering what he promised.

In the meantime, the suburban mayors were having difficulty with Congressman Carney's Mahoning Valley Economic Development Committee. As they describe it, the congressman had to be forced to include them on the committee. Seeing their municipalities having little influence in the Carney–Democratic effort, the suburban mayors (though Democrats themselves) fell back on the Republican backing offered by Governor Rhodes. In March, six months after the shutdown was first announced, the governor visited Campbell, Struthers, and Lowellville with his cabinet. He arranged to have an economic development consultant, George Wilson, paid by the state, come to assist the municipal officials of Campbell, Struthers, and Lowellville in charting an economic development program of their own. In April, this effort developed into a formal economic development agency under the name CASTLO.

The federal government also took notice of the shutdown announcement. Edward Jeep, the acting director of the EDA regional office in Chicago, was instructed to visit Youngstown, together with another representative of the Commerce Department, Loren Wittner. Jeep, who was new on the job and knew little about Youngstown politics, participated in the Carney meeting and arranged financing for MVEDC.

Ironically, while MVEDC was being set up in Youngstown, Bill Sullivan – together with the Reverend Edward Stanton, treasurer of WREDA, and Frank Leseganich – was knocking on doors at the EDA and other Commerce Department offices in Washington. Sullivan had traditionally been the EDA's link to Youngstown and had two projects under contract with EDA at the time of the shutdown announcement. WREDA had also, months before, submitted a proposal for a $1 million community "insurance" fund, against which communities might borrow in the event of a sudden economic hardship such as a major industrial shutdown.[3] On the Friday after Black Monday, the Commerce Department had little to offer. The WREDA contingent was astounded to discover how little some Washington bureau staffers knew about the level of financing in the steel industry. At one point, a $7 million fund was pointed to as a solution – until the Youngstown contingent provided the information that this amount would scarcely cover half the costs of relining a single blast furnace. Commerce Department officials, though sympathetic, simply had no programs to deal with a situation like that in Youngstown.

The WREDA visit to the Commerce Department underlines two important points. First, despite the political moves aimed at WREDA, Sullivan remained a Youngstown spokesperson trusted by the Commerce Department. As the Campbell Works revitalization effort developed over the next eighteen months, officials at the EDA in particular stayed in touch with Sullivan.[4]

Second, the conversation at the Commerce Department underscores the fact that, in September 1977, not only were there no specific programs applicable to the Youngstown situation, but also the government had no policy whatever regarding the steel industry. Only in months to come would official Washington begin to take notice of the burgeoning steel crisis.

Religious Responses

The religious community's response to the steel shutdown announcement was likewise set in motion during the week following the Monday shutdown announcement. The birth of the Ecumenical Coalition of the Mahoning Valley can be dated from a phone call. Reverend Charles (Chuck) Rawlings, staff person for church and society issues in the regional office of the Episcopal Church in Cleveland, picked up an early afternoon edition of the newspaper on Monday, September 19, headlining the Sheet and Tube shutdown. Rawlings carried the news to Bishop John Burt. The phone call followed, from Burt to Bishop James Malone, head of the Catholic diocese in Youngstown. Malone was out of town at a meeting, but returned the call the next day.

Bishop Burt wanted to express his concern over the situation in Youngstown, which was part of his northern Ohio jurisdiction. He knew the city intimately, having served as pastor of St. John's Episcopal Church on Wick Avenue. Burt was also active in his national church's Coalition of Urban Bishops. The phone call was not out of the ordinary. Burt and Malone had worked together in the Ohio Council of Churches, in which Malone was just ending a term as president. In the past few years the Catholic and Episcopal bishops had developed confidence in each other; they shared similar views about the role of the church in social affairs. It was a simple matter to arrange a breakfast meeting for the following Monday in Youngstown.

Chuck Rawlings served as a kind of stage manager in those first few weeks, cueing on stage different players in the opening scene of the Coalition drama. An energetic, articulate man, deeply committed to the cause of social justice, Rawlings described himself as one of a generation of Protestant clergy (some on the staffs of national church offices) who saw the problems of American cities as rooted in the foundation of economic and social arrangements. He thought that Youngstown presented an opportunity for the churches to deal with the urban–industrial crisis at a more fundamental and indeed revolutionary level than seemed possible in a larger city such as Cleveland. In the course of the week, Rawlings got in contact with Richard Barnet at the Institute of Policy Studies in Washington. Barnet had previously been a resource person for Rawlings's church work. Rawlings also contacted church people in Youngstown with whom he was acquainted (e.g., Reverend Edward Weisheimer, pastor of Central Christian Church). The main question for mounting a serious, church-based effort in Youngstown, Rawlings felt, was the role that the Catholic bishop was willing to play.

Bishop Malone rather quickly took the initiative. On the Sunday following the Sheet and Tube announcement, Malone went to preach the sermon at St. John's Church in Campbell, where many of the parishioners were Sheet and Tube Workers. Malone also left word for Father Edward Stanton, the social action director on his own diocesan staff, to clear his calendar and be present at the meeting scheduled for Monday morning.

One week after Black Monday, about a dozen clergy from several denominations sat down to breakfast at the rectory of the Catholic cathedral. Meeting with them were Richard Barnet from Washington and Staughton Lynd, who described himself as representative of a Quaker meeting. The meeting was simply exploratory, the purpose being to open the question of what effects the Campbell Works shutdown would have on the lives of the people in the church pews and what kind of pastoral response was called for from the religious community. No answers were forthcoming at this initial session, but the religious leaders agreed to continue the discussion. As leader of the largest religious group in the Youngstown area, Bishop Malone was acknowledged as coordinator of these efforts. Father Edward Stanton, who had been in Washington the previous week when plans for the first clergy meeting were being laid, came to the Monday session on orders from Bishop Malone. On the one hand, Stanton was the obvious person to be in charge of Catholic representation in such an effort. As diocesan director of social action and human development, the whole set of problems related to the steel shutdown was clearly in his area. Furthermore, Stanton had the right connections. He was known around Youngstown as a "labor priest," who was popular in the union halls and knew the labor officials. And he was also acquainted with people in the business community and steel management, both through pastoral ministry and through his association with the WREDA. On the other hand, Stanton was skeptical about what a church response to the steel shutdown would accomplish and had nothing to do with organizing the initial meeting. As he described his reaction, he had no interest in spending the next two months writing suggested sermon outlines and pious statements that would only fill up file drawers and wastebaskets. Nevertheless, as the Catholic bishop's staff person, he was unavoidably involved. When it became apparent that the clergy leaders were committed to action, and not just talk, Stanton was hooked and was named coordinator of staff-level activities.

Three days later, on September 29, Stanton, Rawlings, and a number of local pastors held a follow-up meeting, this time including Steve Redburn, director of the Center for Urban Studies of Youngstown State University, and representatives from WREDA. The meeting moved in a number of directions: Staughton Lynd speaking about possible litigation, the WREDA representative discussing that agency's loan fund proposal, Redburn pointing to coordination of human services, Rawlings saying that the condition of the steel industry in general might dictate changes in the production activity of Youngstown. There eventually emerged a general consensus that the group should try to clarify and express the moral concerns of the shutdown; they decided to draft a statement for presentation at a community meeting in the Struthers Field House that evening. They then broke up into several task groups to develop recommendations on such questions as coordination structures for the group, public education, and counseling and human services coordination for the unemployed.

The following Monday, October 3, Bishop Malone again chaired a meeting of the religious leaders, this time at First Presbyterian Church, at which the groups reported back. They recommended that the clergy take an active role in mustering present social service agencies; volunteers for assisting in crisis counseling might work through the Human Needs Committee of the Mahoning Valley Association of Churches. The public education committee recommended that a number of public seminars be held; the clergy might have a role in this, but only as a cosponsor with other groups, such as the university or the local media. The committee on economic conversion and long-range planning had no definite proposals at this point, but would meet with a group in Washington at the Institute for Policy Studies on Thursday, October 6. Finally, the participants decided to set up an informal coordinating group within the religious community.

Within a week of the shutdown announcement, a loose coalition was emerging, including most of the major Youngstown religious groups: Catholic, Presbyterian, Episcopalian, Methodist, Baptist, Church of Christ, Disciples of Christ, and the Jewish community. (Lutherans would become active in the Coalition at a later date.) Bishop Malone was acknowledged as chair of the informal coordinating group.

At this point the clergy's concept of their role was twofold: (a) to articulate the moral issues involved in the Sheet and Tube shutdown and (b) to facilitate other agencies, both public and private, in responding to the short-term and long-term needs of the community and its people. It seems clear that, on the whole, religious leaders in Youngstown initially thought of themselves as filling a supporting role.

The first hint of any larger role emerged out of consultations over the next several weeks with two liberal research groups in Washington. Rawlings had contacted the Institute of Policy Studies (IPS) immediately after the shutdown announcement. A communication from IPS dated October 1 indicated that the Institute was very interested in the Youngstown problem. Richard Barnet (1974) had already done research on the effects of disinvestment decisions by large corporations on unemployment in local communities. An IPS arm, the Conference on Alternative State and Local Public Policies, was about to publish a study by Ed Kelly, research director of the Ohio Public Interest Campaign: "Industrial Exodus: What States and Cities Can Do About Plant Closings." Furthermore, the Institute had worked with senators and representatives in drafting legislation dealing with plant closings and was in contact with scholars studying Western European responses to local economic disinvestment. The Institute offered its services, particularly in dealing with the longer-term aspects of the shutdown.

At about the same time, Staughton Lynd had a long telephone conversation with Gar Alperovitz, codirector of a second Washington research group, the Exploratory Project on Economic Alternatives. Alperovitz was an economist and political analyst and had been a fellow of the Institute for Policy Studies. Several years before the events in Youngstown, he had set up the Exploratory Project with private foundation support to do in-depth analysis of the American political economy, as well as develop programs that would model alternative economic structures. Lynd and Alperovitz had coauthored a slim volume in 1973, *Strategy and Program: Two Essays Toward a New American Socialism*. In that book, Staughton Lynd had urged that it was time for the socialist movement in America to forget its internecine quarrels and organize public support around concrete programs at the grass-roots level:

As such movements come into being and begin to grow, they (we) must be serious about being an alternative government. . . . Democracy, we must say again and again, can only survive as libertarian socialism, in which economic as well as political decision-makers are elected and the people take more part in decisions of every kind.

To be serious about being an alternative government we must be able to talk concretely about how a socialist society would deal with problems which oppress people now. Recognizing that much can only be resolved in the midst of experience, still we should begin to gather experience from other countries and spell out in specifics what a socialist approach to public health, a socialist system of education (if any), workers' control in particular industries under socialism, and the rest, might look like. (Lynd and Alperovitz 1973: 47–8)

Alperovitz, in his contribution, likewise urged that "Americans interested in fundamental change begin to define much more precisely what they want" (ibid.: 49). Alperovitz argued that nationalization of industry on the Soviet and East European – or even the British – models was not a solution:

Historically, a major radical starting point has been socialism – conceived as social ownership of the means of production primarily through nationalization. Although the ideal of socialism involves the more encompassing values of justice, equality, cooperation, democracy, and freedom, in practice it has often resulted in a dreary, authoritarian political economy. Could the basic structural concept of common ownership of society's resources for the benefit of all ever be achieved, institutionally, in ways which fostered and sustained – rather than eroded and destroyed, a cooperative, democratic society? (Ibid.: 50)

Alperovitz was looking for an answer to the problem in social ownership by *local* communities:

When small, territorially defined communities control capital or land socially (as, for instance, in the Israeli kibbutz or the Chinese commune), unlike either capitalism or socialism, there is no built-in contradiction between the interests of owners or beneficiaries of industry (capitalist *or* local workers) *as against the community as a whole*. (Ibid.: 60)

Alperovitz was developing this theme in relation to the industrial exodus being felt in older urban centers of the Northeast and Midwest, suggesting that local community ownership of abandoned industries might be a solution. Lynd, who was very much on the scene in Youngstown, suggested to Alperovitz that the Exploratory Project might well find in Youngstown a place to try out his ideas.

The Institute for Policy Studies, the Exploratory Project, and the Youngstown religious leaders came together at a Washington meeting arranged by Rawlings on October 6. Participants from Washington included Richard Barnet and Marcus Raskin from the Institute, Alperovitz and his assistant Roger Hickey from the Exploratory Project, and Michael Maccoby from the Harvard University Project on Technology, Work and Character. Nat Weinberg from the research department of the United Auto Workers represented organized labor, though no one from the United Steelworkers national office was present. Several representatives from national church offices for social affairs represented the Episcopal and United Presbyterian Churches, as well as the National Council of Churches. From Youngstown came four clergymen (Rawlings, Stanton, John Sharick – presbyter executive of the United Presbyterian Church, and Ed Weisheimer – pastor of Central Christian Church), Gerald Dickey – secretary of the Brier Hill steelworkers local, and Jeff Brown of WREDA.

In a wide-ranging four-hour discussion, the meeting covered a spectrum of issues: the importance of discovering the facts about Lykes's acquisition of Sheet and Tube and the shutdown decision, Youngstown as a typical instance of urban–industrial crisis, the problems of human welfare as an issue of justice, ways in which the Youngstown situation was indicative of both the internationalization of the economy and pattern of corporate decision making that adversely affected local communities. Four strategic emphases were singled out: (a) to discover the facts about the shutdown through research and litigation, (b) to educate the community about those facts as well as about larger economic issues affecting its welfare, (c) to press forward with direct worker welfare and relief measures, and (d) to develop a longer-term conversion/economic stabilization project. The group did not attempt to set up a program. It was decided that the circumstances of the Youngstown closing and the development of a longer-term solution should be explored at more length. The participants recommended instead that these questions be dealt with at a two-day closed conference to be held in Youngstown later in the month.

In the weeks between the Washington meeting and the Steel Crisis Conference eventually scheduled for October 28–9 at First Presbyterian Church in Youngstown, a four-person steering committee emerged to plan the conference and in general coordinate the clergy efforts. The two key figures on the committee were Stanton and Rawlings, both diocesan (i.e., regional-level) staff people with expertise in church-based social action, representing respectively the Catholic and Episcopalian Churches. By the end of the month both were released by their bishops to work full time on the Youngstown steel crisis. At this time, the Reverend Gene Bay, pastor of First Presbyterian Church, turned over his church's important role to his relatively new associate pastor, Robert ("Bert") Campbell. Campbell, who had worked his way through the seminary as a steelworker in Pittsburgh and who had been called to the ministry at First Presbyterian partly because of his experience in urban community organizing, became the third member of the committee. The fourth member was the Reverend Donald Walton, Methodist pastor and Youngstown district superintendent for his church.

There was a potential cleavage in the Steering Committee from its inception. Rawlings, who lived in Shaker Heights and worked out of the Episcopalian Church's Cleveland office, chose to become involved in Youngstown because he saw the situation as symptomatic of a larger national issue. His personal strategy was to attack the national issue by working in Youngstown. Rawlings's concern was that people in Youngstown might fail to perceive the connection between their problem and what was happening elsewhere in the country and thereby miss an opportunity to deal effectively with either the local or national issue. Rawlings's understanding of the situation and his approach to it were complemented by his personal style. An energetic, articulate man with a deep capacity for moral concern, Rawlings liked being committed to and working on a cause. Out of his concern for what corporate capitalism was doing to the cities, he adopted Youngstown.

In contrast, Stanton was born and raised in the Youngstown area. As a priest, he had served in parishes in Warren and Youngstown's inner city, developing strong roots and wide contacts in the area. He was far more interested in the concrete problem of restoring jobs in Youngstown than in mounting a national cause. Where Rawlings was a man with a vision, Stanton was more a pragmatist and reality tester; as a skilled negotiator, he knew and appreciated the process of giving on one point to win on another.

The reports that Rawlings and Stanton wrote for Bishop Malone (as chairman of the coordinating group) within days of the Washington meeting reflect their different angles of vision. Stanton, in a memo dated October 10, described the Washington meeting as calling for "some sort of a national effort . . . looking at how communities can have a more definite say in any planning that will involve their economic future." He tended to downplay the connection of Youngstown with a national movement:

My suggestion would be that funding for such a program be sought from national church bodies and/or the Department of Commerce through an EDA planning grant and that local participation in the Mahoning Valley consist of making available any resolutions and information we have to whatever national group (probably the Institute for Policy Studies) that would be doing the major work.

Furthermore, he felt that any clergy action should be of "limited scope," focusing on the moral aspects of the question in the context of public education. He stated to Bishop Malone:

I feel that it would be a mistake for the clergy to seem to be somehow separated from the rest of the community and the people we are all dedicated to serve. I feel that too much prominence given to a clergy group separated from and only relating to the rest of the community would give a wrong image.

Rawlings, however, in a memo dated October 7, was impressed with the larger picture:

There seemed a unanimous consensus that we were addressing deep sea changes in the nature of economic life in both our own country and in the entire world; that the search for alternatives, for innovation, was of the highest priority among public policy questions today.

"Youngstown," he wrote, "presented an opportune chance to focus on a national issue."

All present were careful in wishing to avoid an exploitation of the human needs of people affected in Youngstown for the sake of a national project. On the other hand, it was recognized that in relationship to a pervasive trend over the last ten years, Youngstown represented a "heart attack" around which it may be possible to rally national, intellectual, and research resources as well as national funds from the ecumenical community.

In this and a follow-up memo dated October 11, the outline of a national campaign began to emerge. It would be based on a three-cornered coalition of the Youngstown clergy (who would provide local leadership), the national church offices (which would provide funding for the campaign, as well as national political and media connections), and one or more Washington consulting groups (which would provide technical expertise and advice).

The tension between national and local interests at this early stage should not be overstated. But it is clear that this factor was present from the beginning.

Steel Crisis Conference

The immediate task for the last weeks of October was preparation for the Steel Crisis Conference at First Presbyterian Church, to begin on Friday afternoon, October 28. Invitations were sent out over the signatures of Bishop Malone and Richard Speicher, the executive director of the Mahoning Valley Association of Churches. It was to be a closed conference, with participation limited to about fifty. Invitees were largely from three areas: (a) Catholic and Protestant Churches and Jewish congregations in the Youngstown area, (b) regional and national church offices, and (c) "expert resource persons" from the Institute for Policy Studies and Exploratory Project for Economic Alternatives (Washington) and the WREDA (Youngstown). The design for the conference was worked out largely by Reverend John Sharick, regional Presbyterian executive.

The opening session on Friday afternoon, October 28, was a "fish bowl" exercise, in which the resource persons were invited to address the following questions: (a) What are the facts about the Sheet and Tube shutdown? (2) What is the condition created in Youngstown? (3) What general conditions (national and world-wide) cause such situations?

There are no transcripts from the conference. However, participants report the following outstanding impressions. They remember the three principal speakers as representing a range of opinion from left (Marcus Raskin) to center (Gar Alperovitz) to right (William Sullivan). Raskin spoke first. Sullivan answered by saying that his differences with Raskin were encyclopedic; though he did not offer a point-for-point rebuttal, it was clear that the two were approaching the Youngstown problem from opposite directions. Alperovitz, a skilled speaker, was able to take a center position. He asked the group if it might be possible for the religious community in Youngstown to take a somewhat revolutionary path. The traditional role of the religious community in situations of social dislocation, he said, had been to deal with the people who were hurt by the situation on an individual basis. In this case, he thought it might be possible for the religious community to mount a collective response, focusing on the cause of the dislocation itself. Alperovitz's challenge resonated with the thinking of many in the religious community. As Stanton would put it, "Social action is not just putting on band-aids; it's finding the son-of-a-bitch who inflicted the wounds."

The conference moved through a series of well-orchestrated sessions to identify four tasks and begin blocking out strategies for dealing with them. First was the task of public education, on both a local and national level. The conference decided to issue a joint "pastoral letter" from the religious community that would both identify the moral issues involved in Youngstown and provide a sense of hope and call for action to the community. These themes would also be addressed in a full-page ad in local and national newspapers. Second was the proposal to work toward the coordination of local community with national interests in the development of a national steel policy, particularly emphasizing the retention of basic jobs in severely affected communities throughout the nation. Third was the task of developing a Youngstown project linking national-level church bodies and perhaps other national-level agencies with an organizing effort in Youngstown. Last was the task (to cite the language on the public record) of "examination of the possibility of sponsoring a feasibility study on the acquisition and operation of the Campbell Works of the Youngstown Sheet and Tube Co. by a community–worker group or the conversion of the property to some other use" (Youngstown *Vindicator*, October 31, 1977).

The Steel Crisis Conference in October marks the point at which uncertain and inchoate efforts of the religious leaders came together in an organized structure with at least a general sense of purpose and several immediate tasks to accomplish.

By the end of Friday's evening session, Bishop Malone was already sure that the conference would call for a follow-up of some sort. Even the relatively simple task of putting together the pastoral letter and placing an ad in the *New York Times* would require both coordination and funds, and the thrust of the conference indicated that the effort might escalate well beyond that level. Therefore, Malone had Stanton arrange a Saturday morning breakfast meeting of bishops and judicatory officials. At the meeting, Malone asked the participants if they were willing to provide financial backing for the project. Each one present put $500 to $1,000 of discretionary funds on the table and pledged to seek further funding from the national church offices.

That meeting likewise led to the designation of a formal two-tier structure for the nascent coalition to carry on the work of the conference. An executive committee composed of church officials at the regional level (diocese, judicatory, presbytery) would be responsible for policy making. Bishop Malone was designated as chair of this committee, with the Presbyterian executive Reverend John Sharick as vice-chair. Other members of the committee would represent the religious communities providing funds: Bishop John Burt (Episcopal Diocese, Cleveland), Rabbi Sidney Berkowitz (Rodef Shalom Temple, Youngstown), Bishop James E. Thomas (East Ohio Conference, United Methodist Church, Canton), and Reverend William K. Laurie (Ohio Conference, United Church of Christ, Columbus).

The meeting also gave official recognition to the Steering Committee as the operational arm of the Coalition. The committee continued to consist of the four who had been coordinating the crisis response from the religious sector (Rawlings, Stanton, Campbell, and Walton). But Stanton and Rawlings were now released by their bishops to work full time on the steel crisis, and Bert Campbell was authorized by the session of First Presbyterian Church to devote one day per week to the Coalition.

Immediately after the conference, the Steering Committee moved to put the conference resolutions into effect. One of the first tasks was to draft a pastoral letter stating the position of the interfaith religious community. That task moved with surprising facility. Suggestions were channeled through Stanton to John Carr, a staff person at the Catholic bishops' national office in Washington.[5] For Carr, who had participated in the conference at First Presbyterian, it was a relatively simply job to put in straightforward, nontheoretical language what the group wanted to say. (The pastoral letter is discussed at length in the following chapter.) Within weeks the statement was ready and quietly circulated around Youngstown. Individual clergy were invited to authorize the document with their signatures. According to Bert Campbell, virtually no one was aware that more than three or four close associates were supporting the clergy statement. When the response came in, the Steering Committee was amazed to count 260 signatures (with others coming in too late to be included in the publication of the statement). It was printed and released on November 29, about two months after the first layoffs took effect.

In the meantime, the Steering Committee moved ahead with its exploration of the feasibility of doing something with the Campbell Works. A meeting with Tom Cleary, vice-president of Sheet and Tube and a long-time Youngstown resident, revealed that Lykes had for some time been trying to sell all or part of the Sheet and Tube steel operations, but no buyers were to be found. Since this avenue had already proved to be a dead end, there was no need for the religious coalition to explore it any further. This left the Coalition with the alternatives of buying the steel mill themselves and bringing it back into production or overseeing its conversion to some other productive use.

Father Ed Stanton remembers that the tentative language of the October conference regarding the Campbell Works accurately reflected the clergy's mood of hesitation. On November 1, he says, the religious leaders would have been glad to turn that project over to anyone who would step forward. No one did. A Coalition memo of November 19, 1977, notes with resignation:

Despite the flurry of rumors there is no evidence of interest in acquisition of the Campbell Works by either off-shore or domestic producers.

Against this background, the most promising approach appears to be an employee ownership scheme coupled with an introduction of new technology.

Any consideration of putting the shut-down portion of the Campbell Works back into operation – under community-worker ownership or any other mode – would have to begin with the question of whether the old facility could turn a profit, however modest. To obtain a first-run reading on the economic feasibility of a reopening, the Coalition made use of Stanton's connection with WREDA. The latter had established mutual trust and a good working relationship with Sheet and Tube executives through its work on the pollution study several years before, as well as the subsequent blast furnace and unit-train studies still in process. One of WREDA's consultants on these projects, the Philadelphia steel engineer George Beetle, was familiar with the Sheet and Tube facilities. Because of these connections, WREDA was able to engage Beetle on very short notice to begin an economic feasibility study by mid-November. The company proved very cooperative on this endeavor, providing Beetle with office space and full access to the company's computer and its operational data. Under these favorable circumstances, Beetle was able to deliver a report to the Coalition within thirty days. WREDA and the Coalition split the $30,000 cost of the study.

In his report, made public on December 16, 1977, Beetle stated, "Reopening the closed facilities of the Campbell Works and re-suming steel production is a realistic objective." The project would take money – a great deal of it: Beetle estimated $535 million in capital investment from 1978 to 1985. Beetle insisted that speed was essential; operations would have to resume within nine months in order for the Campbell Works to regain its share of the commercial steel market. In a covering letter, Beetle (1977) noted:

We have found it possible over the past several weeks to carry out these investigations only at a relatively general level of detail. We have not been able to probe as deeply as may be necessary before firm decisions on a reopening can be made, because of the need to establish basic principles for analysis of sales revenue and production costs attri-butable to defined product groups.

Although our work necessarily has been general, we believe that we have been able to develop a proper understanding of the relationships involved, and that our conclusions are as well-founded as circumstances allow.

The Washington Connection

As the Beetle study was getting under way, movement began in the federal government. The federal response to the steel crisis in Youngstown actually proceeded along two relatively separate tracks. In the first instance, Washington regarded what happened in Youngstown as an *industrial* crisis and focused on what the federal government might do for the ailing steel industry. A White House steel conference in mid-October shed some light in government circles on the general problems of the industry. Anthony Solomon, then undersecretary of the treasury, was appointed head of a federal task force to draw up a comprehensive program for the president.

The Youngstown situation figured seriously in the preparation of the "Solomon report." Representatives of the Coalition met with Solomon in Washington on Saturday morning, November 19. Solomon told the Coalition that their project of reopening the Campbell Works would be eligible for the program of federal support that he intended to propose, if it looked economically viable. On Tuesday, November 22, Solomon told Bill Sullivan that money would be available for the Campbell Works "if a hard-nosed feasibility study shows it's possible" (*New York Times*, November 26, 1977). Early drafts of the Solomon report mentioned the Youngstown problem in particular. Though specific reference to Youngstown was edited out of the final version presented to the president on December 6, the report did note:

The impact of a plant closing on a community is much broader than the direct job and income loss and is particularly severe when the bulk of the smaller businesses in a community are heavily dependent on the plant. Unfortunately, this is the case for several of the communities where recent cutbacks or shutdowns have occurred.

The impact is further aggravated because the recent plant cutbacks or shutdowns tend to be concentrated regionally. Eight of the 16 plant closings and cutbacks and 78% of the resulting job losses occurred in a region which includes parts of the states of Ohio, Pennsylvania, and New York. (Solomon 1977: 29)

Two lines of action recommended in the Solomon report were particularly pertinent to the Campbell Works. First, Solomon recommended a "system of trigger prices . . . which would be used as a basis for monitoring imports of steel into the United States and for initiating accelerated anti-dumping investigations with respect to imports priced below the trigger prices" (ibid.: 13). The "trigger price mechanism" was intended to provide the Treasury Department with a device for monitoring steel imports more closely and for initiating antidumping investigations without prior industry complaint. This measure was intended to provide marginal plants such as the Campbell Works with increased protection from the "dumping" of foreign steel. Second, in order to help the industry meet its enormous costs of modernization, at the same time it was saddled with heavy environmental costs, the report recommended a steel loan program, to be administered by the Economic Development Administration in the Commerce Department. Solomon's recommendation was that the federal government provide $1 billion in loan guarantees for steel modernization, although in the actual implementation, the amount ultimately made available was $500 million. Thus, the signals from Washington in late November and early December encouraged the Coalition to believe that their efforts to restore the Campbell Works to steel production would ultimately be assisted by Washington as part of an overall program of steel revitalization.

In the meantime, another federal agency, the Department of Housing and Urban Development, was becoming interested in the *urban* ramifications of a Campbell Works reopening. One current of thinking at HUD, to some extent led by Robert Embry, was that the agency should take a more prominent role in urban economic development. Anne Wexler, then at HUD, had worked previously for Alperovitz's Exploratory Project and was sympathetic with his ideas. Furthermore, HUD Secretary Patricia Harris was chairperson of an interagency committee reviewing the Carter administration's urban policy. Alperovitz's idea of using Youngstown as a "model demonstration project" meshed well with the new thinking at HUD. The agency, for its part, found attractive the prospect of promoting a Youngstown project as a step into urban economic development, hitherto controlled by the Commerce Department.

In the early weeks of December (at the same time the steel loan program was being firmed up), it appeared that HUD would be willing to provide a planning grant for a study to follow up the initial feasibility report by George Beetle. Alperovitz was able to arrange for a $300,000 HUD grant for his National Center for Economic Alternatives (an economic consulting arm of the Exploratory Project) to develop a worker–community ownership plan for the Campbell Works. In the official announcement of the grant on December 30, 1977, Secretary Harris stated: "This commendable community support is precisely the sort of local effort we are looking for in developing new Federal strategies to support areas like Youngstown that are determined to help themselves when faced with devastating plant closings" (*HUD News*, December 30, 1977).

During the weeks of November and early December the religious coalition developed rather quickly from an ad hoc religious action group into something like an economic development agency in its own right. Increasingly the energy and attention of the Coalition was focused on reopening the Campbell Works. The logic of the Coalition strategy included three major elements.

First, a reopening began to appear feasible. The Beetle study indicated that, if the open hearths were replaced and the rolling mills updated, the plant could produce steel at a modest profit. At the same time, the new federal loan guarantee program gave promise of providing some of the capital required. And the new trigger price mechanism promised to limit the "dumping" threat from foreign steel producers, giving the old plant an extra margin for profitability.

Second, in the Youngstown context, a reopening would provide a "quick fix" for the Valley's immediate problems. It would rehire the very workers laid off in the shutdown without putting them through job retraining, as well as cut the time they might have to depend on unemployment benefits. Furthermore, a reopening strategy had considerable advantages over a diversification strategy; it would take several years to bring in sufficient new industries to replace the number of jobs and the capital investment lost at Campbell. And local control of the reopened plant through some form of worker–community ownership would help to free Youngstown from dependence on out-of-town corporate decisions.

Third, in the national context, a successful reopening would have important ramifications in at least three policy areas. For one thing it would demonstrate the viability of "brownfield" revitalization in the steel industry, countering the assumption that building a modern steel plant would necessarily mean abandoning many of the communities where workers lived. For another, it would counter the tendency toward contraction in American steel and the attendant problem of dependence on foreign steel (similar to dependence on foreign oil). Finally, it would use federal dollars for investment rather than for welfare.

By early December, the Coalition had decided to act. At that point, the terminations at the Campbell Works were reaching a peak. The fear was that "two to three times that many jobs in other industries are being endangered if not wiped out" (Youngstown *Vindicator*, December 13, 1977). In the meantime, no other significant short-term action to restore jobs appeared on the Youngstown horizon. EDATA remained devoted to infrastructure planning. WREDA lacked the resources to assume leadership. MVEDC and CASTLO were perceived as political instruments of their creators and, in any case, were not yet sufficiently organized to lead a major development effort. The Chamber of Commerce was more interested in diversification than in trying to rebuild the steel industry. The general belief in the Chamber of Commerce was that, if private business could not run the mill, no one could. The union was doing a good job of providing unemployment benefits, but its leadership had made it clear that no action to regain steel jobs in Youngstown would be forthcoming. As members of the Coalition looked around in the weeks before Christmas 1977, theirs was really the only game in town. They screwed their courage to the sticking place and, with part bluff, part prayer, and part realism, announced on December 12 that they were going to reopen a steel mill.

Until this point, the religious leaders had deliberately kept their distance from Youngstown party politics. For one thing, the religious leaders were hearing from rank-and-file steelworkers that they did not trust the politicans to act in the workers' best interests. For another, the Coalition preferred to adopt a stance of political neutrality. But when the Coalition emerged as the possible recipient of a $300,000 federal grant, with the ultimate possibility of controlling a half-billion-dollar investment financed in large party by federal loan guarantees, the Coalition very quickly became a political actor.

In Washington, when officials at the EDA (charged with administering the steel loan program) heard that HUD was about to award a research grant to Alperovitz for work in Youngstown, EDA Deputy Director Hal Williams called a meeting at the Commerce Department for everyone involved in the Youngstown project. The meeting took place at the Commerce Department on December 20, eight days after the Coalition's announcement of its plan and four days after the release of the Beetle report. EDA Director Robert Hall was present, and Robert Embry headed a contingent from HUD. Congressman Carney came, and the

Ohio senators were represented. From Youngstown came Mayor-
elect Richley and representatives of MVEDC, WREDA, and the
Coalition. The question from EDA was which of the apparently
competing groups Washington should back. The Washington
meeting revealed a competition between MVEDC and the Coalition for control of the prospective research grant from HUD,
with Jim Griffin (former United Steelworker district director and
now, at Carney's invitation, a major force in MVEDC) voicing
criticism of the Beetle report and the mill-reopening project. The
outcome of the meeting was that federal officials pledged their
support but in effect told the Youngstown representatives to go
home and decide with which group Washington should negotiate.
In a subsequent press conference Congressman Carney repeated
Griffin's criticism of Sullivan's work and said the Coalition's
project was "ill conceived and ill advised."

Bishop Malone, chair of the executive committee, called the
congressman and asked for a meeting the next day in the bishop's
office. Those present remember the occasion as a classic confrontation. Each side took thirty minutes to present the reasons
it should be the lead agent and recipient of the federal grant.
Malone spoke first, Carney second. When the congressman
finished speaking, Malone resumed, "Gentlemen, as I was saying
..." And that settled the question. Later, Stanton struck a deal
with Jim Griffin whereby MVEDC would be responsible for
the implementation, if and when the federal loan guarantees were
forthcoming.

On the following day, December 23, the Ecumenical Coalition
of the Mahoning Valley became a legal entity. A mailgram was
sent to the Commerce Department and HUD:

In response to Mr. Hall's pledge, that as soon as one local entity had
been established to begin planning for the possible modernization and
activation of the closed portion of the Campbell Works of the Youngstown Sheet and Tube, the government would act by the end of the year
to release at least $300,000 in planning money, we wish to inform you
of the following: we are today establishing the Ecumenical Coalition
of the Mahoning Valley, Inc. This organization, with our full support,
will be the point of contact and single entity to receive all planning
money. It will be actively and cooperatively supported by the Mahoning
Valley Economic Development Committee, Inc., a group of prominent
citizens selected by Congressman Carney and chaired by the Mayor of
Youngstown.

The mailgram was signed by Congressman Carney, Bishop Malone, Frank Leseganich, and the mayor-elect of Youngstown, J. Philip Richley.

The mailgram also designated Gar Alperovitz's National Center for Economic Alternatives to manage the planning process. The contract for the HUD grant was finalized on December 30. There is one important detail regarding the contract. HUD was afraid that the General Accounting Office might object to giving a grant of this magnitude to a new organization with no track record. Consequently the contract was signed directly between the government and Alperovitz. Minutes of the Coalition Executive Committee meeting of January 13, 1978, note: "The Executive Committee discussed in detail the rationale for the HUD grant going directly to the National Center. It was agreed that we probably had no alternative but to accept the unusual process."

By the end of 1977, a little more than three months after the first exploratory breakfast meeting, the religious coalition was a new political force on the Youngstown scene. Its position as lead agent was recognized. Money for planning was in the pipeline. Other funds from the national denominations were on the way to provide for a staff. At the beginning of the new year, the Coalition effort moved into high gear.

CHAPTER V

Religion and Urban Economic Crisis

The phone call from Bishop Burt in Cleveland to Bishop Malone in Youngstown furnishes a convenient starting point for the Coalition story. And yet, dramatically satisfying as that event might be for beginning a narrative, it hardly explained the series of events that led to the Ecumenical Coalition.

On the one hand, the Coalition certainly was a new and different type of social organization. Nothing like it developed in the other steeltowns caught by the massive job terminations of 1977. As well, both the scale of the religious groups' involvement in such a project for local economic development and the nature of their leadership as a political agent for the local community were probably unprecedented.

On the other hand, it is possible to emphasize an opposite theme – to represent the Coalition as consistent with a tradition of concern in the churches for urban socioeconomic problems. Some members of the Coalition (Bishop Malone, for example) preferred to see the Coalition's thinking and action as rooted in and consistent with church tradition.

Actually, both themes are correct. The Coalition was new and different. At the same time, the Coalition effort did have strong roots within the intellectual and cultural context of the Catholic and mainline Protestant churches. An explanation of how and why the Coalition came into existence must take both factors into account. The Coalition was a product both of history and of structural factors at a particular time and place.

102

Religious Tradition and Urban Community

In the 1980s, it may hardly seem necessary to argue that religion has the potential for being a force in public life. At the national level, religious leaders have quite visibly intervened in (or interfered with, depending on one's point of view) public affairs. One Protestant minister was a serious presidential candidate in 1984; others influenced national politics through the Congress and/or campaigned in 1988 as presidential candidates. Conservative Protestant groups in particular have demonstrated a strong potential for political organizing. The American Catholic Bishops have – in two controversial pastoral letters – questioned the role of nuclear arms in American defense policy and have finalized the third draft of a critique of the American economy. Assertions are made that the Jewish community has had a powerful impact on American foreign policy in the Middle East. Few observers of the American scene in the 1980s would feel compelled to argue with the statement of the president of the American Association for the Sociology of Religion in 1978 that "religion has not disappeared as a significant social factor in American life" (Gannon 1978: 293).

The role of religion at the local community level, however, may be less obvious. Despite what he saw as a declining interest on the part of sociologists, Gannon urged (in the same address) that religion remain a "constitutive component of (family-residential) communities."

Earlier studies of urban communities clearly show religious groups serving local needs: rituals bring people together in fellowship; leaders mediate between their flocks and such impersonal outsiders as police or welfare agencies.

In assessing the strength of these bonds, it would be a serious error to view the religious influence as residual. Few social institutions can demonstrate as enduring an influence as that of religion. (Ibid.: 285, 293)

Gannon reminded his fellow sociologists of "the rich tradition of urban research which at least indirectly attests to the strength of religious solidarities" (ibid.: 295).

Peter Berger and Richard John Neuhaus (1977) have called attention to the role of religious institutions as a "mediating structure" – one of "those institutions standing between the individual in his private life and the large institutions of public life" (2). The church is only one of several such structures (including the family, neighborhood, and voluntary associations) that can serve as centers of political dialogue and political advocacy, "empowering" individual citizens in their dealings with the "megastructures" such as corporations, government, and larger labor unions. This process is seen as crucial for American public life:

Without institutionally reliable processes of mediation, the political order becomes detached from the values and realities of individual life. Deprived of its moral foundation, the political order is "delegitimated." When that happens, the political order must be secured by coercion rather than by consent. And when that happens, democracy disappears. (Ibid.: 3)

This concept of the church's political role is delineated by Wogaman (1980):

Speaking of the church's role as a mediating institution, I do not mean that the state ought to confer official status on the churches as political institutions or anything like that. Rather the church, along with many other kinds of mediating institutions, should be considered a place where political dialogue can occur, where people can confer about what values are important in the political process and by what strategies their chosen policies might be implemented. (94)

In the United States, both the Catholic Church and the mainline Protestant churches (for the most part, those belonging to the National Council of Churches) have had historical experience as mediating structures dealing with serious sociopolitical problems. In the nineteenth century, for example, slavery was a problem calling for reflection within and action by the churches. As the industrial revolution became part of the American experience, the churches began to focus on urban–industrial problems. That concern has found a somewhat different theological formulation and ecclesial style in the two traditions. But it is safe to say that a knowledge of the church's historic social theology and social mission forms part of the intellectual baggage acquired in seminary education, whatever the personal social stance or philosophy of the individual minister or priest.

Protestant Tradition

In the Protestant tradition, concern for public affairs and for social reform was an important current from the Puritan founding through the antislavery Abolitionism preceding the Civil War. After the war, satisfied by the triumph over the evil of slavery, Protestantism enjoyed a sense of security about its exercise of moral vision over American society (May 1949: pt. 2). That spirit was reflected in a sermon preached by Henry Ward Beecher to his middle-class Plymouth Church congregation in Brooklyn in 1869. In addressing the "jealousy about ministers mixing in public affairs," Beecher forthrightly affirmed the minister's

right to go into every part of society. He has a right to give advice. He has a right to whisper, if whispering is the proper method. He has a right to thunder, if thundering is the proper method. And if I do these things, no man can say, "It is none of your business." It *is* my business. Everything that is done under God's sun is my business. (In Cross 1967: 162)

The self-assurance of post–Civil War Protestantism was shaken toward the end of the nineteenth century by the new problems of America's rapidly growing cities. Charles Stelzle, of the Board of Home Missions of the Presbyterian Church, identified the cities of America as "the great storm centres of our country." He saw industrial capitalism as "centring in the city forces which may some day undermine every institution which stands for the peace and the prosperity of the nation" (Stelzle 1907: 20–1).

The filthy slum, the dark tenement, the unsanitary factory, the long hours of toil, the lack of a living wage, the backbreaking labor, the inability to pay necessary doctor's bills in times of sickness, the poor and insufficient food, the lack of leisure, the swift approach of old age, the dismal future, – these weigh down the hearts and lives of vast multitudes in our cities. . . . It is in meeting the needs of these that the Church will be severely tested in coming days. (Ibid.: 22)

The Church likewise could not forever ignore the attempts of labor to organize in the face of industrial power. The railroad strikes, the labor troubles in the Pennsylvania coal mines, the rise and fall of the Knights of Labor, the Homestead strike, the Pullman strike, and the Haymarket riot forced a reassessment of post–Civil War complacency. "Confronted by an increasingly angry and articulate labor movement which had little use for the Church, the churchmen's 'optimistic theory had to be reconsidered in the light of burning box cars'" (Carter 1956: 10).

At the same time, intellectual developments began to encourage Protestant theology in new directions. German biblical scholarship, in uncovering the social setting of the Old and New Testament revelation, invited theologians to reflect on the relationship between scriptural text and the socioeconomic situation from which it emerged. And the rise of modern social science gave scholars new conceptual methods for understanding the social forces that affected the Church's mission.

In responding to these developments, the traditional Protestant concern for public affairs developed both a new pastoral strategy and a new social theology. The pastoral strategy became centered in the "institutional church." The new theology was articulated as the "Social Gospel."

The institutional church. The rapid population growth and changing urban geography of the nation's established industrial cities created problems for the older "downtown" Protestant churches. As country dwellers and new European immigrants poured into the inner city, the older churches faced a crisis: They either moved with their congregations to the suburbs or adapted to the new constituency around them. Charles Stelzle (1907) commented:

The most superficial study of religious work reveals the fact that in almost every large city most of the great church "missions" which were once so successful have either gone out of existence altogether, or else they are being conducted upon a much smaller scale than formerly. There is scarcely a church mission in the United States but what is making a struggle for its existence – at least in comparison with its former glory.

. . . As the social conditions of the people changed, the mission failed to adjust itself to these changing conditions. As new needs arise, the mission went on, blind to its opportunities, with the result that other forces took its place in the hearts of the people. It lost its spiritual grip, because it failed to enlarge its own life and vision, by taking on the life of its constituency. (145–6)

Stelzle's remedy for this situation was for the city church to adopt a new pastoral strategy and style. It should recognize the "social question" as a religious question, establish relations with organized labor, develop new agencies to work in city slums, establish social centers, develop programs for city children. The city church should become an "institutional church." He quotes Josiah Strong, minister of the Central Congregational Church in Cincinnati:

The institutional church succeeds because it adapts itself to changed conditions. It finds that the people living around it have in their homes no opportunity to take a bath; it therefore furnishes bathing facilities. It sees that the people have little or no healthful social life; it accordingly opens attractive social rooms, and organizes clubs for men, women, boys and girls. The people know little of legitimate amusement; the Church, therefore, provides it. . . . Such a church we call "Institutional." (Ibid.: 177)

By the 1920s, Protestantism could point to a number of success stories among downtown churches. Harlan Paul Douglass (1927), as part of an extensive research project conducted by the Institute of Social and Religious Research, published a study of thirty downtown Protestant churches, from New York to San Francisco. All manifested to various degrees the "institutional" style:

Most of the case studies that make up this volume have been concerned with the brave second thoughts of churches that are making the best of bad situations. The pattern of circumstance and behavior that has been met over and over again is somewhat as follows: a desirable urban neighborhood goes bad; the church either flees, or gallantly sticks to its post, and by hook or crook manages to survive; in so doing it sometimes adapts itself to the particular needs of the locality in some part of the area of its service. (414)

One of the cases, though, was distinctive. Olivet Institute Presbyterian in Chicago did not undergo adaptation, but was founded as an "institutional church." "Its story is not that of evolution into a broad ministry of seven-day-a-week Christianity, but rather of such a ministry adopted from the outset. . . . The name Olivet Institute indicates an institution that is not merely a church" (ibid.). Olivet's physical plant occupied fifteen buildings, with less than one-fourth of its budget devoted to strictly "religious" work. "The total enterprise thus constitutes a sort of superchurch, particularly in the aspect of its exceptionally broad and basic social ministries" (ibid.: 415).

In the "institutional church," Protestantism found one way of coping with the problems of a rapidly urbanizing society.

The Social Gospel. The "social question," which Protestant pastors met face to face in the cities, did not go away when they moved from the streets into the study. One current in Protestant theology attempted to integrate the new social reality into theology. The effort had profound effects on theology itself.

Pastoral ministry in the city was a catalytic experience for several key spokespersons in the development of Social Gospel theology. Josiah Strong authored an important book identifying the industrial city as the central crisis for the nation and the church (*Our Country: Its Possible Future and Its Present Crisis*). Strong was also the dynamic organizer of a series of national conferences on the issue, the last of which was held at the Chicago World's Fair (1893). Walter Rauschenbusch, before becoming a professor of church history, spent eleven years ministering to a German Baptist congregation near Hell's Kitchen in New York City. That experience was the inspiration for three books that made him perhaps the foremost American Protestant thinker for two decades: *Christianity and the Social Crisis* (1907), *Christianizing the Social Order* (1912), which prescribed reforms for American capitalism, and *A Theology for the Social Gospel* (1917). Reinhold Niebuhr, the theologian who moved beyond the Social Gospel into a theology of political realism, served as pastor at Bethel Evangelical in Detroit from 1915 until he departed for Union Theological Seminary in 1928. Though Niebuhr's congregation was middle rather than working class, he knew workers in the Ford factories and served in the larger civic life as chair of the mayor's Commission on Interracial Relations and member of the Industrial Relations Commission of the Detroit Council of Churches.

As a theological movement, the Social Gospel articulated in theological terms the social passion of the urban minister. The Social Gospel was clearly linked to the reform currents of the Progressive Era. Historian Donald Meyer (1960) notes that the pastors "were a kind of register of the penetration of the religious community by ideas from more secular headquarters" (2). Meyer himself leaves open the question of which came first, secular reform or Social Gospel. But his exhaustive study tells a rich and complex tale of "religion itself, as challenged by politics."

The intellectual origins of the Social Gospel theology might well include the economic, political, and social ideas of Progressivism. But the new theology also depended on and was linked to the new biblical criticism coming from the German universities. Research into Near Eastern languages, literature, and history provided Christian theologians with a new understanding of the relationship between scriptural text and its social setting. The discovery was aided by the emergence of modern sociology as an independent discipline and instrument for social analysis. Armed with these new critical tools, some scholars went so far as to reinterpret the mission of Jesus as the founding of socialism. Such an endeavor was rather quickly seen as overambitious. The attempt, however, illustrates the rediscovery in Protestant theology of the *social* dimension in the Church's mission.

A key insight of the Social Gospel theology, especially as articulated by Rauschenbusch, was that the essence of the Christian message had been held captive for sixteen centuries by its own success in converting the Roman Empire. After the time of Constantine, theology and Christian mission were free to preach only to the individual. But in the twentieth century, the true message of Jesus was being rediscovered. For Rauschenbusch, the Social Gospel literally marked a decisive turning point in history: "It would mean a real difference, in politics, in economics, in society generally. The new field for Christian action was the social system; it was society that was to experience Christian conversion" (ibid.: 15).

Although Rauschenbusch died shortly before Armistice Day, the Protestant idealism he articulated came to a peak just after the end of World War I. Methodists organized a three-week centennial celebration at the state fair grounds in Columbus, Ohio; they rejoiced in 1 million paid admissions and collected subscriptions of $140 million. The Disciples of Christ renewed their own Men and Millions Movement. Presbyterians, also meeting in general assembly at Columbus, issued an invitation for a Protestant ecumenical union. In response, the Interchurch World Movement was born, with the program of developing a worldwide religious survey to enable "the complete evangelization of all of life" (ibid.).

The ecumenical fervor of the postwar years had been prepared by the launching of the Federal Council of Churches in 1908. At that point, the foundation for interchurch dialogue and cooperation was the social action agenda.

It is an indication of how far the Social Gospel had permeated the Church that in those days it was the one issue upon which groups as diverse as the Episcopalians and the Quakers could agree sufficiently to permit it to be used as a basis for ecumenical union. (Carter 1956: 11)

The social agenda was also a priority for the Interchurch Movement. In fact, its commitment to action for social change was to produce Interchurch's outstanding accomplishment – as well as lead to its undoing.

As the new ecumenical movement was getting organized in 1919, steelworkers went on strike in response to U.S. Steel's antiunionization activities. The U.S. secretary of labor and officials of the American Federation of Labor asked the Interchurch Movement to investigate. A team of investigators, headed by a former captain of Army Intelligence on General Pershing's staff, was sent to Pennsylvania. The study was both comprehensive and professional. The draft was submitted to and approved by a three-person committee, including John D. Rockefeller, Jr. The "1919 Report" was released in two parts. An initial report, published in July 1920, focused on excessive hours; it triggered an attack on the twelve-hour shift in industry that was backed by President Harding himself. A second report, published in 1921, provided an intensive investigation of the steel situation in Pennsylvania, including attitudes of the press and the state government, U.S. Steel's use of labor spies, and tactics of union organization. Since none of this information had been given to the general public, the report broke the conspiracy of silence in the secular press. It remains an important document in American industrial history.

The president of U.S. Steel, Judge Gary, inspired an attack on the Interchurch report by the American Iron and Steel Institute and in the *Wall Street Journal*. The strike ended with steelworkers going back to work a twelve-hour day. But Judge Gary was ultimately forced to concede; U.S. Steel completed the switchover to a three-shift work day in 1923.

The Interchurch Movement, however, was no longer around to celebrate the victory. After the steel strike investigation, the financial support envisioned for the movement (1 billion dollars was the goal) never materialized. Partly for lack of funds, partly because of the weight of its ambitious goals, the Interchurch Movement collapsed.

The Social Gospel found both rejection and acceptance in American business circles. Judge Gary, a Methodist, remained the prize pagan. Visited by a delegation from the Federal Council of Churches during the steel strike, he refused to be converted. Later, officials of his company would charge the Interchurch team investigating the steel strike of being tainted by Bolshevism.

John D. Rockefeller, Jr., was the prize convert. He took

opposition to Gary in approving the steel strike report. When strikes and violence occurred at his Colorado Fuel and Iron Company, Rockefeller inaugurated a shop committee plan that was hailed as a model of Christian stewardship and imitated by other corporations. (When the plan failed to realize the industrial democracy that it promised, Rockefeller was willing to revise the plan in 1927.) There were other examples, too. Arthur Nash, when his Cincinnati textile company earned a million-dollar dividend, gave one-third of it to the workers; he himself instigated unionization of the plant by the Amalgamated Clothing Worker Union. The Dutchess Bleachery Mill (where "earnest Christian layman" Harold Hatch was chairman of the board) included representatives of both the work force and the local community on the board of directors. John J. Eagan (a member of the Federal Council of Churches Commission on Race Relations) bequeathed his American Cast Iron Pipe Company to its workers at his death in 1924 (Meyer 1960: 55–85).

These models of virtue were extolled in conferences and in the religious press. Not only did they provide examples of ethical action; they represented the ideal of a new world, a society structured on the pattern of the Gospel. But preaching the Social Gospel in the board room was not always effective. One Protestant pastor in Detroit concluded:

Realistic laymen were, and have remained, more largely untouched by the whole movement than is generally supposed. I was during all this period the minister of two churches whose congregations included men of status and force in highly industrialized cities. I do not think they shared the official social passion of the communion to which they belonged, knew much or cared much about it. That they knew no more was probably the fault of their minister. But, as far as they did know, their response lacked warmth. The more conservative were politely hostile. (Meyer 1970: 75)

Business leaders – whether receptive to the Social Gospel or not – were still in the pews (even Judge Gary was a practicing Methodist). But labor was not there at all – a source of both guilt and anxiety to Social Gospel proponents. Three strategies were adopted to bridge the gap.

First, the churches took the initiative in carrying the Gospel to the workers by founding special "labor churches." One form of this effort was directed simply at converting the unchurched workers to the traditional faith, giving them an alternative to

Bolshevism. The Methodist Church in particular devoted funds for a special mission of this type to workers in Pennsylvania. An alternative was the founding of the Labor Temple by Charles Stelzle in New York in 1910. The Labor Temple abandoned any Protestant affiliation in order to be a religion of community service (Meyer 1960: 80).

The second strategy was labor diplomacy, engaging in dialogue with labor organizations. The AFL proved adept at this type of contact, speaking in church pulpits and praising the interest of Social Gospel leaders as a sign of encouragement to the labor movement. The "labor sermon" approach did not always work, however. A proposed series at five churches in Detroit was partially blocked by church boards, fearing to alienate industrialists who backed the open shop.

The third strategy was to be present and provide assistance at strikes. One form of this strategy was to investigate and report on strike situations, as in the steel strike of 1919. In one famous case in Lawrence, three ministers actually became leaders of a thirty-thousand-worker textile strike. Officials of the United Textile Workers wished to accept a cut in wages, but the workers objected. When the UTW pulled out, the workers were left with only an inexperienced strike committee for leadership. There was real danger of violence; machine guns were issued to the police. Into this breach stepped three young ministers, A. J. Muste, Harold Rotzel, and Cedric Long. Under their leadership, the strike was eventually settled. Other Lawrence clergy failed to support the strike, however. In the end, all three strike leaders left the active church ministry, loosening in their own lives the connection between the Social Gospel and the Church.

By the end of the 1920s, the idealism of a decade earlier had largely disappeared; it was clear that the Social Gospel vision was not to be easily realized. Events of the 1930s threw into question the whole possibility of a synthesis of "Gospel" and "society" in the existing sociopolitical order. First, the Depression pushed Social Gospel thinkers toward socialism as the only hope for a good society. This left them with the problem of reconciling the ethic of Marxist class struggle with the ethic of Christian love – a task that took its toll in anxiety and confusion. In addition, the failure of Prohibition revealed the danger of attempting to absolutize the Protestant vision of a Gospel-based society in politics. Finally, the coming of war challenged the Social Gospel preference for pacifism, forcing liberal and progressive Protestants to search for a more realistic ethic of violence. Meyer summarizes the dilemma:

Under pressure, social-gospel politics moved in one of two directions, toward sectarian myth or toward expedient compromise. The sectarians managed to protect some of the critical quality of their idealism, but at the expense of relevance. The others . . . worked closer to relevant realities, but with the loss of the cutting-power of their religious word. (Ibid.: 227)

It was the task of Reinhold Niebuhr to propose a way out of this dilemma. Two factors are important for understanding Niebuhr's theology. First, he was and remained a practical pastor, never far from the experience of ethical decision making. He was keenly aware of the practical failures of the Social Gospel. Second, Niebuhr – unlike the earlier Social Gospel theologians – had read Karl Barth. The great German theologian's commentary on the Letter to the Romans was published in 1918; Niebuhr himself wrote on Barth in the late 1920s (see Niebuhr 1977). Barth saw in the German experience the danger of canonizing any political arrangements as a Christian society. His critique rang through European theological circles.

Niebuhr's task as theologian was to salvage the idealism of the Social Gospel, while refining it in the crucible of experience. The result found formulation in his book *Moral Man and Immoral Society* (Niebuhr 1932). His basic thesis was that good men, in working to establish the good society, might have to choose means they would prefer not to employ. It might be necessary to oppose power with power. Niebuhr was also realistic about ends. It was too much to expect the good society to embody an ethic of love. The best that could be hoped for was justice, which provided a more relevant standard for politics than love.

Niebuhr's political realism of the 1930s was very different from the Social Gospel of the early 1900s. "The Christian social consciousness of the followers of Reinhold Niebuhr would hardly have been recognizable to the followers of Walter Rauschenbusch, either in its social or in its Christian characteristics" (Carter 1954: 220). Implicit in the older Social Gospel was the assumption that the world could, once and for all, be Christianized. Niebuhr represents a definitive break with this perspective. The Kingdom of God would not be realized in America, any more than in Germany. Niebuhr's achievement was to preserve the traditional faith as a basis for Christian ethical action. The tone was far more pessimistic than the Social Gospel had been. But it can be argued that Niebuhr saved for Protestant theology a way to think in religious and ethical terms about the hard realities.

The historian of American religion Sidney Ahlstrom (1972) evaluates the Social Gospel as follows:

The men who felt deeply about issues and wanted reform – or even social revolution – found agencies and platforms in the churches where they could speak, organize, publish and act. How positive a response they got from the rank-and-file membership is another question. The revival of social concern and the great increase in liberal pronouncements by church groups of various types seems not to have brought Protestant churchgoers to a position in advance of the American electorate, though it probably brought many to a broader understanding of the issues and of the need for social change. (786)

Catholic Tradition

At the time American Protestants were beginning to focus theological reflection and church organization on urban–industrial problems, the Catholic community in America was faced with a complex of growing pains: building new churches and finding priests to assimilate the huge number of immigrants from Catholic Europe, launching a separate parochial school system as an alternative to public education, coping with ethnic divisions among American Catholics (particularly between the Germans and the Irish). For the most part, Americans were too busy to stop and reflect on what was happening in their church; when they did, their reflection brought them into conflict with the Roman Church's traditional self-understanding.

As Catholicism was sinking roots in American soil, the Roman Church in Europe was undergoing a deep transformation. As industrial capitalism took on social welfare aspects around the turn of the century, a new theology and pastoral strategy began to emerge. In theological terms, the Catholic Church began to interpret social welfare liberalism as a missionary field open to conversion. Its new pastoral strategy was adaptive (rather than defensive).

The older thinking died hard, however, and the transformation occasioned some ecclesiastical schizophrenia. One theoretical formulation of the new church self-understanding was dubbed "Americanism" – though it found articulation primarily in France. These ideas were condemned in the Vatican encyclical letter *Testem Benevolentiae* (1899), a reactionary resurgence of the traditional thinking. This encyclical, condemning Americanism as a heresy, had the effect of dampening creative theological reflection in America for virtually the next half-century. According to Father Walter Ong (1957), American Catholics "were so chastened, . . . that they turned more industriously than ever to developing 'know-how' and letting theory be" (22).

Within the whole Americanism affair, however, there was one important victory for the Catholic Church in America. It concerned the Church's stance toward organized labor. The majority of Catholic immigrants settled in the cities of America as industrial workers. They naturally became involved in early efforts to organize trade unions. One such effort, the Knights of Labor, fell afoul of Vatican restrictions on Catholic participation in secret societies – a prohibition aimed at European, particularly French, Freemasonry. The Canadian archbishop of Quebec twice forbade Catholics from joining the Knights of Labor, a ruling upheld on both occasions by the Vatican. The "secrecy" practiced by the Knights was at least as much a practical matter (to keep critical information from leaking to employers) as it was ritualistic. In 1887, Cardinal Gibbons of Baltimore, an aggressive friend of organized labor, presented a memorial to the Vatican minimizing the danger to Catholic workers' faith and insisting that even an apparent alliance between the Church and the powerful rich would alienate Catholic wage earners from the Church and drive them into the camp of revolution. Gibbons prevailed, - and his action tightened bonds of sympathy between the Catholic Church and conservative trade unionism. The Church's openness to organized labor was reaffirmed in the encyclical *Rerum Novarum* of Leo XIII in 1891. This early alliance between the Catholic Church and American labor may have been a significant factor in preventing the emergence of a revolutionary labor movement in the United States (Abell 1968: 143).

After World War I, while the Social Gospel thinking in the Protestant churches was culminating in the investigation of the 1919 steel strike, the Catholic bishops were developing a distinct pastoral strategy of their own regarding industrial relations. Amid the postwar labor strife and talk of radical change, an American priest, John A. Ryan, penned an essay entitled "Social Reconstruction: A General Review of the Problems and Survey of the Remedies." A committee of bishops of the National Catholic War Council (shortly changed to National Catholic Welfare Conference) adopted the statement, which became known as the Bishops' Program of Social Reconstruction. It was issued on Lincoln's birthday, 1919.[1]

The bishops' program was more a practical than a theoretical document. The position staked out by the bishops lay midway between the British Labour Party's postwar Social Reconstruction Program, on the one side, and conservative American trade unionism, on the other. The bishops' program rejected the Fabian Socialists's call for "immediate radical reforms, leading ultimately to complete socialism" (Catholic Bishops of the United States 1919: no. 4). Not only did the document view the "collectivist organization of industry" in the United States as a practical impossibility, it also voiced a fundamental objection in principle: "Socialism would mean bureaucracy, political tyranny, the helplessness of the individual as a factor in the ordering of his own life, and in general social inefficiency and decadence" (ibid.: no. 33).

While the British program was seen as too radical, the bishops also criticized the American Federation of Labor for being too conservative. The bishops faulted the American labor organization for its failure to "demand or imply that the workers should ever aspire to become owners as well as users of the instruments of production" (ibid.: no. 6). Worker copartnership was one of the fundamental principles of social reconstruction:

The majority must somehow become owners, or at least in part, of the instruments of production. They can be enabled to reach this stage gradually through cooperative productive societies and copartnership arrangements. In the former, the workers own and manage the industries themselves, in the latter they own a substantial part of the corporate stock and exercise a reasonable share in the management. (Ibid.: no. 36)

Though this constituted a call for radical change, the bishops clearly intended something different from socialism:

It is to be noted that this particular modification of the existing order, though far-reaching and involving to a great extent the abolition of the wage system, would not mean the abolition of private ownership. The instruments of production would still be owned by individuals, not by the state. (Ibid.: no. 36)

Among its recommendations for improving labor conditions and social welfare generally, the bishops' program included advocacy of a minimum legal wage, government housing for workers, and social insurance.

The bishops' conference set up a Social Action Department, headed by Ryan, the author-architect of the program. Ryan's efforts at implementation, however, were not immediately successful. First, American labor organizations, stung by some bad experiences with worker ownership arrangements in the Knights of Labor phase, were not interested in the worker ownership approach to industrial arrangements (though they were glad to have Ryan's help in fighting the "open shop"). Second, there was considerable opposition to the program from conservative Catholics (especially Germans who did not accept Ryan's views and those of the Irish at Catholic University as the only orthodox interpretation of Pope Leo XIII's principles). Ryan was even "banned in Boston" by Cardinal O'Connell for his support of the child labor amendment (McShane 1986: 269).

Despite Ryan's efforts, the bishops' program had minimal impact on public policy in the 1920s. It was left to Franklin Roosevelt and the New Deal to realize some of the concrete proposals advocated in the program.

In the Depression era, the American bishops again voiced their sympathy with working people and their problems:

Unemployment is the great peacetime physical tragedy of the nineteenth and twentieth centuries, and both in its cause and the imprint it leaves upon those who inflict it, those who permit it, and those who are its victims, it is one of the great moral tragedies of our time. (Catholic Bishops of the United States 1930: no. 3)

In 1933, the bishops called for "rigorous application of moral principles to big corporations." They advocated "smaller units of business and production," admonishing that "local communities should take pride in them" (Catholic Bishops of the United States 1933: no. 72).

Before World War II, the economic statements of the Catholic hierarchy represented a continuing concern for the welfare of working people, who represented the large majority of the

Catholic constituency in America. Articulated in these documents is a constructive criticism of the American political economy, including recognition of the rights of labor to organize, to receive fair wages, and to hold jobs, the responsible role of government in its welfare and tax policies, and the moral character of economic life.

Essentially, the American bishops called for a correction of the American economy, based both on their analysis of the needs of their people and on an emerging Catholic theology of social justice. The pastoral strategy was adaptive, aimed at opening up opportunity within the American system, rather than calling for any radical transformation.

One significant effort on behalf of labor came from the Jesuits. In a number of major industrial and port cities – Boston, Philadelphia, New Orleans, St. Louis, San Francisco – Jesuit priests instituted "labor schools" to train workers in union organization and industrial relations. One such institution still flourishes; the Labor Guild of Boston has 1,200 members (management and trade union officials, attorneys, labor relations professionals) and publishes the most comprehensive guidebook on Massachusetts employment law.

The 1960s initiated a new period of transformation, both in worldwide Catholicism and for the American Catholic Church. The election of Pope John XXIII and the Second Vatican Council brought deep and far-reaching changes both in the Roman Church's internal order and in its stance toward the non-Catholic world. One dimension of the transformation (perhaps the most fundamental) was a new self-understanding of the Church's mission built on the problematic of justice. In the post–Vatican II Church, justice is more than a virtue studied in the category of moral theology. It is a foundational vision for all of theology. This new Church self-understanding – of potentially profound significance – began to take shape in the documents of the Vatican Council, in the encyclical *Populorum Progressio* (The development of peoples, 1967), and in the International Bishops' Synods of 1971 and 1975.

On the western side of the Atlantic, this new self-understanding of the Church coincided with significant developments for American Catholics. The election of the Irish Catholic John F. Kennedy as president in 1960 both symbolized and helped to effect the "arrival" of Catholics in the American middle-class mainstream. At the same time, the Kennedy era brought a new awareness of "the other America" – the permanently poor – and a new concern for the denial of civil rights to blacks and other minorities.

The American bishops, in addressing widespread poverty and racism in their society, addressed American Catholics no longer as the underclass, but on behalf of the poor and nonwhite minorities. In 1970, the bishops established the Campaign for Human Development to provide seed money for antipoverty programs and hoped their actions would effect in the nonpoor "a conversion of heart, a growth in compassion and sensitivity to the needs of their brothers in want" (Catholic Bishops of the United States 1970). These were inklings of a new understanding of the Church's mission and a new pastoral strategy.

American Churches in the 1960s and 1970s

Two major themes in religious developments at the national level were important for shaping the possibilities of religious action in Youngstown. First was the strengthening of interfaith relations between the Protestant and Catholic communities in particular. The Catholic renewal initiated by Pope John and the Council signaled a theological opening that led to important steps in Protestant–Catholic ecumenism at the grass-roots level.

The second theme was the mutuality that Protestant and Catholic Church people discovered in their reaction to three sociopolitical crises that dominated American public life in the 1960s and 1970s. First, the civil rights revolution had strong organizational links to the religious sector, particularly in the black Protestant churches, but also brought forth strong activist elements in white Protestantism and Catholicism. Second, opposition to the Vietnam War found Catholics and Protestants in the same demonstrations and forging links in such organizations as Clergy and Laity Concerned. Finally, the Watergate episode had important implications for American religion. Even conservative religious leaders predisposed to support the political establishment found themselves asking uncustomary critical questions. Interestingly, it was a Catholic priest – the Jesuit Father Robert Drinan, who – as congressman from Boston – presented the first bill of impeachment in the House of Representatives against President Nixon. The subsequent election of Jimmy Carter as president in 1976 was furthered in no small measure by his public religious stance and by his skill in using church networks in the early months of his presidential campaign.

Religion was profoundly involved in these three social crises. For the most part, church leaders at the top were hesitant to take strong sides in these controversies. But by the mid-1970s, significant elements in both Protestant and Catholic churches had been sufficiently shocked (or at least discomforted) by national events that a deep shift had been created in the position of the churches vis-à-vis the American establishment. Until now, Catholics had largely refrained from criticizing the "system" because their big drive was to become part of it. Protestant churches, for the most part, had provided the American establishment with its moral justification. But in the 1970s, it became thinkable for basically conservative and respectable church leaders to entertain serious criticism of the American system.

As national life returned to normal in the mid-1970s, the churches had within the ranks of their clergy at local and middle-management levels a small, but identifiable cadre of people who shared a generally liberal viewpoint, who were willing to make connections between religion and public policy, and who had learned something about the organization of political protest. Their concern for the relationship between church and society was not simply turned off and filed away until the next national crisis.

One focus for the social energies of the Protestant churches was rediscovery of the city, which some Protestants saw as a reaction to the geographic and intellectual suburbanization of American Protestantism. Catholics, who were strongly concentrated in the urban areas of the Northeast and Midwest, had maintained somewhat stronger cultural links with the cities, but had largely let lapse the strong ties with labor that were characteristic of the organizing phase in the 1930s and 1940s.

Beginning in 1975, a year when unemployment jumped to 8.5%, official statements from both Protestant and Catholic church bodies reflected a new concern by national church leadership for economic justice in general and urban unemployment in particular.

On November 20, 1975, the U.S. Catholic Conference issued "The Economy: Human Dimensions; A Statement of the Catholic Bishops of the United States." The bishops called for an end to unemployment and directed attention to principles drawn from the "social teachings of the Church" – among others, the principles that economic activity should be governed by justice; that opportunities for work should be provided for all able and willing to work; that development planning belongs to all people, not just a few; that government should promote the economic activity of its citizens and safeguard their rights (Catholic Bishops of the United States 1975).

The 1976 General Conference of the United Methodist Church issued "Unemployment: 1976 General Conference Statement." In a ten-point position statement on full employment, the Methodist body stated, "Every citizen of the United States has a right to meaningful, useful, rewarding employment contributing to the public good at a wage that is supportive of an adequate standard of living with human dignity."

Also in 1976, the 188th General Assembly of the United Presbyterian Church USA commended a statement by its Task Force on the Impact of U.S. Economic Power. The general question addressed by the study was, "From our Christian perspective, what should society expect an economic system to do?" The study, entitled "Economic Justice within Environmental Limits: The Need for a New Economic Ethic," provides historical background on the church's economic concern and looks at the ideology and values underlying the U.S. economic system. A followup study explores neighborhood-based models for job creation.

The 11th General Synod of the United Church of Christ, basing a concern for high unemployment rates on history, scripture, and theology, called for the denomination to "reaffirm the God-given right of all persons to useful and remunerative work, together with the responsibility to provide for themselves and their dependents." The synod authorized an educational program and allocated $100,000 to fund it for two years.

The Division of Church and Society of the National Council of Churches published a position paper entitled "Work Without Want", which surveyed the unemployment scene in the United States and presented principles for a "National Program of Economic Security" (Ross 1976).

It would be a serious mistake to assume that such statements of national church bodies are always translated into action by local congregations. But neither are they meaningless. At the least, they represent the initiative of sufficient concerned individuals within a denomination to put the issue on the church's agenda. They also provide a policy statement guiding the disposition of some program funds at the national level. And they can publicize issues through the denominations' communication networks, especially their news publications and programs of adult education.

Actions at the national and international levels of theological formulation and church administration do not always penetrate to local congregations. But the local churches sometimes do act on the ideas and models developed at the cutting edge. This was the case in Youngstown.

Religion and Urban Community in Youngstown

Important elements in the religious sector in Youngstown were at least in accord with, if not actually ahead of, trends at the national level. Three factors stand out as particularly important.

Catholic Church

The first is the position of the Catholic Church in the Youngstown area. Since the Catholic immigration of the early twentieth century, Catholics have comprised the largest religious group in Youngstown. In 1978, they still constituted 68% of the population of Mahoning County. Generational change and suburbanization have lessened the ties between ethnic cultures and Catholicism over the years. But Youngstown in the 1970s still had parishes that were designated informally (if no longer officially) as Slovak or Italian. And the mutual reinforcement of traditional religious and ethnic cultural patterns persisted with striking force.

An important aspect of traditional Catholicism in Youngstown was the multifunctional social role of the clergy. The priest in an ethnic parish often had a variety of functions in addition to his role as leader of prayer and worship. He was marriage counselor for adults and disciplinarian for unruly teenagers. He was school administrator, resident intellectual, and interpreter of the larger society for newcomers. He was a broker for the interests of his people with government officials. And he took a strong role in economic life where necessary. Father Edward Stanton remembers that, as late as the 1940s, a new immigrant in Hubbard (near Youngstown) went first to the parish priest, who took the newcomer to the mill to arrange for a job. (Youngstown priests were not always on the side of labor: Bishop Malone remembered that in the "little steel" strike in Youngstown in the 1930s, priests crossed picket lines to go into the mill and say Mass for the strike*breakers*.) Of course, rising educational levels and the integration of Catholics into American culture as a whole have tended to delimit the social role of the pastor. Nevertheless, the idea that the clergy should be concerned about jobs and the social and economic welfare of their people is an old and familiar principle to local residents.

It is possible to discern in the social position of Catholicism in Youngstown a kind of "modernity of tradition." It was precisely the vigor of traditional Catholicism, and particularly the traditional social role of the priest, that gave legitimacy to the "modern" leadership role assumed by the Catholic clergy.

A second aspect of the paradox is that, within the traditional and parochial setting of Catholic Youngstown, two clergymen emerged with unusual "secular" skills and abilities: Bishop James Malone and Father Ed Stanton.

Malone would need only to exchange his clerical collar for a "power tie" to pass for the ideal U.S. senator. Handsome, silver-haired, and smooth-mannered, Malone meets people easily and has a legendary memory for names. A former school superintendent, he was at the time one of the few Catholic bishops to have earned a Ph.D. in a secular field (education). He is an articulate speaker and has an unusual ability to grasp the essentials of a problem in a few minutes and then lay it out for the press in perfectly quotable paragraphs. Despite his gentle manner, Malone has a powerful public presence and a commander's toughness under pressure. Having won a bout with cancer, he does not scare easily.

Malone's father was a Youngstown steelworker. He recalls that, during the "little steel" strike, his father

went on strike like most of the other men. History tells us that the companies hired strikebreakers, with the emphasis on "break." One day my dad came home from picket duty with a gash in his head. His wound and all it stood for left me with the lasting conviction that the church's witness on behalf of justice can't be overplayed. (Malone 1981)

Father Ed Stanton was on Malone's staff as diocesan director of social action. Stanton had worked summers in a steel mill while in the seminary, was close to steelworkers and known as a union man. As treasurer of WREDA, Stanton was also acquainted with the management side of the industry through the agency's work on the pollution study and other projects. Where Malone was the perfect front man, Stanton took the role of the heavyweight. A large man with a brusque and incisive manner, Stanton could amply anchor one side of a negotiating table. He was savvy and street smart, but a good enough diplomat to cultivate connections and know-how to use them skillfully. Stanton liked the conflict of politics, and one time almost ran for the City Council. But he was even more the conciliator, a role that drew out his ability to identify and articulate issues. In the Youngstown public school teachers' strike of 1973 (the first major teacher walkout in the country), both sides sought out Stanton after reaching an impasse; the strike was ultimately settled with his mediation in a meeting room at the Catholic cathedral. Later, serving as the court-appointed arbitrator in another teachers' strike in Trumbull County, he took the last-best offer of both sides and literally overnight scissors-and-pasted together an eighty-eight-page labor contract that both sides agreed to the next day without a change.

Stanton and Malone had an implicit understanding of the theory of Catholic social action, based on a straightforward reading of their church's normative documents. When Stanton first took the job of social action director on Malone's staff, the guidelines for his new position were agreed on in a five-minute stroll with the bishop across the cathedral parking lot. Stanton said he would do nothing more or less than follow the statements of the Vatican and of the American bishops – to which Malone obviously subscribed.

Malone, in a private interview, volunteered that the best articulation of his own thinking about the practical social role of a Catholic bishop could be found in a statement to the American Bishops' Conference by the Jesuit theologian Avery Dulles (son of the late secretary of state John Foster Dulles).

Dulles's talk is a highlighting of and commentary on two documents, the encyclical *Development of Peoples* of Pope Paul VI (1967) and the statement of the Catholic Bishops' Synod of 1971, "Justice in the World." The encyclical is the more abstract theological document, famous for its declaration that "the new name for peace is development." The synod document is the more concrete. Its central thesis is expressed in an often quoted sentence: "Action on behalf of justice and participation in the transformation of the world fully appear to us as a constitutive dimension of the preaching of the Gospel, or in other words, of the Church's mission for the redemption of the human race and its liberation from every oppressive situation" (Catholic Bishops' Synod 1971).

Dulles (1975) elaborates on the Church's dilemma of locating its pastoral strategy between the general and the particular:

If it sticks to generalities, the Church alienates those who want to see the Church denounce specific evils with prophetic vigor, with some cutting edge and bite.

If, on the other hand, the Church does espouse particular solutions to political, economic, or social problems, then the Church is accused of wandering into areas in which it has no special competence and of preaching conjectural human theories in place of the Gospel of Christ. And so, it alienates good Christians whose prudential judgments on practical issues differ from those who purport to speak for the Church.

Dulles does not say that bishops should refrain from taking "positive initiatives in applying the Gospel to the social, political and cultural problems of the day." He does warn the bishops to avoid the wrong kind of authoritarianism and suggests five cautions: (a) Get the advice of competent experts. (b) Make known how a decision has been reached, perhaps pointing to studies that have been commissioned. (c) Use a rhetoric inviting thoughtful agreement, without threatening those who dissent. (d) Make it clear that Church members are free to disagree if they have reasons or authorities of equal or greater weight. (e) Do not merely speak, but "be prepared to follow up [your] words with appropriate actions" (ibid.).

First Presbyterian Church

A second key factor on the local scene in Youngstown was the First Presbyterian Church and its program of revitalization. Founded in 1799, "Old First" became known in its formative period (1875–1935) as the "management church." (It should be recalled that 60% of the "iron barons" were Presbyterian.) In 1955, the congregation decided not to relocate in the suburbs, but to rebuild on Wick Avenue, one block north of the downtown business center; the new church building was completed in 1960. The decade following brought not growth, but decline – for city and church alike. The church faced a crisis of identity; it had made a commitment to staying downtown, but had little idea of what a downtown church should be or do.

In 1972, the pastor retired, giving the church an opportunity to initiate a self-study and search for new leadership. Eugene C. Bay was called as pastor in May 1974. Bay was assured that First Church was serious about trying to discover and undertake ministries appropriate for a "downtown" church. Particularly in order to bolster the church's urban and social thrust, Robert Campbell was called as associate pastor in the fall of 1975. Campbell brought unusual capabilities and experiences to the Presbyterian pastorate. An antiwar activist in the Vietnam period, he had worked for eight years as a steelworker and had four years of experience as a union grievance committeeman. Together, Bay and Campbell set out on a long-term program that would reconsider the church's internal structure and ministry, as well as consciously develop its mission for the city.[2]

Bay and Campbell decided that the model for development would be that of a "Protestant cathedral," not so much trying to gather all into its fold as exercising a ministry of "summoning and sending." Four primary thrusts were identified: worship, theological reflection, pastoral care, and reflection on and response to social needs and issues. The four points were tightly interwoven. Through its worship, the pastors wished "to offer the community an understanding of the gospel different from the personalistic, other-worldly interpretation which dominated the Youngstown religious landscape. The Reformed tradition offered another perspective" (Bay and Campbell 1979: 16).

But to achieve this goal, it was necessary to upgrade the theological capability of the church's membership:

It was required of the members of the church that they discover for themselves what the Reformed tradition is and how best to give expression to it in the last quarter of the twentieth century. . . . Without skill in theological reflection, their approach to the renewal of worship promised to be faddish. (Ibid.: 17)

Theological capability was fundamental to the success of the entire project. "In order for First Church to assist with the transformation of the community, it had to help that community grapple, not just from sociological perspectives, but from theological perspectives, with the issues before it" (ibid.).

Theological as well as environmental reasons called for attention to social needs and issues. "The Reformed tradition," according to the pastors, "has to do with the totality of life." They saw in the ministry of John Calvin in Geneva an inspiration for the ministry of First Church:

Calvin was "preacher to the city" as well as preacher to a Sunday congregation. A week in Calvin's ministry was as likely to include an argument with local merchants over interest rates as a discussion with church elders over the proper form of the Communion service. He was as likely to be seen in a meeting of the town council . . . as in his own study at night writing Bible Commentaries. And he was as likely to be discussing with a manufacturer a scheme for getting jobs for unemployed Protestant refugees as he was to be preparing next Sunday's sermon. (Ostrom and Shriver in ibid.: 18–19).

Operationalizing the social witness aspect of First Church's revitalization began with the formation of a Church and Society Committee, which developed its own "job description": "First, it should become aware of social needs and issues and choose from among them a few requiring additional study. Second, after study, it should recommend action by the church. Third, the committee should be the educator of the congregation regarding social needs and issues" (ibid.: 146).

The committee and the pastors together focused energy on revitalizing the city. Particularly important was the inauguration of a series of Sunday morning forums. In the fall of 1976, a series was held on the topic "Downtown – Future Possible." One presenter in that series was Mr. Arthur Young, member of First Church and president of the downtown Mahoning Bank. Having first approached his topic with some reluctance, Young admitted that he had become a "convert to what was possible." "Mr. Young emphasized that what was needed in the Mahoning Valley was a strategy group of community leaders who were above political and business partisanship and who were willing to strategize about the revitalization of the entire metropolitan area" (ibid.: 156).

The school desegregation suit also provided the church another opportunity for community education with a series on school desegregation. (Meanwhile Bay and Campbell were instrumental in organizing Educational Opportunity Youngstown, in which they headed two of the three subcommittees.) In the spring of 1977, a series on labor–management issues was initiated, including talks on the Protestant work ethic by Dr. Richard Stone, the Catholic theory of profit for the common good by Father Edward Stanton, and the practice of labor–management cooperation in the steel pollution case by Mr. William Sullivan. In the fall, an additional forum brought Attorney Staughton Lynd to First Church for a discussion of the plight of the rank-and-file worker who was often neither cared for by his company nor represented by his union. Lynd addressed the obligation of the steel industry to the Youngstown-area community. His presentation, on Sunday, September 18, was headlined on Monday's paper – immediately below the story of the Sheet and Tube shutdown:

Management has as great a responsibility to its work force as it does to make a profit, Lynd said. "When industry asks for a no-strike pledge (a reference to the steel industry's Experimental Negotiating Agreement), the union can legitimately ask for some guarantee that its members won't be laid off."

It is wrong for a company to come to town, allow families to depend on it for a livelihood, and then leave simply because it thinks it can make a larger profit elsewhere, Lynd stated. It must acquire a greater sense of social responsibility. It must reinvest its profits where it earned them. (Youngstown *Vindicator*, September 19, 1977)

Bay and Campbell (1979) stated of their work at First Church: "Part of the purpose of this project was to determine if and how one downtown church could exert a redemptive influence on the city of Youngstown" (144). In the steel crisis that began on Monday, September 19, their two years of work met a very real test. The important thing is that First Presbyterian Church was able to play a key role in the religious response to the steel shutdown because of what was already under way.

Interfaith Relations

A third key factor is the development of interfaith relations in Youngstown-area religious groups. Here Youngstown manifested in the 1970s a development at the grass-roots level that mirrored, and even went beyond, religious developments at the national and international level.

Among Protestant churches, the focal point for ecumenism was the Mahoning Valley Association of Churches, which was founded in 1916. Membership in the Association was by individual congregations rather than by denominational affiliation; hence personal and parochial factors were an influence on ecumenical participation, along with theological persuasion. Approximately one hundred congregations in the Youngstown area belonged to the Association. Participation in this local ecumenism largely mirrored the national scene; congregations belonging to the Association were predominantly from the "mainline" churches (e.g., Episcopal, Presbyterian, Methodist, Lutheran), whereas the more evangelical and fundamentalist congregations remained unaffiliated.

Serious Protestant–Catholic relations date from the Second Vatican Council in the 1960s. When Bishop Malone returned from Rome, he found Protestant leaders vitally interested in the newer, open stance of the Catholic Church. Programs of shared worship and exchange of pulpits were initiated and have become an accepted tradition. Catholic congregations did not join the Association of Churches, but in the past two decades, representatives from the Catholic diocese have cooperated with the Association at a task-force level. In the early 1970s, the Association set up a Committee on Human Needs to monitor specific local questions on welfare rights, housing, and the like; Catholic (along with Jewish) representatives have met with this committee from its foundation.

Christian–Jewish relations seem to depend not on any single event, but on the growth of informal personal contacts. A key figure in the Youngstown story was Rabbi Sydney Berkowitz of Rodef Sholom Temple. A long-time resident of Youngstown, Berkowitz not only was active in Youngstown religious circles, but had a respected reputation in civic affairs, particularly for his community development work on Youngstown's near north side. A measure of Berkowitz's security about his standing in Youngstown is revealed by an anecdote about the name eventually given to the religious coalition. When it appeared in early November 1977 that a formal organization would be set up, the name "Ecumenical Coalition" simply emerged. Father Ed Stanton, sensitive to Jewish feelings about the term "ecumenical" as applying more strictly to relations among the Christian churches, asked Rabbi Berkowitz if the organization (in which Berkowitz was already an important participant) should not be termed the "Interfaith Coalition." Berkowitz replied: "No, Ed, let it go down as 'ecumenical.' It sounds sexier that way."

A major instance of interfaith relations in Youngstown moving beyond the polite stage came in 1976 with the desegregation suit filed by the Department of Justice against the Youngstown school system. When the suit was instituted, religious leaders decided to join forces in order to prepare the community for a possible court order mandating school busing to achieve integration. The religious leaders of all faiths joined together in a new organization, "Educational Opportunity Youngstown," to explore ways of defusing a potentially explosive situation before the court order was handed down. The then Catholic auxiliary bishop of Youngstown, William Hughes, was elected chairperson of the group. For the first time, religious leaders in Youngstown joined forces on a serious issue affecting the community. As it turned out, the federal court did not order busing, as expected, but only the exchange of a few teachers. The religious coalition was not really tested in this instance, but a model for concerted action was developed.

In summary, the internal dynamic of the religious sector in Youngstown was characterized by two trends, corresponding to trends in major religious bodies at a national and global level. First, the churches were increasingly inclined to take action in the sociopolitical sphere. And second, they were increasingly inclined to adopt a cooperative, interfaith strategy.

Emergence of the Coalition: Structural Factors

In Chapter III, the proposition was advanced that the steel shutdown announcement of Black Monday precipitated a local crisis that manifested characteristics comparable to the effects of a natural disaster and that the analogy might be helpful for understanding the emergence of the Coalition. One current in disaster theory focuses on the organizational response to disaster. The crisis situation as it was perceived in September and October 1977 in Youngstown included four structural factors that were conducive to the emergence of an interfaith religious action as an element of response to disaster.

1. The Ecumenical Coalition was an emergent group that came into existence when other traditional structures for crisis management were perceived as ineffective. Workers and others affected by the shutdown were left without any clear leadership to hear their demands (for jobs rather than welfare) and to champion their cause (for short-term and not more laissez faire long-term

economic solutions). Neither organized labor nor the political sector (where crisis-management leadership might have been expected) responded directly to the workers' situation. In this "political vacuum" (to use the phrase of Bishop Malone), the Coalition emerged as a political actor asserting a domain for action.

Thomas R. Forrest (1978) suggests that, in an emergent group, two specific positions are key – leadership and boundary positions:

Leadership involves the coordination and integration of the group by making decisions which commit the entire group to certain courses of action. On the other hand, boundary positions are concerned with relating the group to its environment. Their mediating transactions represent the group to other organizations and environmental groups, legitimizing the group and its activities, procuring resources, and providing an entrance point at which input resources can be channeled into the group. (108)

The early success of the Ecumenical Coalition in establishing its domain can be attributed, at least in part, to the way it filled these two positions.

2. Russell R. Dynes (1978) noted the important function of leadership in giving legitimacy to emergent organizations. "An organization can . . . gain legitimacy by the character of its leadership. If its leaders also occupy positions of power and influence in other parts of the community structure its claim to legitimacy is readily validated" (52). In Youngstown, the Coalition was led by the highest-ranking regional-level religious leaders. People such as Bishop Malone, Bishop Thomas, Bishop Burt, Rabbi Berkowitz, and Reverend Sharick enjoyed considerable prestige in the Youngstown area. Their prestige was transferred, through their direct involvement in the Executive Committee, to the newly emergent Coalition. The Coalition's goals and strategy gained weight because of the prestige of its leaders:

3. As boundary personnel, the Coalition was able to employ at the Steering Committee-level people from within the church structure who had important links to other organizational structures:

Individuals who occupy boundary roles between organizations facilitate the exchange of information and resources. . . . Some hold positions in two or more organizations. Still others provide the link between organizations primarily through their previously established friendships, which come to have special significance during the emergency periods (Ibid.)

Three of the original four members of the Steering Committee were particularly capable of functioning as boundary personnel. Ed Stanton, who became staff director of the Coalition, was treasurer of WREDA – a link that provided important resources for the Coalition in its first months. Both through his pastoral ministry and his work at WREDA, Stanton was acquainted with steel industry executives. Both Stanton and Bert Campbell had strong links with the steelworkers union. Campbell, through his pastoral ministry at First Presbyterian, had connections with the Youngstown financial community. Charles Rawlings had worked with the Institute of Policy Studies and technical advisory and action groups at the national church level.

As the Steering Committee was expanded, new members brought other connections. Staughton Lynd provided access to legal services as well as the original link with Gar Alperovitz and the National Center. Ed Weisheimer, pastor of Central Christian Church, had as members of his congregation a Sheet and Tube plant superintendent sympathetic to the reopening, as well as one of the few people in the Youngstown business community to do volunteer work for the Coalition.

4. Research on the organizational response to a natural disaster shows that churches have a comparatively high prestige ranking (Figure 5.1). In the emergency phase (when physical safety is the paramount need), the police have the highest ranking. But as the disaster response moves into the recovery phase, the police return to everyday duties and the social service role of the churches becomes increasingly salient. The churches are ranked second only to the National Guard, which tends to be remembered for its dramatic role in providing security (Wright 1978). In Youngstown, the prominent role of the churches in the recovery phase after the initial shock was consistent with the pattern of response to natural disasters.

In a disaster, external linkages beyond the community – of both a horizontal and a hierarchical type – tend to increase. "In large scale disasters, regional and national headquarters of local organizations send representatives into the community" (Wenger 1978: 36). The Youngstown church groups, more than any other sector, were able to draw on external linkages as resources. In the

Time ──────▶

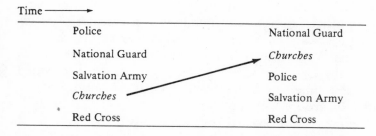

Figure 5.1. Prestige in disaster response; scale ranking changes over time. *Source*: Wright (1978).

labor sector, union links from the locals and the Youngstown district to the national steelworkers union were not particularly strong or effective. In the political sector, many national politicians came to Youngstown a year after the shutdown to campaign for Congressman Carney; they were not perceived as being particularly helpful to Youngstown, and in fact Carney was defeated.

Church linkages, on the contrary, proved effective. The national church organizations provided more than $350,000 to fund a local staff and program. The church offices also provided a communications network that gave the Coalition effort high visibility around the country. National church conferences passed resolutions supporting the Coalition, and national leaders occasionally lobbied on the Coalition's behalf.

In the period from September to December 1977, the Ecumenical Coalition functioned as an emergent organization for the purpose of crisis management. Two other structural factors were important in explaining the emergence of the Coalition as a church-backed organization:

1. Youngstown was the right size for such a movement. It was neither too large nor too small. In a larger metropolitan area (e.g., Chicago) the shock of a five-thousand job shutdown would be dispersed throughout a much larger regional economy. The shutdown would have a smaller impact on the relevant economic area, and it would be less likely to provide an organizing point for a community-wide movement. In contrast, the Youngstown area was small enough that five thousand jobs made a big difference.

But neither was the Youngstown area too small. In particular, Youngstown was large enough to be the location for several regional-level church offices. In the Catholic community, the "see" city of a diocese (where the bishop resides and the cathedral and diocesan offices are located) functions as the center of activity; outlying areas are clearly peripheral. It was key to the religious effort that Youngstown was the see city; the steel crisis was too close for the Catholic bishop to ignore, even had he wanted to. At the same time, the presence in town of the leader of the largest religious group, who also turned out to have the capabilities of a Malone, was a decided organizing advantage.

The same is true of the Presbyterians. Not only was First Presbyterian Church a strong anchor for a local movement, but the office of the Eastminster Presbytery (the regional division) was also in Youngstown. John Sharick, the Presbytery executive, provided strong connections at the national church level, as well as his own expertise in group dynamics. The Methodist judicatory, though not in Youngstown, was located nearby in Canton. The regional Episcopalian center was in Cleveland, which was close enough to permit serious front-line involvement.

Size was also a factor in the secular communications resources that became important for the Coalition. The city of Youngstown was the central city of a metropolitan area, with a major daily newspaper, three television stations, and eight radio stations. Because it was located at the center of the metropolitan area, the Coalition effort attracted more attention than it would have had it been in a city of the same size on the periphery of a larger area.

2. The particular structure chosen by the Coalition – an interfaith action committee structurally separate from the churches themselves – proved an apt structure for drawing on the resources of the churches, yet shielding the Coalition from potential opposition within the churches themselves. In this respect, the Coalition structure reflected a pattern that had already been successful. An American church historian has written of the problem of the churches' role in social reform movements:

The American churches can affect public policy only by their powers of persuasion. Yet at the same time, they are dependent upon voluntary support for their continued existence as institutions. The minister who champions an unpopular cause runs the risk of bringing economic disaster upon his congregation by the departure from it of those who are alienated by his views. The same dilemma exists at successive levels of any denominational hierarchy. One solution, common in the early nineteenth century, was to organize efforts for social reform into separate voluntary associations – temperance and abolition societies, for example – encouraged by but not officially identified with the denomination. In this way, those who were moved to work for social reform could do so under religious auspices, while those who opposed it did not necessarily feel disposed to withdraw their support from the denomination on that account. (Powell 1967: xvii–xviii)

In Youngstown, the coalition structure of the churches' effort gave the organization some insulation and independence from the individual church groups, but it allowed for a rather complex variety of contributions to the effort at local, regional, and national levels. The resources provided to the Ecumenical Coalition by various religious groups will be examined in the following chapter.

The Purpose of the Coalition: The Pastoral Letter

The explanation offered thus far for the origin of the Ecumenical Coalition of the Mahoning Valley has been essentially an exercise in sociological and political analysis. By taking the Coalition apart in this fashion, to examine the rare (and perhaps unique) set of circumstances that were conducive to this phenomenon, one runs the risk of analyzing away the heart and spirit of the Coalition. The author has found himself remembering Wordsworth's admonition, "We murder to dissect." In this process, it is possible to lose sight of the very qualities that made the Coalition interesting – a band of daring, quixotic preachers, tilting at the corporate powers on behalf of their people.

To keep the story from becoming just another boring scholarly treatise, it is necessary to touch the Coalition at another dimension. The Coalition was different, not because it demonstrated some skill at manipulating community power; many local organizations have accomplished that. The Youngstown Coalition was different because of the character and the quality of its purpose. That purpose, and its spirit, are captured most clearly in the pastoral letter of the Coalition, written in November 1977.

Such a document might normally be presented as an appendix to this kind of study. In that position, though, it might too easily be ignored; it might seem – literally – an appendage rather than a centerpiece document for understanding the events in Youngstown. It is therefore reproduced in full at this point, in the middle of the story. (The circumstances of the document's origin are related in Chapter IV.)

The "pastoral letter" as a literary genre is familiar in many religious groups. It is basically a kind of preaching document, frequently attempting to articulate the faith tradition of the community in new and different circumstances. It typically includes dimensions of theological reflection and instruction, moral exhortation, and pastoral encouragement.

In the Coalition's case, the letter originated from a single event: "Our community was wounded on September 19." It states the facts as well as they could be known: five thousand out of work, perhaps an additional ten thousand jobs lost, community services cut back. The result is the community's "shock, anger, and genuine fear" – to which the letter is addressed.

The letter tries, first of all, to interpret this event, to say what it means for the community. Though it recites the social, economic, and political factors that led to the shutdown, its central purpose is to insist that these causes do not constitute the whole story. There is a category of meaning – the "human dimension," a context of moral value – counterposed to the Lykes decision. "Human beings and community life are higher values than corporate profits." Basic to the entire document is the thesis that economic life takes place within a moral context: "Corporations have social and moral responsibilities."

The case is important primarily for the people involved in Youngstown. But it is important for "other cities across the nation" because it is symptomatic of "a way of doing business in this country." The crisis is not just economic; it is moral as well. It does not just deal with the community's pattern of income and expenditures; it touches the community's soul – how it identifies and lives with good and evil.

The foundation concept of the document is justice. "Our God is a God of justice." The concept is rooted in the revelation about God in the Hebrew scriptures, a God who stands beside the oppressed. For Christians, justice is also rooted in the life and teaching of Jesus, who "identifies himself with the poor and victims of injustice." Justice – in the Judeo-Christian tradition of social teaching – insists that "the purpose of economic life is to serve the common good and the needs of people." Furthermore, justice requires that those in authority over economic resources act as stewards – using those resources not simply for their own benefit, but for the good of the community.

These religious themes lead to the principle that "economic

decisions ought not to be left to the judgment of a few persons with economic power, but should be shared with the larger community which is affected by the decisions."

The analysis of the situation in Youngstown recognizes its complexity. "We do not come with simple or easy answers." Even though the letter asserts that the Lykes corporation failed to meet the fundamental moral criteria of corporate responsibility, "the Lykes Corporation does not bear the sole blame for this crisis." Steelworker wage demands, inefficient railroads, national trade policy, labor–management relations – all can bear part of the blame for what has happened. The letter does not indulge in scapegoating. The point rather is to "address this crisis," as well as "the attitudes and forces which created it."

The pastoral strategy calls for a cooperative effort. The intent of the religious initiative is "to provide a common ground and an impetus for community efforts." The religious leaders "seek to avoid political rivalry and organizational conflict" (emphasis in original). Three courses of action are projected. First, public education will "raise the moral and human dimensions" of the crisis and of corporate responsibility. Second, both short- and long-term solutions will be sought for unemployment and for remedying the pattern of economic and investment decisions in the Valley. Third, the Coalition will join with others to advocate national policies for retaining a healthy steel industry in the places where workers live.

The letter invites the community to move beyond its initial shock and anger, to see in the crisis an opportunity, not just to put its economy on a more just and firm foundation, but to "renew the ties of common purpose and concern which can help us to become a better and more just community."

The text of the letter, dated November 29, 1977, is as follows:

A Religious Response to the Mahoning Valley Steel Crisis

Introduction

Our community was wounded on September 19. On that date, the Lykes Corporation announced its decision to close most of its Youngstown Sheet & Tube operations at its Campbell facility and several departments at Brier Hill and relocate its offices. This decision is costing our Valley a great deal in human suffering, economic health and lost confidence and vitality. Five thousand of our neighbors will be out of work. An additional 10,000 jobs may be lost in the ripple effects of this decision. In addition, several local communities may be forced to cut back on essential services at a time when they are most needed. This blow to our community has generated shock, anger, and genuine fear.

We in the religious community are profoundly disturbed and troubled by this decision and its tragic consequences. We, therefore, wish to share with you our reflections on what these events mean for us and our community.

We are not experts in steel production or economic matters.

We do not come with simple or easy answers. Rather, we come as pastors deeply concerned about the pain and fear now present in our community. We need to examine the causes of this crisis and how we might act to alleviate suffering. We also need to consider how we might be able to restore economic health in our Valley and how we can strive to insure that this distress will not happen again.

We believe that this action by the Lykes Corporation has meaning far beyond its own troubled financial affairs and even beyond the fate of its 5,000 local employees. This decision raises profound issues of corporate responsibility and justice. It poses an enormous challenge to the Youngstown community and to the nation.

We say this because the decision is the result of a way of doing business in this country that too often fails to take into account the human dimensions of economic action. Other companies are faced with similar decisions in this community and other cities across the nation. As religious leaders, we cannot ignore the moral and religious aspects of this crisis.

Some maintain that this decision is a private, purely economic judgment which is the exclusive prerogative of the Lykes Corporation. We disagree. This decision is a matter of public concern since it profoundly affects the lives of so many people as well as the future of Youngstown and the Mahoning Valley.

The costs of this decision are overwhelming. The loss of jobs, income and production is enormous. No less clear, on reflection, are the human and community consequences of these losses – the strains on marriage and family life, increased depression, alcoholism and alienation, as well as lost confidence, ambition and self-respect. It is especially hard on older workers who have given this company many years of service and who will find it exceedingly difficult to obtain new jobs. It exacerbates an already serious unemployment problem. It also threatens related industries and businesses as well as the tax base of several of our communities. This closing has already contributed to greater distrust and antagonism between various elements in our community. Behind the statistics and headlines lie individuals, families and communities left vulnerable and fearful by this decision. This is not in any sense a purely economic problem.

What happened on September 19 is clear. A company shut down a steel works and began laying off 5,000 workers. There are many explanations for why it happened. Some say that a conglomerate in deep financial trouble, faced with large capital costs for modernization and environmental protection, shut down an unprofitable steel mill. Others say that poor management, declining product quality, inadequate investment and absentee ownership resulted in a decision to close the mill. Still others believe that the steel industry has embarked on a strategy of concentration and reducing productive capacity in order to take full economic advantage of steel needs in the future and make the industry more profitable. Other analysts suggest that our present crisis is not simply the result of individual action. It is also a reflection of broader forces which have contributed to a significant loss of jobs in our region and the decline of tool, basic metals and other manufacturing. Our problems have been intensified by patterns of investment and relationships between capital and labor which have favored other regions and industries above our own. We suspect that each of these explanations contains some elements of truth. We know that each of them raises serious moral issues.

Moral Dimensions of the Crisis

What is the religious dimension of this? Why have we, as local representatives of the Catholic, Protestant, Jewish and Orthodox faiths, decided to issue this message and embark on a program of education and action to deal with this crisis? We enter this complex and controversial situation out of a concern for the victims of the shutdown, out of love for our Valley at a time of crisis and out of a conviction that religious faith provides essential insights on our problems and possible remedies.

Within the religious community, we are blessed with a rich resource in dealing with issues of economic and social life. The Scriptures point to important values which form our response: God's concern with the liberation of His people, the importance of work and stewardship. Our God is a God of justice. "The Lord, Who does what is right, is always on the side of the oppressed" (Ps. 103:6). His message is very direct: "Cease to do evil. Learn to do good. Search for justice. Help the oppressed" (Isaiah 1:16–17). For those who are Christians, the life and ministry of Jesus lead us to similar concerns. Jesus came "to bring good news to the poor, to proclaim liberty to captives and new sight to the blind and to set the downtrodden free" (Luke 4:18). He very clearly identifies Himself with the poor and the victims of injustice. "Whenever you did it for one of these, the least of my brothers, you did it for me" (Matt. 25). Our common religious tradition summons us to respond to our neighbors' needs and to work for justice.

In addition, our Judeo-Christian tradition has articulated a highly developed social teaching with direct relevance to issues of economic justice. This tradition insists that economic life ought to reflect the values of justice and respect for human dignity. The purpose of economic life is to serve the common good and the needs of people. This tradition also emphasizes the dignity of the human person and identifies those basic human rights which demand to be respected. These rights include the right to useful employment and to decent wages and income, the right to participation in economic decisions and even ownership, the right to bargain collectively, among others. These rights carry with them the responsibility to labor honestly and productively for the common good. These corollary responsibilities apply to employee and employer alike. Our social teachings further lead us to the conviction that government is required to preserve and defend human rights when private action fails to insure them. Economic institutions, although they have their own purposes and methods, still must serve the common good and are subject to moral judgment. We are convinced, in short, that corporations have social and moral responsibilities.

We believe that the performance of the Lykes Corporation, in this instance, fails to meet this fundamental moral criteria. We say this not to condemn individuals, but to examine a system in which persons feel compelled to make such harsh decisions and to do so in secrecy. We believe that industrial investment decisions ought to take into account the needs and desires of employees and the community at large. In its refusal to invest in new equipment or necessary maintenance, the Lykes Corporation failed to do this. Human beings and community life are higher values than corporate profits. In its decision to close the steel works, we believe that the Lykes Corporation followed a different course. Our common faiths teach us the value of stewardship of material and human resources. We believe that the Lykes Corporation failed the test of stewardship in the management of this company and its resources.

Our traditional teaching points out that economic decisions ought not to be left to the judgment of a few persons with economic power, but should be shared with the larger community which is affected by the decisions. In the suddenness, the totality and the secrecy of this decision, the Lykes Corporation ignored this principle. Corporations have a social responsibility to their employees and to the community, as well as a responsibility to shareholders. By their abandonment of Youngstown, the Lykes Corporation has neglected this corporate social responsibility. We deplore not only the decision to close the steel mill, but also the manner in which the decision was made, the way it is being implemented, and the pattern of neglect which led to it.

At the same time, the Lykes Corporation does not bear the sole responsibility for this crisis. Local, national and international forces are at work which create the environment for such actions. Locally, a preoccupation with our own individual interests and a lack of concern for our common good may have contributed to our present problem. It is possible, for example, that an excessive concern with higher and higher wages and better and better fringe benefits may have contributed to the situation which now confronts us. We wonder whether labor and management have worked together as well as they could to solve their common problems. Perhaps, production costs have been raised by the failure of railroads to overcome their jurisdictional and territorial conflicts as well as work regulations which make efficient and direct transportation of steel and raw materials impossible. Nationally, the failure to formulate a comprehensive national policy to retain and support the manufacture of basic steel is a serious failing which helped to bring about our present state. Internationally, the willingness of some foreign steel producers to "dump" steel at below market prices into the United States has contributed to our difficulties.

However, our response to this crisis cannot be based on a search for scapegoats. We should not permit the evasion of responsibility by those whose decisions and policies primarily created this situation. We were disturbed by the Lykes Corporation's attempt to focus responsibility for their action upon environmental laws, imported steel and governmental efforts to keep down the cost of steel. While these factors may have contributed to this decision, it is worth noting that the amount of steel imported into the United States has remained relatively constant for the past ten years. We also understand that industry expenditures on pollution abatement equipment as a percentage of total capital expenditures have remained relatively constant over the last five years and that steel prices have risen more rapidly than the consumer price index. We say this not to minimize these problems, but to point out that other factors may also be responsible for the decision.

A Response to the Crisis

The religious community has a responsibility to address this crisis, the suffering it entails, and the attitudes and forces which created it. We are faced with a choice between resignation and despair or firm acceptance of our responsibility to act in accordance with our beliefs. Our situation in Youngstown is an opportunity as well as a serious problem. It is an opportunity to give witness to our religious principles of justice, to alleviate pain, and to create new models of concern and involvement. For this reason, representatives of various religious congregations in the Mahoning Valley have been meeting to formulate a creative and focused response. This common message is a first product of our ongoing collaboration.

In the face of this crisis, we need unity, common purpose and coordinated action for the good of the community. Time is short. We in the religious community attempt to respond to this crisis with no vested interests or hidden concerns other than the welfare of our community. It is our intention to provide a common ground and an impetus for community efforts without substituting for other legitimate interests. We do not wish to take the place of leaders of industry, union leaders, business representatives and government officials. Rather, *we seek to avoid* political rivalry and organizational conflict. Motivated by pastoral concern, we wish to raise issues, serve our community and call upon these and other groups to play their essential roles in restoring and rebuilding the economic vitality of our Valley.

We wish to cooperate with other groups and individuals seeking remedies to this crisis. We are eager to join our efforts to those of the workers and their unions, political officials, responsible business and corporate leaders, and other members of the Mahoning Valley seeking to restore the economic health of our community.

First, we will initiate programs of education. We will seek to continue to raise the moral and human dimensions of this crisis, clarify the causes of our problems and emphasize the need for diversification in our regional economy. We will also attempt to help national leaders and organizations understand the dimensions of our crisis and the national and international forces which contribute to it. We will work with the national religious community to develop programs which emphasize corporate responsibility and the relationship between economic decisions and social justice. What we do in this area could serve as a focus for national education and action within the religious community.

In this context, it is important to remind ourselves that our problems are not unique. Recently, some 20,000 steelworkers across the country have lost their jobs as a result of plant closings. In our nation, nearly seven million people are out of work, according to government statistics. Millions more have given up looking for work out of frustration. In parts of our own area, unemployment is a way of life rather than a recent threat. In our concern for the victims of recent layoffs, we cannot neglect the critical problems of those who are unemployed because of discrimination, lack of skills, lack of mobility, or simply a lack of jobs. As we fashion a specific response to this particular shutdown, we also commit ourselves to the ongoing and related struggles for full employment and equal opportunity for all people. Our current distress should strengthen the resolve of each of us to work toward an economy which provides a job for every person able and willing to work.

Secondly, we will seek short and long-term remedies to the crisis and its consequences. We strongly support efforts to aid laid-off workers and their families in coping with the economic, social and emotional trauma of joblessness. We will seek to intensify social service efforts in our own institutions and to deploy them in new ways to meet the enormous needs of the victims of the shutdown.

More significantly, we are prepared to assist, in whatever way we can, the efforts to save the jobs of the workers affected by the shutdown. The skilled steelworkers of the Valley and the facilities of the mill, despite its age, constitute major resources for the region and the nation. To allow the workers to scatter and to stand by and watch the mill deteriorate further would be a tragic waste. We fully support proposals for interim maintenance of the Campbell Works. In addition, we have begun a process of seriously exploring the possibility of community and/or worker ownership of the Sheet and Tube plant or other positive alternative use of the facilities to employ the workers. We have decided to help fund a feasibility study to examine the potential purchase and operation of the facilities by workers and/or the community. In pledging our support of such efforts, we recognize that this would be a serious undertaking. However, the idea of worker and community ownership is not foreign to our religious and national traditions. It ought to be explored as a creative response to abandonment of the mill by outside interests.

We also call upon other major employers in the Valley, especially other steel companies, to pledge publicly, community and employee consultation in future economic and investment decisions affecting employment and community life. The failure of Lykes to share its problems and options with the community and its abrupt decision to shut down cannot be repeated. We will seek pledges as a good faith gesture on the part of the industrial and investment community. We believe that they would contribute to a significant reduction in anxiety and distrust.

The decision of the Lykes Corporation to close its Sheet and Tube operation does not terminate the Corporation's responsibility to the Mahoning Valley, even though merger or other alternatives are being discussed. Litigation against the company is being contemplated by other organizations and individuals. In addition, we hope that Lykes will fully cooperate with the efforts of those seeking to provide minimal maintenance for the mill and those exploring the feasibility of operation under different auspices. In particular, we believe that Lykes has a moral responsibility to respond generously to a genuine and realistic program to reopen the mill under community, worker or public ownership. In setting a price for the purchase of the mill and in cooperating with potential new managers, Lykes has an obligation to assist in efforts to repair the extensive damage which has come from its decision to close the mill.

Thirdly, we in the religious community will join with others to advocate an effective national policy to retain in our region, basic steel and the jobs related to it. This will include administrative and legislative action to:

- provide federal aid for modernization of existing steel facilities in severely impacted areas where steelworkers already live;
- government purchasing policies which provide preferential treatment for mills and communities in deep financial trouble;
- encourage increased use of steel to meet human and community needs;
- seek changes in economic policies which unfairly pit region against region for jobs and economic growth, encourage the development of conglomerates and neglect the needs of older and urban communities.

We will join with others in advocating new policies and greater urgency in responding to the deterioration of our steel making capability. We will meet with officials of the Carter Administration and the Congress, as well as leaders of state and local government, industry and labor, and point out the human and community dimensions of the crisis and the need for prompt and compassionate action to relieve our distress. We believe that Youngstown can serve as a model for cooperative action and governmental aid to assist workers and the community to save jobs and economic strength. In the past the federal government has acted to provide large-scale assistance to private corporations in financial difficulties. Clearly, the needs of our community are at least as compelling and worthy of a response. In fact, we believe that this situation offers an even greater opportunity to renew and revitalize the confidence and productive capacity of an entire community. It is our profound hope that the federal government will join in partnership with our community to fashion a new road to economic health and well-being for the Mahoning Valley – and to do so in a manner which can suggest new directions for other communities as well.

We call upon the members of our community to join together in a comprehensive plan of action to develop the will, the resources and the commitment to revitalize our Valley. This effort will require the cooperation of every sector of Youngstown: churches, synagogues, labor, business, financial institutions, government, and other organizations and individuals. In this common effort, we can rebuild far more than our economic capacity, we can renew the ties of common purpose and concern which can help us to become a better and more just community. This will not be easy, but the suffering of our people, the precarious position of our Valley, the teaching of our faith and the ideals of our nation require a determined effort to respond to this crisis.

These educational, economic development and advocacy efforts must be accompanied by our constant prayers and vivid recollection of the realities of hope, regeneration and redemption. As religious people, we have ample cause for hope even in the midst of suffering. By our concern, by our application of religious principles to this crisis, and by our commitment to action, we are carrying on the Judeo-Christian tradition which is "to do justice, to love mercy and to walk humbly with God" (Micah 6, 8). In so doing, we discover the basis for hope. As the Prophet Isaiah said:

> Look, you do business on your fastdays,
> you oppress all your workmen and strike the
> poor man with your fist.
> Let the oppressed go free,
> and break every yoke,
> share your bread with the hungry
> and shelter the homeless poor,
> clothe the man you see to be naked
> and do not turn from your own kin.
> Then will your light shine like the dawn
> and your wound be quickly healed over. . . .
> If you do away with the yoke,
> the clenched fist, the wicked word,
> if you give your bread to the hungry,
> and relief to the oppressed,
> your light will rise in the darkness,
> and your shadows become like noon.
> You will rebuild the ancient ruins,
> build upon the old foundations.
> You will be called "Conciliator,"
> "restorer of households."

(Isaiah 58)

CHAPTER VI

Launching a Movement

Bert Campbell, associate pastor of First Presbyterian Church and key member of the Coalition Steering Committee, was often asked, "What is the Ecumenical Coalition?" That question, he says, admitted a variety of answers. Sometimes the Coalition was simply the four members of the Steering Committee. Sometimes it was the whole organization: Executive and Steering Committees with the paid and volunteer staff. Again it might mean the entire organizational response of church and temple – at local, regional, and national levels. Or it might include all the people and organizations, both in Youngstown and across the country, who had provided some measurable support.

What was the Ecumenical Coalition?

The Double Agenda

At first, the Coalition was an emergent group. Two rather different dynamics contributed to its emergence. One was the dynamic of crisis response in the local community. The second was a recently sharpened sense of sociopolitical urban mission within the religious sector. Together, these two dynamics help explain how the Coalition came to be.

There is little or no evidence that the religious leaders who formed the Coalition's Executive Committee originally intended the Coalition to be anything more than an emergency crisis-management group. They were busy people; this project would mean extra work on top of already full schedules. They had the political sense to realize that stepping beyond their traditional

146

roles in church administration would be controversial; they might well antagonize some church members who preferred that priests and preachers stay out of business and politics. Even as he was releasing Ed Stanton from his diocesan job to work full time for the Coalition, Bishop Malone thought that the churches' direct involvement would be wound up in a matter of weeks. At the outset, the bishops and judicatory leaders had no intention of taking the driver's seat in a major urban development project.

At the opening of 1978, however, the Coalition had become more than an emergent group. In the three months following the exploratory meeting on September 26, 1977, the Coalition evolved from a vague idea to an organization with a program and operational budget of three-quarters of a million dollars, developing a project involving a half-billion dollars. The agreement with the Department of Housing and Urban Development on December 30, 1977, marked a watershed in the Coalition's development. Until that time, the Coalition had been principally concerned to establish its domain – the sphere of activity in which it could legitimately operate. With the HUD contract, the Coalition obtained legal and political recognition. It faced a new set of tasks, involving rather different dynamics.

By that time, it was clear that the Coalition would not restrict itself to a social service strategy traditionally characteristic of religious social action. Instead, the Coalition had opted to focus its energies on economic redevelopment. The economic redevelopment strategy in turn involved a choice about the kind of entity the Coalition was to become. As the Coalition's Washington consultants began work on the Campbell Works plan and the Steering Committee in Youngstown set about hiring a staff and opening an office, the Ecumenical Coalition became an organization with a double agenda. The focus on the Campbell Works gave the Coalition the character of an economic development agency, with the task of starting up a business. But since the key element in the Campbell Works project was federal government financing, the Coalition effort took on a particularly political dimension. The assumption was that political pressure would be useful, and possibly a necessary condition, for convincing the Carter administration to put federal dollars into Youngstown. In addition to being a lead agent for economic development, then, the Coalition also felt the need to become a political movement.

The development and movement aspects of the Coalition were

strongly interdependent. On the one hand, the plan for reopening the Campbell Works depended on the success of the political effort in getting funds allocated to Youngstown. On the other hand, the political movement needed a credible economic development plan with likelihood of success in order to attract strong public support. Both elements of the Coalition needed each other.

But the development and movement aspects of the Coalition were quite different. These two agendas more or less dictated a division of labor among the Coalition personnel. Stanton became responsible chiefly for the economic development aspect of the Campbell Works reopening plan and negotiations with the corporation and government. Rawlings was associated principally with the movement aspect – the development of a campaign to generate public support for the Coalition. Rawlings, late in the Coalition effort, warned the author that there were really "two Coalitions."

The two prongs of the Coalition effort were sufficiently different to serve as the organizing points for this analysis. Chronologically, the major activity took place first on the campaign front, from January through September 1978. The plan and negotiation aspects of the Coalition effort became prominent roughly from the summer of 1978 through April 1979. A chronology of the Coalition is provided in Table 6.1.

This chapter details the Coalition's effort to mount a political movement. Chapter VII deals with the development of the plan for the Campbell Works and negotiations with the corporate owner. Chapter VIII details the negotiations with government and the final decision on the Coalition proposal.

Organization of the Coalition

As it moved into a new phase, the Coalition retained essentially the two-tier structure that had been formalized at the Steel Crisis Conference in October (Figure 6.1). The Executive Committee was the policy and decision-making board. The Steering Committee was responsible for implementing the Coalition program; it also prepared the agenda for the Executive Committee. A new addition to the Coalition structure in January 1978 was a hired campaign staff. Though technically the staff was a kind of third tier, principal staff members actually functioned more as members of the Steering Committee.

Table 6.1. *Chronology of events: Ecumenical Coalition of the Mahoning Valley*

Date	Event
1977	
September	
18	Board meeting of Youngstown Sheet and Tube
19	Campbell Works shutdown announced
19–23	Steelworkers meet with clergy
21	Governor Rhodes visits Youngstown
22	Youngstown: meeting of representatives from Commerce Department with Youngstown Sheet and Tube executive and government officials
22–3	Washington: meetings at Commerce Department, Sullivan and Stanton (WREDA) and Leseganich (USWA)
23	Washington: steelworkers march to White House and Capitol Billet mill and open hearths at Campbell close
26	Youngstown: clergy breakfast meeting on steel crisis
October	
6	Washington: clergy meet with Institute for Policy Studies and Exploratory Project for Economic Alternatives
28–9	Steel Crisis Conference at First Presbyterian Church, Youngstown (begins and sets goals for Coalition)
November	
3	Washington meeting to explore HUD grant
16	Coalition and WREDA initiate economic feasibility study for Campbell Works reopening (Beetle report)
19	Coalition meeting with Anthony Solomon, Treasury Department, regarding federal steel program
29	Pastoral letter of Coalition issued
December	
4	Solomon Report to President Carter: recommendations for steel loan guarantee program
12	Coalition announces plan to take over Campbell Works
16	Beetle report for Coalition and WREDA released: Campbell Works reopening is feasible
20	Washington: meeting with HUD and EDA, attended by MVEDC, WREDA, Coalition, congressmen, and USWA
22	Meeting of Bishop Malone and Congressman Carney regarding control of HUD grant
30	HUD contract ($335,000) finalized with NCEA
1978	
February	
16	Save Our Valley campaign opened
April	
2	Mayor Richley proposes Steel Research Institute

Table 6.1. (*Cont.*)

Date	Event
April	
11	NCEA interim report released
17	Coalition meets with antitrust division of Justice Department regarding Lykes–LTV merger
21	Meeting with Thomas Graham, president of J & L Steel regarding purchase of Campbell Works
May	
12	Bishop Malone testifies before Senate Anti-Trust Subcommittee
June	
11	Save Our Valley campaign goes national; New York office announced
20	Edgar Speer (chairman of U.S. Steel) calls Coalition effort "Communist plot"
21	Attorney General approves Lykes–LTV merger
July	
26–7	NCEA presents community–worker corporate model to community meetings at First Presbyterian Church
September	
14	NCEA final report released
27	White House meeting: coalition presents NCEA plan
28	Coalition hosts national conference in Youngstown
October	
14	CASTLO meeting at White House; questions Coalition plan
18	White House letter to Coalition: decision on Campbell Works deferred; new market study required
November	
3	Coalition meets with J & L Steel; purchase price to be named in 30 days
5	Governor Rhodes pledges $10 million to Coalition from Illinois state funds
7	Election: Lyle Williams defeats Congressman Carney in 19th District, Governor Rhodes reelected
8	Ohio Senator Metzenbaum asks Attorney General to suspend approval of Lykes–LTV merger pending serious negotiations with Coalition
17	Coalition receives firm price offer from J & L Steel (Lykes–LTV)
December	
5	Lykes–LTV merger approved by stockholders at meetings in New Orleans and Dallas
1979	
January	
29	City of Youngstown submits UDAG proposal for $17 million on behalf of Coalition

Table 6.1. (*Cont.*)

Date	Event
March	
11	Ohio state grant for $10 million approved by State Senate Finance Committee
21	Washington meeting with EDA
30	Coalition informed that plan for Campbell Works is rejected
April	
5	Coalition meeting; Campbell Works project terminated
June	
1	Coalition's option on Campbell Works property expires
6	J & L Steel announces plan to sell Campbell Works property

Structure: Denominational Representation

As Figure 6.1 indicates, the Ecumenical Coalition was literally a coalition of religious groups, with denominational representation as the basis for membership. In the Executive Committee, denominational representation was formal and explicit. Voting membership on the Executive Committee was limited to regional officials of the religious groups providing funds for the Coalition effort. In the Steering Committee, the principle of representation by denomination was not as strict, but it was operational. The original four members of the Steering Committee (Stanton, Rawlings, Campbell, and Walton) represented different religious denominations. As the Steering Committee was enlarged, new members were added to represent still other religious groups.

Denominational representation seems largely to have been taken for granted and never seriously questioned within the Coalition. The structure developed in this fashion largely because the denominational groups were the source of operating funds for the Coalition effort. And it was simply assumed that those groups funding the effort should have ultimate responsibility for the way their money was spent. Forming the Coalition around the principle of denominational representation, however, had several limiting consequences. First, nonreligious groups (e.g., the union unemployed workers, business or economic development groups) did not really fit into the Coalition structure. In this context, the process of coalition building essentially meant adding

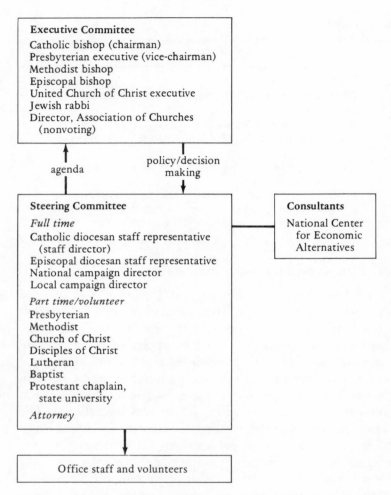

Figure 6.1. Internal organization of the Ecumenical Coalition.

still more religious groups (e.g., the Lutherans) rather than adding functional expertise (e.g., steelmaking or business experience). Second, for all practical purposes, membership in the coalition decision-making structure was limited to clergy or religious professionals. This had an important effect on the kind of knowledge and experience available to the Coalition from within. No one on the Executive Committee had any firsthand experience with the steel industry. On the Steering Committee, only Ed Stanton and

Bert Campbell had some knowledge of steelmaking from inside the plant gates: Campbell from his previous experience as a steelworker, and Stanton from his work in economic development (and summer work in the mill as a seminary student). For expertise in the technology and management of steelmaking the Coalition was almost totally dependent on outside consultants.

As a structure, then, the Coalition was not as well suited to the economic development effort as it was to the "movement" agenda. The structural strength of the Coalition organizational design was its ability to make use of resources within the religious sector in support of a community-based sociopolitical movement.

Religion and Campaign Resources

The Youngstown effort enjoyed one decided advantage over religious participation in the civil rights and antiwar movements of the 1960s and 1970s. In those movements, top church leadership had often been divided and uncertain. Clergy could sometimes count on tolerance but not often on support by the institutional structure. In Youngstown, however, with the full participation and even leadership of the bishops and regional-level officials, an array of resources became available to the community organizing effort.

The Catholic and mainline Protestant churches are organized at local, regional, and national levels. Although the hierarchical nature of the links between these levels differs from one denomination to another, the kind of resources available from the religious structure as a whole forms a coherent pattern. Again, the leadership role of regional officials was key. Their participation had the effect of legitimating the efforts of local church people, as well as tapping into the financial, communications, and political resources of the national religious offices.

Table 6.2 outlines the contributions to the Coalition effort from various levels of the religious structure. (The "Save Our Valley" deposits referred to are discussed later in the chapter). Local congregations for the most part provided "in kind" rather than cash resources. Their pastors often provided contacts with key persons in the community. Their physical facilities, suitable for public meetings of all kinds, were available whenever needed. First Presbyterian, because of that church's involvement and also because of its central location, frequently provided meeting facil-

Table 6.2. *Church contributions to the Ecumenical Coalition*

Nature of contribution	Local churches	Regional jurisdictions	National denominations
Professional staff			
Released time			
Full time	—	Stanton and Rawlings	—
Part time	Campbell	—	—
Part of regular activity	Sermons, church organizations	Communications Office, Catholic diocese	National Council of Churches/U.S. Catholic Conference
In addition to regular activity	Local pastors (Steering Committee)	Bishops and executives (Executive Committee)	
Use of physical plant, other services	Meetings	Stanton's office and secretary	National campaign office
Funding			
Direct grants	Some (small grants to $1,000)	Some funding	Major funding ($350,000)
Save Our Valley	Deposits to $50,000 each	Deposits to $40,000 each	Deposits to $300,000 each
Communications and promotion	Church newsletters and announcements	Access to local media	National denomination press and communication

ities, though important functions were also held at Boardman United Methodist and Central Christian Churches. First Presbyterian Church donated one day per week of Bert Campbell's salaried time to his work on the Steering Committee. Other congregations did not object to their pastors spending time on Coalition business on a more informal basis, either as members of the Steering Committee or on incidental projects. Very little of the direct funding came from local congregations, though some made significant savings deposits in the "Save Our Valley" campaign (described later).

Regional-level offices contributed heavily in terms of professional time. Members of the Executive Committee – all regional-level administrators – experienced major demands on their time, covering both in-town and out-of-town meetings and presentations. Malone gave Coalition business top priority, allowing Stanton to call on him in spite of almost any other previous commitments. The Catholic and Episcopalian dioceses continued to pay the salaries of Stanton and Rawlings, while releasing them to work full time for the Coalition. The regional offices also acted as the major source of funds for the Coalition's operational expenses, either contributing funds themselves or serving as conduits for funding grants from the national denominational offices. National church offices provided the principal financial support. The Catholic Campaign for Human Development, for example, provided $100,000 through the Catholic diocese. A financial report of October 31, 1978 (one year after the origin of the Coalition at the Steel Crisis Conference), shows the following contributions by denomination:

Catholic diocese	$63,325
Episcopal diocese	54,600
United Methodist	40,658
United Presbyterian	27,850
United Church of Christ	8,500
Disciples of Christ	5,500
Jewish Federation	1,000

At this point, the Coalition had received and spent almost $230,000. (The planning grant from HUD, paid directly to the National Center for Economic Alternatives, was in addition to these operational expenses.)

Staffing the Campaign

As the Coalition moved into its new phase, it was clear that people would be needed to staff some sort of campaign or public publicity effort. Around the beginning of 1978, the problem of staffing was addressed both by adding new members to the Steering Committee and by hiring campaign staff. At the same time, the Coalition also decided to retain an attorney.

The Steering Committee was in many ways the key to the Coalition's operation. It was in the Steering Committee that questions of objectives and strategy were deliberated and recommendations forwarded to the Executive Committee. The Steering Committee was also responsible for staffing the Coalition effort, either through members of the Steering Committee itself or by providing for a staff, both paid and volunteer. Basically, whatever the Coalition actually accomplished had to be performed, or at least organized and monitored, by the members of the Steering Committee.

The original Steering Committee of four members (Stanton, Rawlings, Campbell, and Walton) was more or less balanced in composition. Stanton and Rawlings, as the two diocesan staff persons working full time for the Coalition, were clearly the key personnel. Stanton's identification lay much more with the local Youngstown scene and with the economic development agenda. Rawlings, from Cleveland, was much more concerned about the national political implications of the Youngstown situation. Campbell and Walton functioned somewhat as middle men, holding together the Coalition's double agenda and the Steering Committee's two principal members.

The constellation of the Steering Committee was altered, however, when Rawlings took the initiative in doubling the size of the committee. (Campbell says that the additions to the Steering Committee were made without his knowledge.) Four church people who were particularly sympathetic to the Coalition effort began meeting with the committee in January. Joining the committee were Reverend Edward Weisheimer, pastor of Central Christian Church in Youngstown; Reverend Dianne Kenney, Protestant chaplain at Youngstown State University; Reverend Robert Taylor, pastor of Howland Community Church in Trumbull County; and Reverend David Stone, director of a Baptist urban mission in Campbell. The new members added strength primarily to the movement aspect of the Coalition, broadening its ecumenical base in Youngstown.

Rawlings was also instrumental in the selection of a campaign director and the designation of Staughton Lynd as attorney for the Coalition. As a candidate for the campaign director position, Rawlings introduced Richard Fernandez, a United Church of Christ minister from Philadelphia. Fernandez's most recent position had been with the Institute of World Order, but he had acquired some prominence in the anti–Vietnam War movement as the director of Clergy and Laity Concerned, a church-based peace group. Fernandez was clearly the most able and experienced candidate, and was hired for the position.

In January, the Coalition also decided to retain Staughton Lynd as attorney. After being very active in the early weeks of the organizing phase, Lynd had been relatively uninvolved in the October conference and the negotiations with Alperovitz and the government. As it became apparent that the Coalition would need legal counsel on a regular basis, Lynd's name naturally came up.[1] Lynd had many qualities that made him the ideal legal representative for the Coalition. A recognized scholar and intellectual, Lynd was passionately dedicated to social justice and the cause of the disadvantaged. In a letter of December 14, 1977, Rawlings recommended to Bishop Malone:

Staughton Lynd is one of our best assets for the tougher battles that I think lie ahead as big Steel may frown on the development of competition that they do not easily control. Staughton is needed by the Coalition because he has the scholarship, discipline and spiritual dedication to help us greatly. Moreover, he has worked very, very hard for us already.

Staughton Lynd's designation as attorney for the Coalition, however, was the subject of some discussion. A straightforward and selfless man in his personal style, Lynd nevertheless had a lightning-rod quality that seemed to attract controversy. One problem in terms of the Coalition effort was the strong antipathy toward Lynd at steelworkers union headquarters in Pittsburgh. McBride forces resented Lynd's "meddling" in steelworker union national elections and other affairs in East Chicago, when he was not a member of the union. In spite of this potential difficulty, the Coalition did formally designate Lynd as its attorney, as Lynd himself speculated, "probably because no other lawyer could be found to put in the hours required for the fee available."

Having hired a campaign director and an attorney, the Coalition proceeded to open a campaign office and hire a staff. A storefront campaign office was rented on Federal Plaza, in Youngstown's downtown business district. Furnished in campaign office fashion with folding tables and chairs and a file cabinet, it became the home of the Coalition's publicity effort. John Greenman, a native of Youngstown, was hired as publicity director. Greenman was between jobs, after having just attempted with his friend Dale Peskin to launch a Youngstown-area magazine, an effort that was aborted by the economic uncertainty in Youngstown following the Campbell Works shutdown. (Peskin went on to become a reporter for the Youngstown *Vindicator*, where he was assigned to cover the Coalition.) Marsha Peskin, Dale's wife, became the office manager at the Federal Plaza storefront, overseeing a small secretarial staff and occasional volunteers.

In the meantime, Stanton was named by the Executive Committee as "staff director" of the Coalition. The title was less a job description than an acknowledgment of Stanton's importance to the Coalition effort, a way of saying to the public that Stanton had a particularly responsible role in the enterprise. He was ultimately in charge of hiring and directing the campaign staff and was perhaps the principal spokesman in the local campaign effort. But Stanton's major function within the Coalition was not "staff direction." It was rather the role of principal contact person and monitor for the economic development effort.

Stanton's role of brokering a new business enterprise off the ground involved a different set of dynamics than did running a campaign. Instead of seeking publicity, he sometimes had to confer with steel executives or labor officials out of the spotlight; the requisite confidentiality for these exchanges was difficult, if not impossible, to achieve in the downtown storefront. While the campaign demanded warmhearted enthusiasm, negotiation often demanded a different mood – one of cool-headed, hard-nosed economic rationality. For these reasons, Stanton elected to keep his office at the Catholic diocesan headquarters, about four blocks across the tracks and up the hill from the campaign office.

The physical separation between the two offices helped to create an information gap that augmented the difference in personal styles between Stanton and Rawlings, as well as the different dynamics involved in the Coalition's two agendas. The campaign staff sometimes felt that they did not know or understand what Stanton was up to. But the briefings that Stanton tried to provide on steel technology, finance, and so on often proved too tedious and time-consuming for the Steering Committee and campaign staff. At the operational level, then, there were in some ways "two Coalitions," which increasingly tended to operate at arm's length from each other.

Bert Campbell, in reflecting on the early development of the Coalition, recalls that he set for himself the task of "keeping Stanton credible with the radicals." Campbell's political sense told him that Stanton – because of the importance of the Catholic Church in Youngstown and because of Stanton's position in the community – would be key to the success of any large-scale religious-based effort. But he was also aware that Stanton's basically pragmatic approach would continually have to be reconciled with the more revolutionary approach of Rawlings and others.

For the most part, the reconciliation was successful. John Sharick, vice-chairman of the Executive Committee, said that the Coalition was stronger for the different approaches and viewpoints present in the Steering Committee. By the time proposals reached the Executive Committee, they had been thoroughly talked through, examined from every angle. And even though its members did not always think in exactly the same way, the Coalition generally succeeded in speaking with one voice. Very few people outside the Coalition itself were ever aware of any difference of opinion or philosophy within the group.

From Action Group to Social Movement

The Ecumenical Coalition clearly originated as an elite action group of religious professionals. Emerging in something of a leadership "vacuum," the group was able to establish with the federal government its legitimacy as a lead agent in Youngstown for dealing with the unemployment caused by the steel shutdown. At its October organizational conference the Coalition had named four rather broad goals: public education regarding corporate responsibility, development of national policy to retain jobs where workers live, coordination of a model steel retention policy for Youngstown, and examination of the feasibility of reopening the Campbell Works or converting it to some other use. By January, those four goals had become concretized in the

Campbell Works project. Reopening the Campbell Works became for all practical purposes the Coalition's single program for accomplishing the broader goals.

The idea of reopening the Campbell Works did not come from the unemployed workers themselves. (Gerald Dickey, to whom it was first attributed, worked at Brier Hill rather than at Campbell.) Nor was the idea associated with any groundswell of enthusiasm among the workers or any other group in the community. As a program for action, the reopening idea had to be sold to people in Youngstown.

Furthermore, the reopening strategy was situated in a national political context. The reopening depended not only on the economic viability of the proposal, but on political pressure. In order for Washington to give the proposal serious attention, the Coalition had to demonstrate strong backing in the Youngstown area, as well as support from other regions for allocating federal funds to Youngstown.

Both to build support in Youngstown and to put pressure on Washington, the Coalition had to become more than an elite action group. The Coalition had to become a political movement.

A theory of social movements is useful for understanding the shape of the new challenge the Coalition faced in January 1978. A *social movement*, say the Fainsteins (1974) in their study of such phenomena in American cities, is "an emergent group which proposes to innovate and depends for its success upon the conversion of a social collectivity into an action group" (238). A *political movement* is one type of social movement that tries to alter the pattern or process of distributing resources, to have an effect on (ultimately governmental) decisions determining who gets what where, how, and when. Typically, a social movement emerges from the interaction between (a) a collectivity that feels that it has been unjustly deprived, (b) a set of ideas that apportions blame and offers solutions, and (c) the leaders and spokespersons for the incipient movement. "When the interaction reaches a level such that members of the collectivity become organized into an action group, we say that a movement has formed" (ibid.: 247).

In Youngstown, all of the elements for a social movement were present. The workers who lost their jobs in the shutdown were shocked and angry at having their life chances curtailed by the impersonal decision of an out-of-town corporate owner. The

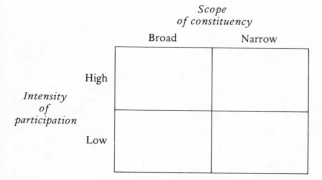

Figure 6.2. Scope and intensity of social movements: I.

ideas embodied in the Coalition's pastoral letter and communicated through both formal sermons and informal conversations articulated what the workers were feeling. The religious leaders told them that they had been wronged, their current distress was not (at least not primarily) their fault, and something could be done about it. The church people became leaders and spokespersons in this new kind of enterprise because they alone – among the possible leadership elements in Youngstown – spoke with authentic concern and dared to take some kind of action.

In Youngstown, though, the interactive process that normally serves as the gestation for a social movement was so short as to be virtually nonexistent. The idea for the Coalition took shape in the clergy's conversations with steelworkers in the first weeks after the shutdown. But the Ecumenical Coalition did not come forth out of the collectivity that experienced or anticipated unemployment. Having emerged as an elite action group of religious professionals, the Coalition now had to fill in the infrastructure, to identify and organize the collectivity for which it was speaking.

In order to develop a social movement in Youngstown, the Coalition had to deal with two questions: (a) What was its constituency? (b) What kind of involvement would be required of the movement's constituents?

These two questions can be considered as cross-cutting dimensions of a simple matrix, providing four strategic options (Figure 6.2). On the one dimension, the Coalition needed to determine the scope of its constituency: Would that be defined narrowly, focusing primarily on the unemployed workers, for instance? Or

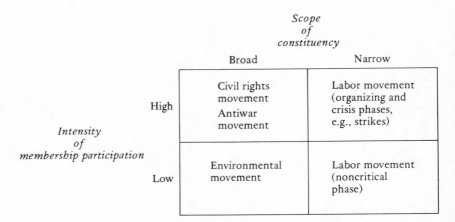

Figure 6.3. Scope and intensity of social movements: II.

would the Coalition focus its energies (also) on the public at large? On the second dimension, the Coalition had to decide what kind of response it wanted. Would participation be relatively intense, characterized by street demonstrations, for example? Or would it call for a "cooler" participation style, placing greater emphasis on the negotiating skills of leadership?

The typology formed by these two dimensions is not merely an abstract exercise. It is useful for identifying important characteristics of some actual social movements and thereby understanding more fully the options for the Youngstown Coalition (Figure 6.3). The civil rights and antiwar movements of the 1960s targeted a broad constituency, extending their scope as widely as possible. A major technique in both movements was to ask people to put their bodies on the line – in freedom marches, sit-ins, and rallies and in willingness to go to prison. The environmental movement likewise targeted a broad constituency, but for the most part the successes, of the environmental movement were won through lobbying and litigation rather than demonstration. Where the civil rights and antiwar movements placed their participants on the front line of action, the environmental movement generally preferred that its adherents stay at home, writing checks for dues and contributions to the Sierra Club, to pay for legal fees and lobbying costs.

Common to both types of movement, however, was a general strategy in the use of resources. They were able to use comparatively meager financial resources to leverage sweeping changes in public policy and the reallocation of the nation's resources. It has been estimated that, at the height of the civil rights movement in the 1960s, the budget of the National Association for the Advancement of Colored People (NAACP) was only a little more than a million dollars (Hardin 1982: 109). For the environmental movement, the political budget for 1977 has been estimated at around $10 million (ibid.: 106).

Compared with the sums available to business organizations (e.g., Mobil Oil in the 1970s was spending more than $1 million a year merely on its op-ed advertisements [ibid.: 106]), the amounts of money spent by civil rights and environmental organizations to influence public policy are paltry indeed. Yet the investment in environmental action, for example, contributed to (if it did not exactly cause) a reallocation of resources calculated in the billions of dollars.

In contrast, the labor movement provides an example of a social movement that has had to target a narrow constituency – ultimately the workers in a single plant or company. Though the labor movement may be happy to enjoy favorable public opinion over a broad scope, more important is the ability to win a certification election or to preserve tight discipline during a strike. In these critical phases (such as organizing or striking), the labor movement places a high premium on worker participation. Once the union is well established, though, a different dynamic sets in. Workers may be asked simply to pay their dues and leave important matters to union leadership. For example, in the United Steelworkers in the 1970s, local unions did not have the right to strike over local grievances, nor did workers have the right to vote on their labor contract. In its style of participation, an established union may resemble the environmental movement rather than the labor movement of the 1930s.

The nature of the Coalition as a social movement and the shape of its campaign would depend to a great extent on the way that the Coalition resolved the questions about the scope of its constituency and the type (or intensity) of participation it would elicit.

The Campaign

By the first of January 1978, the Steering and Executive Committees of the Coalition seem to have been convinced that broad political backing was necessary for a mill-reopening strategy to work. As they read the situation, however strong the economic arguments for reopening the Campbell Works, it would take more than a financial prospectus for the federal government to commit several hundred million dollars in federal loan guarantees. The plight of Youngstown had to be brought forcefully to the attention of the new administration. As a bargaining chip, the Youngstown group felt it could point to local support for Carter in the 1976 presidential election, in which Mahoning County gave Carter the biggest majority in the state of Ohio, a strongly contested state that was crucial for his victory. An essential aspect of Coalition strategy, then, became a political movement targeted at the White House. But no such movement existed, or was about to happen spontaneously. It would have to be created, and by the Coalition. The obvious instrument for creating such a movement was a campaign. It would have to be a nonpartisan campaign, since the Coalition wanted support from both Republicans and Democrats. But it would be clearly political, a kind of public lobbying effort that would, for the present, bypass electoral politics (though the threat of electoral sanction was left standing visibly in the corner, to be used if needed).

The timetable was tight (Table 6.3). Any campaign effort would have to be mounted quickly. The initial economic feasibility study predicted that the chances for a successful reopening of the Campbell Works would be based on its being back in business by the last quarter of 1978. By that time also, benefits for the unemployed steelworkers would be running out; they would have to seek other work and perhaps relocate out of the area. In order to retain the mill's experienced workers, the reopening plan would have to be well on its way by summertime, or early fall at the latest. A campaign effort to firm up local support and put pressure on Washington would have to begin immediately. Consequently, the Coalition would have to devise a campaign strategy around the resources immediately available.

The overall strategy of sending a message to Washington called for a campaign effort that was broad in scope, attracting a wide participation. But four other factors, particular to the Coalition as a group, were also conducive to a broad campaign and political movement.

The first factor was simply the organizational structure. Because of its principle of denominational representation, the mem-

Table 6.3. *Timetable: Coalition campaign strategy*

Date	Action/objective
1977	
September	Shutdown announcement
October	Coalition emerges as organization
November	Beetle report says Campbell Works reopening economically feasible
December	HUD planning grant makes Coalition lead agent for Campbell Works reopening
1978	
January	Campaign initiated; planning work begins
March	Political movement under way, attracting national support
	Negotiations under way with steel company, state and local governments
June	Grant proposals submitted for Urban Development Action Grant and Steel Loan Guarantees
September	Federal funds allocated; purchase of steel mill; renovation work begins
December	Steel production resumes at Campbell Works

Note: In order to meet the recommendation of the Beetle report, to restore production at the Campbell Works within 12 months, the Coalition would have to meet this timetable.

bers of the Coalition – at both Executive and Steering Committee levels – were broadly representative of the community as a whole. Two or three "boundary personnel" had particular contacts with the labor or business sector, but on the whole the strength of the Coalition structure lay in its ability to appeal to the community as a whole, rather than to one sector or another.

The second factor was the moral nature of the Coalition's appeal. The theology expressed in the pastoral letter was oriented toward reconciliation of different elements in the community. An appeal focused exclusively on one sector (for instance, the unemployed workers) ran the risk of further sharpening a conflict situation. The church leaders proved themselves willing to take a strong stand and use strong language on the issue of corporate responsibility. But – particularly at the Executive Committee level – this was always within the bounds of a conciliatory approach.

The third factor was the nature of the resources and support that the Coalition could count on. In January 1978, only two resources could be counted on with any certainty. One was the planning grant from HUD and the consequent investment of time and energy by the National Center for Economic Alternatives (NCEA) in the Youngstown project. The NCEA concept of Youngstown as a "demonstration experiment" for the nation tended to call for broad support. The other firm resource was the funding and program support promised by the religious sector at local, regional, and national levels. The effort to capitalize on these resources drew the campaign increasingly to broaden the scope of its constituency.

Finally, there was the personnel factor – the people who comprised the Steering Committee and staff. Particularly because of time pressure, devising a campaign strategy had to be largely an instinctive process, based on their perception of the situation. That perception would inevitably be colored by their personal philosophies and their past experience. The majority of the Steering Committee seem to have interpreted the Youngstown situation in light of the previous causes in which some of them had worked successfully (i.e., the civil rights and antiwar movements). They tended to identify Youngstown in similar terms – as a situation in which political resources applied over a broad front could leverage significant policy change.

The Washington consultants largely supported this view. They saw the role of the religious leadership as one of developing the political muscle to put their ideas into effect. In an early memo (October 9, 1977), Gar Alperovitz wrote:

At this stage, I believe virtually all of the significant issues in Youngstown are moral and political, not economic. . . . What it would take to turn the situation around in Youngstown is a dramatic local and national moral campaign capable of mobilizing massive political and financial resources; the only way this could be accomplished is by force of the *drama, significance,* and *extraordinary importance of the issue to society as a whole.* (Emphasis in original)

Alperovitz indicated that he was thinking in terms of a "Mississippi Summer" spirit, which would fire the imagination of young people, the religious community, and the media.

Both because of the overall strategy of influencing Washington and because of the particular characteristics of Coalition leadership, it was taken for granted that the coalition campaign would aim at a broad constituency. The campaign would try to target in a special way the union and unemployed steelworkers, as well as the Youngstown-area business community. But the appeal to these groups would be in the context of a larger, community-wide effort.

The intensity of participation – what participants in the campaign would be asked to do – was more an open question. The Coalition did, in fact, try out the "high-intensity" approach with a street demonstration in Columbus, producing one of the few dramatic scenes of the campaign. But more often the television cameras were merely focused on the backs of Coalition members getting on planes to Washington or on interviews with them as they stepped off. For the most part, it was taken for granted that the campaign would be characterized by "low-intensity" kinds of activity. Only at the end of the campaign did any serious discussion arise about moving to a more high-intensity style of participation.

"Save Our Valley": The Savings Account Plan

As Coalition leaders began thinking about a campaign, their principal focus turned toward developing local community participation in and support for the Campbell Works reopening project. A Coalition memo noted:

This demonstration of support is necessary as a symbol both to the community-at-large and to the federal government that the reopening of the Campbell Works is truly a community-based project with a large number of Mahoning Valley residents actively interested and participating in the project. The Ecumenical Coalition feels that (i) without this community involvement, a reopening of the steel mill will generate only limited and short-term benefits, and (ii) the various departments of the federal government will be more inclined to provide assistance if the project has widespread community support.

The problem was to devise a form of community involvement. Simply another petition drive seemed insufficient. Letters to the U.S. president or members of Congress were welcome, but alone they would not carry enough weight to trigger the release of federal funds. Some collective action, demonstrating organized community support, was called for.

Preferably, such a collective action should involve some commitment of financial support. What the project needed was investment capital. The Beetle feasibility study had estimated that more than $500 million would be needed over a seven-year period. That kind of money was not available from Youngstown banks; it would have to come from the federal government and/ or the national capital markets. But if some equity capital were raised in the Youngstown area, the local money might well serve to leverage investment from outside Youngstown. In particular it would bolster the case that Youngstown was trying to help itself and was therefore a worthy candidate for federal grants and loan guarantees.

However, in January 1978, it was far too early for the Coalition to ask citizens of Youngstown to invest in the reopening project. Only a preliminary feasibility study had been finished; the planning work of the NCEA was just getting under way. It was premature to seek direct community investment in a new corporation. (Inquiry with the Securities and Exchange Commission revealed that any such attempt would have been disallowed.) The Coalition decided, therefore, that any plan for enlisting direct community financial support would have to meet the criterion of being "essentially risk free to the community residents until more is known about the feasibility and corporate structure of any corporation formed to operate the steelmill and until full compliance with all state and federal securities laws can be demonstrated." At the same time, it was decided that financial support should *not* benefit the churches themselves: "Any financial support must not be in the form of a charitable contribution or donation to any one of the churches involved." The problem was how to collect money pledges, yet hold the funds in a kind of escrow or trust.

The solution came in the form of a savings account plan. Individual citizens, as well as organizations, were asked to create a special-purpose savings account at participating banks and savings institutions. The savings accounts were regular pass book accounts, with the depositors retaining complete ownership and control over both principal and interest. The special-purpose accounts differed from regular passbook accounts in two ways. First, these accounts were designated "Save Our Valley" accounts, much the same as a "Christmas Club" account has a special designation. Second, the depositor creating a "Save Our Valley" account agreed to permit the financial institution "(i) to place the individual's name on a list of all persons opening such accounts, (ii) to add the individual's deposit to the total deposited in all such accounts and (iii) to relay this information to the Ecumenical Coalition." The Coalition had no access to these funds. But the money on deposit was intended to be a pledge of the community's willingness to provide some financial backing to the steel mill reopening.

As a campaign tactic, the savings accounts would have a double function. First, the act of opening the account, regardless of the amount deposited, would serve as a surrogate vote backing the Coalition effort. The total number of accounts could be used to indicate the number of supporters in the community. Second, the amount of money deposited would be interpreted as an initial index of potential investment capital from local savings.

Bert Campbell was the member of the Steering Committee who was primarily instrumental in making arrangements for the Save Our Valley accounts with local banks and savings and loans. These arrangements were facilitated by two members of Campbell's congregation at First Presbyterian Church: the president of Mahoning Bank (a major commercial bank) and the president of a savings and loan. The counsel for the NCEA in Washington contacted agencies at both state and federal levels for their approval, including the Securities and Exchange Commission, the Federal Reserve Board, the FDIC, the Ohio Department of Commerce, and the Ohio attorney general.

The Save Our Valley campaign was inaugurated on Thursday, February 16, 1978. Reverend John Sharick, vice-chairman of the Executive Committee, opened the campaign with the announcement that the Eastminster Presbytery (composed of United Presbyterian churches in the Akron–Youngstown–Warren area) was depositing $10,000 in a Save Our Valley account. That evening, a rally was held at the Boardman United Methodist Church. Methodist Bishop James Thomas urged: "I charge you in the name of God to let your faith be sound and sure. The nation needs an example, and I charge you to be that example." Some questions were raised: Would the steel market increase? Who would manage the new company? Should the federal government be involved? One steelworker, who had been a grievance committeeman at the tube mill before being forced on pension, said he thought the efforts were a long shot but worth a try. He showed the four hundred people assembled in the church the bank book of his own Save Our Valley account.

Reverend Richard Fernandez, campaign director, was asked by reporters to name a goal for the campaign. Fernandez guessed that it might bring in $6–12 million, with 8,000 to 12,000 depositors.

The response in the initial weeks was relatively slow. The concept of a savings account as a vote of confidence in a community campaign was a new idea that required repeated explanation. A news account in the Youngstown *Vindicator* reflected the popular impression that the "preachers" were passing the collection plate – a view that the paper's own editorial supporting the campaign felt obliged to correct:

In all the talk about "donations" and "passing the plate," misunderstanding may develop. No contributions are involved. The campaign is not asking for donations. There is no commitment to invest in the new company. The purpose is simply to demonstrate how much money will be available for investment if the studies now under way show that it is feasible to reopen the abandoned department of the Campbell plant.

The "Save Our Valley" campaign will not take a penny from anyone's pocket. It will, however, enable advocates of the new steel operation to show, in solid figures, how much support they can expect from the community. The leaders of the coalition ask for support and prayer in their unprecedented project. They should have both. (Youngstown *Vindicator*, February 19, 1978)

In March, the campaign began to pick up momentum when John Greenman was hired to develop publicity. Working out of the Federal Plaza storefront, Greenman produced public service ads for radio and television, rented sixteen outdoor billboards, and published a Save Our Valley newsletter. By the beginning of April, after the campaign's first six weeks, there were 482 deposits, with $426,000 in Save Our Valley bank accounts. In the following two weeks, that amount more than doubled. In May, the Coalition conducted a five-day telephone blitz, with 460 volunteers manning banks of phones set up in a Mahoning County annex building. In making more than 48,000 phone calls, the volunteers collected 7,000 pledges.

An important feature of the savings account campaign was that both individuals and institutions could become depositors. Individual accounts sometimes provided more symbolic than financial backing, as with the $3 account opened by a 12-year-old girl in the opening week. But labor unions, civic organizations, and local and regional church groups provided some large deposits. St.

Patrick's Church (a Catholic parish in the inner city where Stanton resided) deposited $50,000 from the sale of a school building annex. Deposits also began coming in from Ohio regional church offices – among them $10,000 from the state office of the American Baptist Church and $40,000 from the Ohio Conference of United Church of Christ. Local labor unions also placed funds in Save Our Valley deposits. The president of the United Steelworkers local at U.S. Steel's Ohio Works stated:

At the Ohio Works of U.S. Steel, we are operating under many of the same conditions that workers at the Campbell Works experienced before that plant closed. Our deposit of $10,000 is an effort to say to the nation that we're willing to help ourselves restore steel jobs and protect existing ones. (Youngstown *Vindicator*, June 1, 1978)

The executive committee of an auto workers local at GM's Lordstown plant proposed to deposit $10,000; in floor debate on the motion, the opening figure was called and raised – poker style – to $20,000 and finally to $40,000.

From January to June 1978, the Save Our Valley savings account plan was clearly the centerpiece of the Coalition campaign effort in Youngstown. Campaign energies were heavily concentrated in this direction. John Greenman estimates that the Save Our Valley accounts took seven-eighths of his time as public information director and later as compaign director. In contacts with individuals and community groups by members of the Steering Committee and campaign staff, the principal support action that the Coalition called for was the opening of a Save Our Valley account.

By June 1, Save Our Valley topped the $2 million mark with 881 new accounts opened in the last two weeks of May alone. After that point, however, the number of new accounts began to trickle off. John Greenman, on taking over the post of the local campaign director later in the month, decided that the Save Our Valley campaign had largely exhausted its potential market in the Youngstown area and brought the local advertising effort to a close.

National Campaign

As the Save Our Valley campaign was winding down in Youngstown, the Coalition was further broadening the scope of its efforts by carrying the campaign to the state and national levels. On June 11, a national office was opened in New York City. Richard Fernandez, who had directed the campaign in Youngstown, went to New York as national director.

The move to the national level actually began with a meeting on April 13 at the National Council of Churches headquarters in New York. About fifty church officials from the National Council and national denominational offices were in attendance. The timing of the meeting was perfect. Articles about the Coalition and the Youngstown steel problem had been published in the *New York Times*, and Stanton had just been a guest on the "Today" show. The group was primed and ready to listen to the Coalition's presentation. After the Youngstown delegation made its case, William Sloan Coffin (antiwar activist and pastor of Riverside Church) led off the discussion by remarking to Bishop Burt, "You have had greatness thrust upon you, and you have responded in a great manner."

Save Our Valley. One focus of the meeting was to explore the willingness of national church offices to act as "ethical investors" by depositing national church funds in Youngstown. The national offices were already providing operational funds for the campaign effort. Now they were being asked to open Save Our Valley accounts as well. A major reason for opening an office in New York City (in the National Council headquarters building at 475 Riverside Drive) was to coordinate this effort. Ultimately the national church offices did make a significant contribution to the Save Our Valley campaign. The United Presbyterian Church deposited a total of $500,000 from its Board of Pensions and the United Presbyterian Foundation. National offices of the United Methodist Church deposited $360,000. The Riverside Church alone deposited $100,000.

In July, Save Our Valley campaign offices were also opened throughout the state of Ohio, in Akron, Cleveland, Toledo, Columbus, and Cincinnati. In opening the statewide campaign, Bishop Malone indicated the Coalition's reason for going to sister Ohio cities, some of which had also experienced devastating plant closings: "We believe that the self-help plan proposed for Youngstown can be a model for other communities. In that spirit, we call upon the people of Ohio to help make the Youngstown plan a success" (Akron *Beacon Journal*, July 25, 1978). The response in the Ohio cities was not significant; these offices were maintained (and generally staffed with part-time personnel) for only six to eight weeks. They did have the effect of publicizing and helping to increase the visibility of the Youngstown project throughout Ohio.

The final total in the Save Our Valley accounts from depositors – both in Youngstown and around the country – reached $4,091,927.26 as of January 1979. The accounts, including those of both individuals and institutions, numbered 4,138.

The Church Connection

Public relations. The religious sector, in addition to providing operational funds and a major portion of the Save Our Valley accounts, also furnished a national communications network that helped to publicize the Coalition effort. As a result of the April meeting at the National Council of Churches in New York, Philip Newell (Presbyterian Economic Just Issues Program Agency) and John Collins (director, Interfaith Center on Corporate Responsibility) agreed to spearhead a national education program. The Coalition story made headlines and was followed closely in the denominational press. In the Catholic community, for example, it was written up in liberal weekly newspapers and journals – the *National Catholic Reporter, Commonweal, America* – which expressed strong approval for the action by the clergy. Similar attention was provided in other denominational organs, for instance, the Presbyterian *A.D.*

A national conference organized by the Coalition in Youngstown, September 29–30, 1978 (approximately a year after the Campbell Works shutdown), attempted to strengthen this network. About 120 people, many of whom were invited through the religious social action network, attended the two-day conference. The participants listened to presentations of the Coalition's program, talked with steelworkers, heard comments from such observers as Congressman Peter Kostmayer, State Senator Mike Schwarzwalder, and representatives of the Ohio Public Interest Campaign. The mood of the conference reflected the activism of the 1960s. A folk song composed and sung by minister-musician Tom Hunter from California gave the conference a theme refrain, "I'm going back to work in Youngstown, and doin' it in my own way." The speech by Gar Alperovitz at the conference banquet probably stands as the best sermon to come out of the Coalition. Alperovitz talked on the conference theme: "Save Youngstown, Save America." In a low-key, understated style, he exhorted his listeners to "step up to history." The future of America, he said, turned on the potential of Youngstown (and cities like it) to come back. The evening, and the conference, ended with participants folding literature and stuffing envelopes, while singing "going back to work in Youngstown" and (inevitably) "We Shall Overcome."

The church connection developed pockets of relatively well informed, sympathetic observers of the Coalition effort around the country. For example, two hundred social activists at the annual meeting of the Catholic Committee on Urban Ministry at Notre Dame University devoted a half-day to a plenary session on the Coalition. Beyond mere sympathy, such publicity efforts yielded occasional letters to President Carter and other officials.[2]

Stockholder support. The church connection turned up a surprising ally in the Coalition's dealings with the corporate owner of the Campbell Works. A Mankato, Minnesota, branch of the School Sisters of Notre Dame, a teaching order of Catholic nuns, discovered in the stock portfolio of their retirement program a block of four thousand shares of Lykes Corporation stock. The treasurer of the order, Sister Joanna Illg, offered to use the order's stockholder position to aid the Coalition effort. The offer came at a crucial point in the merger proceedings between Lykes and LTV, a Dallas conglomerate. Lykes was forced to hold a stockholders' meeting to ratify the merger proposal. At the meeting, held in New Orleans on December 5, 1978, Sister Illg submitted a stockholders' resolution pledging the company to cooperate with the Coalition efforts to reopen the Campbell Works.

The Coalition and the sisters expected that the resolution would capture at most 10% of stockholder votes. Lykes directors were known to oppose the resolution, and they controlled between 30 and 40% of the stock. Amazingly, Sister Illg's resolution almost passed, gaining 47.8% of the shares voted.[3]

Broad-Scope Strategy

The option for a broad-scope campaign, centered on the Save Our Valley savings account plan, characterized the Coalition's entire campaign effort. In the summer of 1978, campaign energy and resources were increasingly focused beyond the Youngstown area itself, targeted at state and national constituencies. The clear choice in terms of campaign strategy, then, was to pursue an ever broader scope. The danger involved in this strategy was the possibility of spreading scarce campaign resources too thin and of failing to develop a support base of sufficient depth, particularly in Youngstown itself.

Target Constituencies in Youngstown

The Coalition campaign may have been tempted to pursue potential support at the state and national levels because of the difficulties it began to experience in consolidating support within the Youngstown area itself. With its emphasis on the savings account plan, the campaign essentially focused on building a community-wide constituency. Several particular constituencies at the local level were especially important, however. The campaign did devote special attention to gaining support from (a) the local business community, (b) organized labor, particularly the steelworkers union, and (c) the unemployed workers themselves. These efforts met with, at best, mixed success.

Business Community

The Youngstown business community did not give the Coalition notably strong support. That perhaps is not surprising in view of the perceptions in the business community that Youngstown was too dependent on the steel industry, and that the steelworkers were overpaid and their union too powerful (see Chapter IV).

Most prominent business people, such as leaders of the Chamber of Commerce, held back from any public criticism of the Coalition. But at lunch tables and in private conversations, business and professional people – while giving the clergy high marks for their good intentions – often described the Campbell Works reopening as misguided, or worse. Occasionally business skepticism about the Coalition project was based on good information and reasoned critique. Often it was based on partial information and unreflected assumptions.

Typically three points were made by business and professional people. First, they asked what priests and preachers knew about running a steel mill. The answer they clearly expected was nothing. This point was usually made as a way of dismissing the Coalition effort without taking the trouble to examine the project in detail. The comment by an associate professor of business economics at the University of Akron is typical: "It doesn't have a chance in hell. It's really unfortunate, but I can't imagine a group more improperly prepared to run a steel mill than a bunch of nuns from Youngstown" (Lally 1978: 26).

In point of fact, the Coalition never intended to run the steel mill, but to serve as a kind of broker for the interests of the local community in redeveloping the steel property. Management of the mill would be the job of an executive team. Technical and financial advice in the planning and start-up phases was coming from such reputable sources as Paul Marshall, senior partner of Putnam, Hayes, and Bartlett and consultant to the American Iron and Steel Institute; Robert Brandwein, Policy and Management Associates (Boston); George Arnoff, senior partner of the Cleveland law firm Benesch, Friedlander; and the Wall Street investment banking firm of Warburg Paribas Becker. In the later planning phase, important contributions also came from James Smith, assistant to the president of United Steelworkers of America; John Stone, retired vice-president of Youngstown Sheet and Tube; and Frank McGough, engineering consultant and former assistant district manager at Youngstown Sheet and Tube, East Chicago. What may have been the image in the business community of the local minister or parish priest taking over the executive suite of a major steel corporation had little correspondence with reality.

Hidden within this often flippant critique of the Coalition was a serious point. The decision-making structure of the Coalition included no one with real expertise in steel management or corporate finance. Consequently the Coalition did not have within its own ranks anyone capable of evaluating the work of the consultants. Stanton (and to some extent Bert Campbell) attempted to fill this gap, at times through off-the-record private conversations with present and former steel executives. But members of the Coalition, while not pretending themselves to have the requisite expertise for running a steel mill, were overly dependent on their consultants. (This point will be discussed further in the following chapter.) Unfortunately, this serious critical point was generally lost in the "What do the preachers know about . . . ?" rhetoric. In addition, there may have been a general discomfort among business people with the new role asserted by the religious leaders.

Second, some members of the business community saw the Coalition program, unlikely as this may seem, as related to socialist–communist conspiracy. When it became known in Youngstown that Alperovitz and Lynd had written a book advocating a "new American Socialism," it became easy to dismiss the Coalition effort as "socialist" or even "communist." In a Chamber of Commerce speech at McKeesport, Pennsylvania, chairman of U.S. Steel, Edgar Speer, denounced the Coalition effort as "nothing short of a Communist takeover." Literature was circulated within the Youngstown business community describing Alperovitz's Exploratory Project for Economic Alternatives as a "front group for Democratic Party penetration," part of the "effective machinery for consolidating a total Institute for Policy Studies–Wall Street takeover of the Democratic Party." Jeff Faux, codirector, was described as "one of Alperovitz's top 'left cover' corporatist economic warfare planners." Staughton Lynd, among his list of credits, was a "professor at the labor counter-insurgency center, Roosevelt University," now "redeployed to Youngstown, Ohio." According to this view, the innocent Youngstown clergy were dupes of a radical socialist (even communist?) plot to nationalize the steel mills. Community control of industry was seen as a way for government to get its foot in the door, leading to the end of free enterprise.

There were, of course, answers to these charges. Alperovitz could be defended as a respected economist who had worked at the Brookings Institution, the Kennedy Institute of Politics at Harvard, and the State Department. He was legislative aide to Congressman Robert Kastenmeier and legislative director for Senator Gaylord Nelson. In 1976, some sixty members of Congress (including the chairs of both the House and Senate Banking Committees) urged his appointment to the Council of Economic Advisors.

Furthermore, Coalition members began to see that part of their problem with the business community was terminology. Faced with the charge that community–worker control was socialist, Coalition members learned to describe the plant ownership scheme as

an attempt to extend the basic democratic philosophy: Workers and the community should have some say about investment decisions in their community. . . . It's novel perhaps, but is certainly not socialist by any stretch of the term. (Staughton Lynd)

There are some who see it as creeping socialism – it's not. It's the best of capitalism: a lot of people putting their money and labor together. It's like the original Plymouth Colony. It's pure capitalism. (Ed Stanton in Lally 1978: 10)

Once again, the rhetoric concealed an important question. Should the federal government be the guarantor for such a large portion of the investment (some 90%) in the new steel company? While businesses of many types were clearly profiting from federal government tax breaks or subsidies (it was said that the Lykes Corporation had benefited by more than $500 million from federal regulation of and subsidy to the shipping industry), such a massive government investment in a single company represented a new turn in American political economy. (It should be noted that the Youngstown steel crisis predated the Chrysler Corporation bail-out.) In 1978–79, the time of decision for Youngstown, the largest federal loan guarantee to a company in crisis had been $250 million to Lockheed, a major defense supplier. It could be argued that investing $300 million in a Youngstown steel mill was going a major step further, opening the federal government to similar demands from virtually every city in economic trouble. If the Campbell Works reopening represented a viable business proposal, why was it not able to raise a greater equity investment? Unfortunately, this serious question became lost in the red baiting.

Third, members of the business community typically made the assumption that "steel in the Valley is dead" and that "if a private company couldn't make a go of the Campbell Works, nobody can." These assumptions overlooked two things. One was that, in spite of the drastic reduction in steel production and employment in the Valley, firms like Sharon Steel and Commercial Shearing were highly profitable, and Republic Steel was just deciding to put $250 million into upgrading its productive capacity at Warren. The other was that the combination of the corporate structure and management allocation of capital was a major cause of the New Orleans–based conglomerate's failure to make a go of the Campbell Works. The assumption that the Campbell Works was finished as a steel producer had to be reexamined if a new corporate structure and modernized production facilities were to be introduced.

Given the general climate of opinion regarding the Coalition in the Youngstown business community, developing support within this constituency was not an easy task. The strategy devised was to recruit a "Committee of 100," who would be the ground breakers for the Coalition. The initial coordinator of the project, Jacqueline Alfred, had difficulty recruiting business people even to sign a letter of invitation. A dinner coordinated by Alfred and Jim Bennet (a local attorney and member of Ed Weisheimer's Central Christian Church), was held for local business people. By most accounts, it was a disaster; Coalition representatives were able to make few converts.

Finally, in June 1978, four local business people were prevailed upon to sign a letter of appeal to local business firms. They included Arthur Young, president of the Mahoning Bank; William Brown, publisher of the *Vindicator*, and two presidents of local firms, Bert Tamarkin and Charles Stiver. The letter, mailed to 1,347 business firms, assured business people that "business is well represented" in the process of judging the feasibility of the Coalition's plan for the Campbell Works and warned that "business must be as much involved in showing support for the effort as it is in judging the feasibility." They were urged to open a Save Our Valley savings account.

Business people were invited to participate in two public sessions in late July 1978 that reviewed the NCEA proposal for a corporate structure for the new steel company. These meetings (to be considered in the following chapter) were probably the most fruitful collective exchange between the Coalition and the business community. Later in the fall, there were some queries from individual business people concerning whether the Coalition might be reassessing its plans for the Campbell Works.

One problem in the relationship between the Coalition and the business community may very well have been a kind of clergy–lay dynamic that worked to impede communication. Business people may have been unaccustomed to dealing with clergy as colleagues on a business matter. And the clergy may have communicated a sense of moral certitude that made them seem deaf to hard business questions. It is possible that only in instances where both sides took the time and trouble to listen and probe for a common language did real communication take place.

One place where the clergy–lay dichotomy seems to have been successfully bridged was the First Presbyterian Church. Through its revitalization program, the church members as a body had already begun addressing civic problems. Bert Campbell in particular was able to engage church members who were also business leaders in informative discussion about the Coalition's work. These discussions did not always end in agreement with the Coalition's plan. But they did create a climate of understanding and mutual respect. One Sunday, a parishioner handed Bert Campbell a substantial check, saying, "I don't believe you guys will get the Campbell Works open. But you're doing good work. This is to help with your extra expenses."

But apart from the few individuals who responded to the Coalition's appeal, both for financial support and for dialogue, the dominant reaction from the business community can probably be characterized as silent nonsupport.

The Youngstown business community as a whole was rather slow to acknowledge the need for a serious economic development effort. Some (a bank president, for example) felt that the local economy would right itself after a short slump. There was a general feeling that the economy should diversify into other sectors and end local dependence on the steel industry. As their institutional vehicle for economic development, the business community adopted Congressman Carney's Mahoning Valley Economic Development Committee. The development of MVEDC, however, was far too late for the committee to make any direct response to the situation at the Campbell Works. It had neither office nor director before January 1979. Furthermore, it was considered such a political creature that the top three candidates for the director's job turned it down. The person eventually chosen as director was fired after eight months on the job, leaving the agency virtually without accomplishment two years after the Sheet and Tube shutdown.

The Union

Organized labor, particularly the steelworkers union, was a critical target constituency. The Coalition emerged partly as a result of the lack of any official union response other than to arrange for unemployment benefits. But in political terms, the Coalition needed the backing of the steelworkers union. Lack of union support for the reopening effort would have been a telling, if not fateful, blow to the whole idea.

In analyzing the relationship of the union to the Coalition

campaign, it is useful to distinguish between the union structure and the rank-and-file workers facing unemployment through the shutdown. The two are related, but somewhat distinct constituencies.

Union representation at Sheet and Tube was spread over six local unions. The two most seriously affected were at Campbell (Local No. 2418) and Struthers (Local No. 2163). The Brier Hill local was least affected, losing about one hundred workers through job shifts connected with the shutdown. Since so many locals were affected, the task of coordinating a response to the situation fell to the director of the Youngstown District 26, Frank Leseganich.

As a union politician, Leseganich had both friends and enemies. On the one hand, he was on good terms with union headquarters in Pittsburgh. A McBride supporter, he had recently been re-elected district director, even as his district was giving a majority to McBride's opponent, Sadlowski. Leseganich was least popular in Brier Hill, where Sadlowski support was concentrated. In civic affairs, Leseganich was not particularly close to Congressman Charles Carney; though Carney was unofficially the steelworkers' man in Washington, Carney's personal ties were to Jim Griffin, the former district director whom Leseganich had defeated.

In the first week after the shutdown announcement, Leseganich went to Washington with the steelworkers from Youngstown carrying petitions to President Carter. In succeeding weeks, he became largely a follower rather than a leader of events. Leseganich observed the jockeying for position on the part of Congressman Carney, on the one hand, and Governor Rhodes, on the other. His principal concern was to prevent steel unemployment from becoming a political football kicked back and forth by the politicians. For this reason, Leseganich was willing to back the Ecumenical Coalition. He saw it as being led by a priest whom he knew and trusted as sympathetic to labor.

In the showdown between Bishop Malone and Congressman Carney over who would control the planning grant from HUD, Leseganich essentially backed the Coalition. When the letter to Washington was drawn up specifying the Coalition as lead agent in Youngstown, Leseganich could not be reached at his office to sign it. Stanton presumed upon their friendship to announce at the subsequent press conference that Leseganich was a signatory to the letter. (He actually called while the press conference was in progress to say he would be happy to sign, if that prevented Carney from controlling the money.)

Shortly thereafter, Leseganich was startled when Staughton Lynd (attorney for the Brier Hill local) was named attorney for the Ecumenical Coalition. Lynd's designation had important implications for union support for the Coalition effort. At first Pittsburgh had largely allowed Leseganich a free hand in taking a position with respect to the Coalition. But Pittsburgh was decidedly nervous about Lynd. In fact, Pittsburgh interpreted the Youngstown movement as simply another effort by Lynd to meddle in union affairs and embarrass the national union leadership. The attitude in Pittsburgh turned decidedly cautious.

In the meantime, Leseganich was in a difficult position trying to reconcile differences of opinion about the Coalition among the six local presidents. The strongest support for the Coalition was coming from the Sadlowski faction at Brier Hill, the local that had been the least affected by the Campbell Works shutdown. The two locals with the largest job losses were divided. Bill Sferra, president of the Campbell local, was skeptical about the success of the reopening plan, but he was willing to cooperate fully with the Coalition. In contrast, Russell Baxter, president of the Struthers local, was a highly vocal critic of the Coalition. Leseganich himself, who was skeptical that money could be raised from any source to finance a reopening, opted for maintaining a friendly, but relatively hands-off posture.

As the Coalition campaign effort picked up momentum during the spring of 1978, organized labor became targeted as a constituency calling for special attention. Duane Irving, a grievance committeeman at the Campbell local (later elected vice-president), had been involved with the worker ownership discussions and Coalition meetings from the beginning. Having been laid off in the shutdown, he was hired by the Coalition as a labor organizer and, together with Ed Stanton, made the rounds of local unions in the Youngstown area for two and a half months, appealing for support through the Save Our Valley account campaign. Irving was also in charge of other organizing attempts such as a mailing to the ninety-six local unions making up the Youngstown area AFL–CIO, of which Russell Baxter (the Coalition critic) was president. Local unions frequently responded to the Coalition campaign pitch by depositing local union funds in a Save Our

Valley account, but relatively few accounts from individual workers were forthcoming.

In order to carry the Coalition campaign more directly to the workers, it was proposed that District 26 send a fifty-thousand-piece mailing directly to workers' homes, appealing for Coalition support. Frank Leseganich promised to cover the mailing costs, and actually did draft a two-page letter. Recalling the great steel strikes of 1892, 1919, 1937, and 1959, he asked steelworkers to help their fellow USW members in an "emergency every bit as real and every bit as serious as those crimes." In asking union members to open Save Our Valley accounts, Leseganich wrote: "You and I have an unparalleled opportunity to help our fellow members as never before. What's more, we can do it from our living rooms – and it won't cost a dime." The letter, however, was never sent. As the mailing was in preparation, Leseganich received a memo from Pittsburgh (dated May 3, 1978). Jim Smith, assistant to McBride, had reviewed Alperovitz's preliminary report and found it weak. He also recalled the failure of worker-owned enterprises during the Knights of Labor phase in American labor history. Pointing to the long-standing union policy of concentrating on collective bargaining rather than worker ownership, Smith commented:

The time may come when organized labor should take a new look at this whole subject. However, when and if we do, that action will have to be taken by the decision making bodies of the Union, and not by individuals.

In the meantime I would not recommend that the International Union engage in the promotion of such schemes. If local unions wish to do so, or if our members wish to do so, I do not believe that President McBride or other officers would be inclined to interfere, but it is a very different thing for the International Union to place its stamp of approval on such ventures.

Commenting on the NCEA paper's call for the international union to invest in and promote community–worker ownership, he concluded:

The writers of the paper are either ignorant of American labor's bad experience with such schemes, in which case they should have asked for information rather than give instructions, or they know perfectly well what the situation is and are simply seeking to discredit the union in the eyes of those members who wish to see the Campbell Works reopened. I strongly suspect that the latter is the case.

The proposed mailing was never heard of again.

Lloyd McBride visited Youngstown for the first time after the shutdown to give a dinner speech at the District 26 convention on May 13, 1978. His critics in the union were saying that almost eight months was rather late for a show of sympathy and concern. Furthermore, the impression was strong both in the Brier Hill local and among Coalition members close to Staughton Lynd that the international union was opposed to the Coalition effort.

The view from the office tower headquarters in Pittsburgh was different. In the union president's office, the suspicion was that the Coalition effort in Youngstown was being masterminded by long-term opponents of the union administration. Local presidents within Youngstown were divided about whether to support it. The plan being developed by the NCEA looked financially infeasible to the union's economist. A trusted union confidant, Jim Griffin, was backing the Mahoning Valley Economic Development Corporation (in which he was a founding trustee) rather than the Coalition. Consequently, union headquarters was reticent about promoting an effort that could only, in their view, increase the stature of opponents to the McBride administration and raise false hopes among the workers terminated by the shutdown.

The question of Pittsburgh's policy toward the Coalition came up for discussion at the union's national convention in Atlantic City during August 1978. Representatives from Brier Hill had submitted a resolution in District 26 backing the Ecumenical Coalition. This resolution was not, however, supported by Russell Baxter's union (Local 2163), one of the locals most directly affected by the shutdown. The committee preparing resolutions for the national convention wished to combine similar resolutions on plant closings. In the process of preparing the material, the committee also received a resolution from Jim Griffin, the former District 26 director who had worked at Pittsburgh headquarters. Partly in view of the difference of opinion in District 26, partly because of Griffin's Pittsburgh connections, the committee chose to bring to the floor the Griffin resolution backing the Coalition. On the convention floor Brier Hill representatives objected that, if Youngstown were being mentioned, something more serious than the Griffin resolution should be considered. McBride agreed, but the other locals failed to support Brier Hill on the convention floor. The matter was referred to a special meeting of the Youngstown representatives with Jim Smith and a union vice-president. Meanwhile, at a press conference, Gerald Dickey, secretary at Brier Hill, asked McBride about the Youngstown resolution. McBride was understood to answer that he had a plan for restoring jobs in Youngstown. McBride's "secret plan," bannered in the Youngstown *Vindicator*, caused misunderstanding between Youngstown and Pittsburgh for some weeks thereafter. According to Smith, the situation at the convention was characteristic of Pittsburgh's difficulty: "Part of our whole problem in Youngstown was the fact that our members were somewhat fragmented into the different locals. If we had one local union in the whole complex with one elected set of leadership, we would have been able to do more than we did. But that's history."

In September 1978 (a year after the shutdown), the Executive Committee of the Coalition attempted to enlist McBride's support in lobbying the Carter administration at the time when it was expected a decision would be forthcoming in Washington. McBride's reply was noncommittal:

I have your telegram relative to a plan for improving employment prospects and expressing your desire to discuss it with me.

I have expressed my thoughts in this regard to representatives of the Carter Administration, and I have reason to believe that the administration will give serious consideration to my views. I am convinced that no good purpose would be served by my making public the exchanges that have taken place with representatives of the Carter Administration. . . .

I feel we are all working for the same cause and understand the problem in the same light; hopefully, the right solution will evolve from the effort we are all extending. (Letter to Reverend John Sharick, September 27, 1978)

A return letter of John Scharick, vice-chairman of the Executive Committee of the Coalition, again requested a meeting with McBride:

It is my personal hope that in the near future you may be willing to sit down with members of the executive committee of the Ecumenical Coalition to discuss future cooperation for what your letter calls the "same cause" and that we may continue to "understand the problem in the same light." (Letter to Lloyd McBride, October 4, 1978)

But for the time being, there was no meeting with McBride.

The relationship between Pittsburgh and the Coalition began to change markedly later in the fall of 1978. Jim Smith began to take a particular interest in Youngstown. At Stanton's invitation, he appeared with Bishop Malone and Bill Sullivan on the Coalition presentation at Notre Dame. The occasion provided an opportunity for a long and frank exchange of views over scotch the evening before in the Morris Inn, as well as at lunch the next day. Smith also discovered a kindred soul in Bert Campbell, the former steelworker grievance committeeman. It evidently became apparent to Smith that Pittsburgh's early impression of the Coalition as a front for Staughton Lynd was mistaken. In the final months of 1978, Smith became virtually on call for the Coalition. He was closely involved in the later stages of the planning work (to be detailed in the following chapter) and was instrumental in finally arranging a meeting between the Coalition and McBride. On March 16, 1979, as the Coalition proposal was in final consideration in Washington, McBride did write to President Carter endorsing the Ecumenical Coalition proposal. It was much more than a perfunctory letter. Reviewing the problems caused by Sheet and Tube and the need to avert a future steel shortage, he said of the Youngstown project:

Under the leadership of the churches of that area, and the religious community network through the United States, a new spirit of community determination has been forged in the midst of the Youngstown tragedy. Labor, management, and public officials are working together more closely than ever before. They are convinced that by hard work and close cooperation they can rebuild the economic base of their community. To do so they need the sort of basic financial support which only the Federal Government can provide. . . . Needless to say, I am pleased to endorse their request, and I would urge a prompt decision.

Critics of McBride conceded that his endorsement of the Coalition in the last weeks of the campaign showed an excellent sense of timing. He came in late enough not to be identified with the project if it should fail. But he was there to take credit for a last-minute shove, if that was all that was needed to push the proposal over the top.

Unemployed Workers

Of the three specially targeted constituencies in the Youngstown area, the unemployed workers comprised the one group that the Coalition had to win. It might be possible to carry off the Campbell Works reopening without the support of the local business community, and even without the explicit endorsement of the steelworkers union. But it would be hard for the Coalition to argue that it represented the unemployed workers without their visible support. And yet that was increasingly the position the Coalition found itself in.

The collective support from unemployed workers was disappointing. The only significant collective action by workers themselves was the petition drive in the week following Black Monday, when workers stood at grocery stores, banks, and shopping plazas collecting thousands of signatures. Following that initial effort, the workers as a group seem to have largely disappeared. Duane Irving, the labor organizer for the Coalition, admits that there was never any groundswell of support among the Sheet and Tube workers. "I can't figure it out," he said. At a community planning meeting in July, Stanton confessed his disappointment at the relatively few Save Our Valley accounts opened by individual steelworkers.

The total number of Save Our Valley accounts was less than 4,200, indicating that this campaign tactic never caught on among the workers. If each of the workers laid off in the shutdown had been responsible for opening but one account, the total number of accounts would have been significantly larger. Nor did the workers turn out for public rallies. In September 1978, on the anniversary of Black Monday, a rally was called at noon at the downtown Federal Plaza. It is reported that downtown office workers on their lunch break far outnumbered the few steelworkers who showed up. The same thing happened again in March 1979. On a beautiful St. Patrick's Day, the Coalition joined the Brier Hill union in sponsoring a rally. The newspaper estimated the turnout at 250, and witnesses say that estimate was generous. Finally, Stanton estimates that no more than 50 steelworkers in total did any volunteer work for the Coalition campaign.

It would be easy to conclude from the sparse campaign participation by individual steelworkers that there simply was no support for the Coalition. Such a conclusion, however, would fail to take into account the supportive attitudes of workers that were manifested outside the campaign mechanism. In the author's experience of interviewing and spending time with Youngstown residents, hope for the Coalition effort was frequently volunteered without solicitation: for example, from the cleaning lady whose husband had worked at Brier Hill for twenty-five years and the former Sheet and Tube worker pumping gas on Market Street who had tried unsuccessfully to find a steel job in Chicago. There was the steelworker at a conference in Pittsburgh who asked the author to convey to Father Stanton his conviction that "the clergy are all we've got." There was the group of ten to twenty unemployed steelworkers between the ages of 52 and 64 who met every other Wednesday morning for breakfast in Lowellville. None had been able to find other work. "Our best bet," said one, "is if they reopen the Campbell Works." "We're not the only ones in the Valley," said another. "There's a lot that just sit back and don't say nothing" (Youngstown *Vindicator*, March 25, 1979).

Why did so many of the Sheet and Tube workers, even those claiming to experience real difficulty in finding other work, "sit back and say nothing?" Two things seem clear. First there was a complex set of factors in the Youngstown situation that tended to impede campaign participation by the unemployed workers. And second, the low rate of participation by the unemployed in Youngstown is consistent with a national pattern of low political participation by the unemployed in general.

Youngstown factors. Seven factors are important here.

1. It was widely believed among the workers at Campbell that the shutdown was not final. The knowledge on the mill floor was that the hot- and cold-strip rolling mills were not in such bad shape, compared with what workers knew about similar facilities in the Youngstown area and in western Pennsylvania. They felt that the shutdown announcement may well have been just a tactic to bring labor in line, giving the company a freer hand in altering the manning tables, increasing shop floor discipline, and holding the line on wage increases. It was conceded that the blast furnaces and open hearths were probably down for good. But workers thought that, when the steel market picked up again, the company would buy slabs somewhere (nearby Sharon Steel was getting slabs from Poland and Brazil) and start up the rolling mills. Such a conjecture was not totally unreasonable. No less a local steel authority than Bill Sullivan thought that, when the steel market peaked in the winter of 1978–9, the rolling mills might

very well have been cranked up again temporarily – had they not been tied up in negotiation with the Coalition.

2. Workers were influenced by the signals they were getting from union leadership about the Coalition and its reopening project. For at least a year after the shutdown, there was no clear-cut message from the union hierarchy of support for the Coalition. One local president (also the president of the local AFL–CIO) was vocal in his opposition. The district director was halting and uncertain. The national convention maneuvered the Coalition resolution off the agenda. The national president did not think enough of the situation to drive sixty-five miles to Youngstown and refused to talk with the Coalition. It was natural for workers in the mill to follow the lead of people who supposedly knew what was going on and were watching out for their interests. By the time the union did endorse the Coalition, any chance for organizing the workers had already been lost. The workers' passivity vis-à-vis the union hierarchy probably should have been expected. The steelworkers no longer had the experience of being part of a "movement." With high wages and excellent benefits (including such things as full dental coverage and a thirteen-week vacation every five years for twenty-year veterans), the workers had come to use membership in the union much as they would use an insurance policy. Union dues were the insurance premiums that gave the individual worker coverage in an unusual crisis: dispute with the foreman or temporary unemployment in slack times. The union structure did not encourage intense participation; with the Experimental Negotiating Agreement, locals had lost the right to strike over shop floor issues, and only district directors were allowed to vote on the national wage contract. The very structure of the union and its success in providing high wages and benefits left the workers ill-prepared for independent decision making. The steelworkers district director in Youngstown himself stated very aptly: "Our people have become so lax and dependent on somebody else to do it for them, when something doesn't work, they blame somebody else."

3. Particularly without any strong leadership from the union, the workers were afraid of taking any action that could jeopardize their pension rights or unemployment benefits. The company would have welcomed a strike, they felt. That would only have allowed the shutdown to proceed more quickly or given the company an excuse to shut down portions of the mill still operat-

ing. The company clearly had the upper hand; the workers were afraid to do anything that could endanger the little security they had left. This feeling was enforced by the company's foot dragging in the normal grievance procedures as soon as the shutdown plan went into effect.

4. The very success of the Coalition in persuading various union locals to make substantial Save Our Valley deposits may well have worked against individual initiatives by the workers. When the local had already opened an account of ten, twenty, or forty thousand dollars, it set up an "I gave at the office" syndrome. Even workers sympathetic to the Coalition felt that their responsibility had already been fulfilled.

5. Workers had the same questions and doubts as the business community. Workers, too, asked themselves, "How can priests and ministers run a steel mill?" and "If the company can't make a profit here, how can anyone else?" And, just as with the business people, these questions tended to be conversation stoppers rather than requests for information. Combined with the ignorance and misinformation were intelligent questions about the likelihood of capital investment from any source, public or private, about the lack of managerial capacity. The answers they settled on (particularly as they left the workplace and moved out of communication) were often based on secondhand information and opinions.

6. Once the shutdown took place, the workers were no longer an organized group, but simply individuals pursuing an individual calculus of interest. (Since they were divided over several different locals, there was no single group to start with anyway.) The 4200 unemployed workers found themselves in widely different circumstances. Some with transferrable job skills (machinists and millwrights, for example) were quickly reemployed. Others could retire. A few went to college and got white-collar jobs. The unemployed workers lacked the group solidarity to pursue a single purpose. Although a good argument could be made for the importance of reopening the mill in terms of the overall economic and employment picture for the community, that did not always mean that investing in a mill reopening was the best strategy for individual workers. Their circumstances were simply too varied.

Officials at the Brier Hill local were fully aware of this dynamic as they watched what happened to the workers at Campbell. Faced with the shutdown of Brier Hill, they realized that worker efforts focused on keeping the mill open would have to take place *before* the shutdown. The workplace itself was the unifying factor. Once the plant gates closed, there was no more group.

7. Aside from (or along with) all of the preceding factors, there simply was a good deal of worker apathy. The generous scale of unemployment benefits probably did as much as anything to prevent an organized response to the shutdown. According to Bill Sferra, president of the Campbell local, "One of the biggest problems I have to deal with is guys being bored." John McNichol, later one of the cofounders of Steelworkers United for Employment, admitted that, after his hair turned white and fell out within weeks of Black Monday, he just decided to "take the year off and watch the grass grow." (It did not help the Coalition's campaign effort that he made this statement while appearing with Ed Stanton on the local Dan Ryan radio talk show.)

At the time when the Coalition was exerting its greatest campaign effort (in spring and early summer), workers were being well paid for not working. Frank Leseganich, Steelworkers District 26 director, thought the Coalition campaign would have had a better chance with the steelworkers if the Coalition had waited until the benefits ran out and workers started getting hungry.

When the benefits did run out, a grass-roots worker movement finally did appear on the scene. It began with a conversation in the Legal Services Office (where Staughton Lynd was an attorney). In talking with several steelworkers, the director, Bob Clyde, suggested that the steelworkers organize on their own. Len Balluck, a union grievance committeeman at the Struthers local who had worked in the Campbell open hearth shop, and John McNichol, a carpenter at the Campbell Works, began to explore the idea. They asked the Coalition for assistance in getting started and were given a small subsidy for office space and supplies. In March, an organizational meeting and a follow-up meeting in the basement of Ed Weisheimer's Central Christian Church drew a respectable turnout of several hundred workers. Within a month Steelworkers United for Employment (SUE, for short) had a mailing list of more than four hundred. Founded specifically to represent the unemployed, SUE became a strong supporter of the Coalition effort. Balluck in particular was a convincing spokesperson. He accompanied Coalition representatives to Washington, where his sincere and forthright account of how it felt as a worker to be "thrown on a garbage heap" was picked up by the national wire services. Balluck was offered financial assistance for his movement from union headquarters, but he elected to remain independent.

SUE provided important backing to the Coalition in its final phase. But in terms of winning the battle to reopen the Campbell Works, it gave too little, too late.

Organizing the unemployed: theory and research. Steelworker union officials Frank Leseganich and Duane Irving thought that one reason for the limited response to the Coalition campaign was the dynamic of "Let the other guy do it." In simple language, the steelworkers were merely restating the problem of collective action as articulated by Mancur Olson (1945):

> If the members of some group have a common interest or objective, and if they would all be better off if that objective were achieved, it has been thought to follow logically that the individuals in that group would, if they were rational and self-interested, act to achieve that objective.
>
> But it is *not* in fact true that the idea that groups will act in their self-interest follows from the premise of rational and self-interested behavior. It does *not* follow, because all of the individuals in a group would gain if they achieved their group objective, even if they were all rational and self-interested. Indeed, unless the number of individuals in a group is quite small, or unless there is coercion or some other special device to make individuals act in their self-interest, *rational self-interested individuals will not act to achieve their common or group interests.* (2–3; emphasis in the original)

The rational, self-interested individual will – as Olson goes on to demonstrate – try to be a free rider, to gain the benefit of the common good (reopening the Campbell Works) without sharing the cost (opening an account, participating in rallies, volunteering for campaign work). The free-rider principle, as Olson shows, is the reason for compulsory union membership; where union membership is not obligatory, it is in the interest of individuals to enjoy the benefits (wages and working conditions) without paying union dues.

With regard to Youngstown, even presuming that the workers constituted a group (which no longer was the case after the shutdown) and presuming that they all agreed that reopening the Campbell Works was in their collective interest (which they did not), the free-rider principle would still act as a disincentive.

According to the free-rider principle, the failure of such a voluntary approach was to be expected.

Furthermore, research on the unemployed indicates that they are a particularly difficult group to organize. In an important national study, Kay Schlozman and Sidney Verba (1979) found that the stress of unemployment is generally not converted into organized activity in the political process. It would be unfair to the complexity and sophistication of their data to attempt a synopsis of their findings, but their thesis may be fairly represented here by two notes from their book. The first concerns a series of interviews they undertook with people involved in politics to ascertain whether their data were failing to pick up significant activity by the unemployed that might not be so visible to those outside the policy process:

There was virtual unanimity among those with whom we spoke that our conclusion about the political quiescence of the unemployed was warranted. Regardless of the perspective of the informant – leaders of organizations involved in mobilizing the unemployed, government officials, a media observer – the situation looked the same: the unemployed are not an active force. They are, in the words of one government official, "a political zero." (Schlozman and Verba 1979: 264–5)

The second note concerns the authors' comparison of activity organized by the unemployed with activity organized by blacks for civil rights. The authors surveyed the *New York Times Index* for "demonstrations" (including sit-ins, marches, picketing) and "other organized acts" (including statements, speeches, conferences, appeals to office holders) by blacks in the years 1964–6 and the unemployed in the years 1974–6 (Table 6.4). Schlozman and Verba concluded:

The contrast is striking. There was substantially more activity by blacks during the 1960s than by the unemployed a decade later. Especially when we recall that a substantial portion of the activity in the "organized acts" category is undertaken *for* the unemployed by organizations like unions rather than *by* them, it is clear that the unemployed are not a politically organized group. (Ibid.: 264)

The relevant theory and research are not sanguine about the prospects for such an undertaking as the Ecumenical Coalition attempted. It is not surprising that steelworker support remained "disappointing."

Table 6.4. *Organized activity by the unemployed, 1974–1976, and by blacks, 1964–1966*

Organized activity	Number of demonstrations	Number of other organized acts
By the unemployed		
1974	1	7
1975	3	9
1976	1	8
By blacks		
1964	59	8
1965	98	31
1966	70	41

Source: New York Times Index, as cited by Schlozman and Verba (1979), 265. Reprinted by permission of Harvard University Press.

Assessment of the Campaign

The campaign effort by the Ecumenical Coalition was aimed at launching a social movement. The shape of that movement was determined to a great extent by the strategy and success of the campaign. What, then, did the Coalition campaign achieve? What sort of social movement resulted from the Coalition's effort?

Scope

In retrospect, the fact that the Coalition campaign became a broad-scope effort was as much a matter of necessity as of choice. The Coalition simply was not able to build sufficient support in any single constituency (the business community, the union, the unemployed) to serve as a political base. The electorate thus became the target constituency, first in the Youngstown area itself and then more broadly in the state and nation.

In the electorate, the campaign was remarkably successful. The Coalition established virtually universal name recognition in Youngstown. In a survey of 235 workers conducted by Youngstown State University, all but one of the respondents – an auto worker – knew of the Coalition. And through the national media, both print and television, the Coalition story was carried both forcefully and sympathetically to the nation. At the same time,

Table 6.5. *Public perception of effectiveness of agencies and officials in the Mahoning Valley*

Agencies having an effect on unemployment (August 1978)

	Coalition (%)	MVEDC
Is having an effect	63	42
Is *not* having an effect	16	14
Don't know	21	44

Percent responding "_____ is having an impact on unemployment" (February 1980)

Congressman Williams	63
Governor Rhodes	51
Ecumenical Coalition	47
MVEDC	37
County government	35
Youngstown mayor	32
President Carter	29

Source: Office of Congressman Lyle Williams.

the Coalition was able to establish a surprisingly high degree of legitimacy as a lead agent for economic development. A political poll conducted in the 19th Congressional District in August 1978, before the congressional election, found that the Coalition was being taken seriously by the electorate. In the survey, a question was asked about groups or individuals having an impact on the unemployment situation in the Mahoning Valley. By late summer, the Ecumenical Coalition was recognized as a more effective group than the Mahoning Valley Economic Development Commission (Table 6.5). In February 1980, a similar poll, taken nine months after the Campbell Works reopening had clearly failed, shows that the Coalition was still considered an effective force in the Valley. Only the new congressman, Lyle Williams, and Governor Rhodes ranked above the Coalition in the estimate of the electorate in their effect on unemployment. Not only did the Coalition continue to outpoint MVEDC at a time when that agency was finally gearing up and the Coalition had largely ended its activity; the Coalition was also considered more effective than the Youngstown mayor or President Carter. A further question on the survey indicates that, in the view of the electorate, the Coalition not only *did* have a role in economic development, it *should* have such a role. Of those answering that the Coalition was not having an impact (39%), 62% still thought that it should.

The Coalition campaign, then, could claim some success as a broad-scope movement. It established itself in the eyes of the electorate as a legitimate voice. And it had a surprisingly good reputation with the voters.

Participation

The central focus of the Coalition's campaign was clearly the Save Our Valley savings account plan. The one thing people and groups were asked to do, whether in the public at large or in special target constituencies, was to open a Save Our Valley account. As a campaign mechanism, opening a savings account was basically a low-intensity style of campaign participation. It might be the decision of a local union or community group meeting, but it might also be a solitary act accomplished by mail or on one's way to the grocery store.

As a campaign activity, opening a savings account was available to just about anyone, individual or group, young or old, steelworker or car salesperson. It cost only a little time; the return on the deposit was comparable to that of any other bank account (high interest rates generating the switch from passbook savings to money market accounts came later). There was no confrontation involved. And unlike demonstrations in the civil rights or antiwar movements, there was neither the excitement, nor even the danger, of a march or sit-in.

In one sense, the strengths of the savings account plan – its ease, its availability, its politeness – were also a weakness. Little or no follow-up was called for. Opening an account was a rational, cool sort of behavior that was not particularly effective in building solidarity or hardening attitudes or commitment.

But the savings account plan – however soft a commitment it involved – was the one thing the Coalition could do. Community organizing, in the sense of a person-to-person campaign, was beyond the Coalition's resources. The Coalition was never able to obtain a list of the unemployed workers. The two principal union locals had neither the staff nor the inclination to do a person-to-person campaign. And the Coalition's effort to reach workers by direct mail was ultimately blocked by the union.

According to John Greenman, who managed the local campaign, the fundamental strategy ultimately depended on the press and television:

We were on a very fast track, and we sensed that we could manipulate the federal government through the press, and convince the federal government through the press that the whole community was behind us. I think that the federal government, at one point, sensed that there was a strong local, regional, and national reaction to this closing and that they'd better do something.

Rather than a community organizing effort, the Coalition ended up conducting a media campaign. In the end Greenman himself was not convinced that the campaign was building any public consensus, though the political polls showed that Greenman's work had a greater effect than he seemed to realize.

Through the spring and summer of 1978, Coalition members seem to have basically agreed on a low-intensity style of campaign participation, keyed to the Save Our Valley program. There was a tendency within the Steering Committee, however, focused largely around Chuck Rawlings, to turn the Coalition into a national cause. This approach was apparent at the national conference in late September 1978. The conference was even described as a "new Selma" in a news account and editorial in the *Vindicator*.

A Coalition demonstration shortly before (using the same "Save Youngstown, Save America" banner that decorated the conference hall) may have indicated to some that the Coalition was about to embark on a more dramatic, confrontation style. In mid-September, President Carter was to give a speech at Columbus, Ohio. The Coalition asked to meet with the president on this trip, but was refused. The Coalition then took out a full page ad in the *Washington Post* and Columbus papers (with more than three thousand signatures), and the Executive and Steering Committees led a group to Columbus. The demonstration, with bishops carrying signs, had a kind of "made for television" quality. (At one point a state trooper – supposedly guarding the president from the demonstrators – came over to tell Bishop Hughes, substituting for Malone that day, that there was a phone call for him and that he could take it at the trooper command post.) This was perhaps the most dramatic scene of the campaign. The bishops were willing to take to the streets when it seemed crucial – and the demonstration did help to bring about a meeting at the White House within a week. But the Executive Committee clearly preferred negotiation over demonstration as a campaign style.

Later in the winter, when an unfavorable decision in Washington seemed imminent and then was finally delivered, agreement within the Steering Committee about the style of campaign began to fall apart. Rhetoric escalated. At a conference in Pittsburgh, Rawlings castigated the Youngstown business community for being "beset by fear and guilt." He insisted that "we aren't going to take 'no' for an answer." And when Washington's answer was no Rawlings insisted that the Coalition would fight on and threatened electoral revenge. Staughton Lynd proposed at a Coalition meeting to carry the struggle to the streets of Washington. Bishop Malone, however, firmly put an end to such talk; as bishop of "all the people" of the Mahoning Valley, he could not endorse such actions.

As a social movement, the Coalition essentially retained the shape of a broad-scale, low-intensity effort. It never became a new cause, similar to the civil rights or antiwar movement, though some clearly wanted to push it in that direction. In the long run, it was closer to the environmental movement, keeping a rather low participation profile and depending on negotiations at the elite level to achieve its goals.

Linkage

A problem throughout the campaign was the linkage between the movement and economic development aspects of the Coalition. Uncertainty about the economic viability of the plan for the Campbell Works had a limiting effect on the success of the campaign. For the business community, the union, and the steelworkers, questions about the management and capitalization of the Campbell Works plan tended to limit their participation. Yet the campaign could also affect the success of the economic development thrust. The following chapters will take up the development of the plan (Chapter VII) and the process of negotiating it into effect (Chapter VIII).

CHAPTER VII

The Plan

The key to the Youngstown effort was a technical and financial plan, one sufficiently credible to attract investors, gain the support of the steelworkers, and warrant federal grants and loan guarantees.

Through the agreement with the Department of Housing and Urban Development, developing "the plan" became the responsibility of the National Center for Economic Alternatives. For approximately the first half of 1978, the plan was in the process of gestation in Washington. The Coalition in Youngstown focused its energies largely on the campaign, while waiting for the plan fashioned by the experts to descend from the nation's capital. The NCEA was to get feedback from Youngstown on a preliminary report and to hear advice from Campbell workers on improving productivity and from local business people on the structure of the new community corporation. But the division of labor for at least the first six months called for the Washington consultants to do the thinking and the Coalition to do the leg work. From January through September, the posture of the Coalition with regard to the plan was essentially a passive one. Such a posture, it should be noted, was to some extent dictated by the terms of the agreement with HUD. The research contract was signed directly between HUD and Alperovitz. The Coalition was given only a kind of informal oversight and had no contractual authority over the planning process or its result.

In the summer and fall of 1978, the plan developed by the NCEA ran into trouble. From September on, a major revision of the plan was conceived and worked out largely in Youngstown, with the aid of volunteer consultants.

199

This chapter focuses on the development of the plan and, at the same time, on the relationship between the Coalition and its Washington consultants.

WREDA and NCEA

Bill Sullivan and the Western Reserve Economic Development Agency were very much involved in the initial brainstorming about a Campbell Works reopening. Although the worker ownership idea is generally attributed to the steelworker Gerald Dickey, Sullivan was one of the first to take the reopening seriously. His first reaction was "All we know for sure is that yesterday the mill was operating and today it isn't, and it will take a lot of fifteen-job factories to replace it." Sullivan was perhaps the Valley's preeminent generalist on the steel industry, and his Western Reserve Economic Development Agency was facing an increasingly uncomfortable political climate. It was clearly to Sullivan's advantage to position his agency for potential involvement in the disposition of the Campbell Works.

It was also to the advantage of the Coalition to have Sullivan and his agency as a resource. Because of its connections both with the steel company and with steel consulting engineers, WREDA was able to execute an economic feasibility study in less than six weeks of the initial request. That study provided the foundation for the Coalition announcement on December 12, 1977, of its intent to take over the Campbell Works. But shortly thereafter, the smooth relationship between WREDA and the Coalition suddenly hit bumpy going. Objections to Sullivan and WREDA came both from within the Coalition Steering Committee and from Washington.

When the Beetle feasibility study demonstrated that an attempt to reopen the shutdown portion of the mill was justified, Sullivan moved quickly to prevent the Lykes Corporation from selling off the remaining or still-useful machinery from the plant and thereby short-circuiting any reopening attempt. (Charges did surface from time to time that such "stripping" was indeed taking place.)[1] To prevent such a move by the corporate owner and to hold an option on the property while it was intact, Sullivan filed papers of incorporation for the "Mahoning Steel Company" – a paper company with members of his staff listed as officers. On December 15, 1977, he wrote to the chair and chief executive officer of Sheet and Tube:

On behalf of the Mahoning Steel Company, we are advising you of that company's interest in acquiring that portion of the Youngstown Sheet and Tube facilities in Mahoning and Trumbull County not now in operation. . . . We are also advising you of the interest of the Mahoning Steel Company in a first refusal option on the remainder of the Youngstown Sheet and Tube Youngstown district property.

The purpose of this legal move was to hold the property intact. In an internal memo to the WREDA executive committee, Sullivan explained the connection between Mahoning Steel and the efforts of the Ecumenical Coalition:

Concurrent with Mahoning Steel's work, consultants hired by the Ecumenical Coalition will be working on a design for "Community Ownership." Should this effort be successful, the community-owned entity could acquire the Mahoning Steel shell with an exchange of stock and proceed to reopen the operation. Should the community ownership scheme for some reason prove unworkable, Mahoning Steel would be left with the option of seeking conventional financing.

Sullivan has said that he was willing to sell the Mahoning Steel Company to the Coalition for the cost of its incorporation – $50. But the incorporation of Mahoning Steel was understood by Rawlings and Lynd as an effort by Sullivan – in collusion with Youngstown Sheet and Tube and the steel industry – to prevent the Coalition from acquiring the Campbell Works. Pressure was brought directly on Bishop Malone to sever any connections between the Coalition and WREDA. Not only should the Coalition have nothing further to do with WREDA, but Stanton should be forced to resign as WREDA treasurer.

At about the same time, Congressman Carney in Washington was saying that WREDA's economic feasibility study was worthless.[2] Because of Carney's opposition, Sullivan – a Republican – was perceived as a political liability to the Coalition in Washington. Where Alperovitz and his NCEA were politically well connected at HUD, Sullivan and WREDA were no longer considered eligible for federal contracts from such agencies as the Economic Development Agency, which switched its funding to Carney's Mahoning Valley Economic Development Commission.

Malone, on investigation, decided that the criticism of Sullivan and WREDA was unfounded. He took the trouble to call Sullivan at a Christmas party and assure him of his appreciation of

WREDA's work. He asked Sullivan to continue his efforts on behalf of the Coalition. And Malone gave his blessing to Stanton's continuing as treasurer of WREDA. Sullivan did participate in several meetings with Alperovitz, but he differed sharply with the NCEA's philosophy and approach to the Youngstown problem and felt himself a persona non grata. Sullivan shortly withdrew from any formal participation in the Campbell Works project. He did, because of his friendship with Stanton, continue to provide occasional advice (which sometimes showed up in Coalition statements and speeches). Later in the Coalition effort, Sullivan did – when asked – publicly express reservations about the technical and economic work of Alperovitz and the NCEA, though he continued to support the general thrust of the Coalition effort as an important public service to the Mahoning Valley.

In retrospect, the loss of Sullivan to the Coalition effort had important consequences. With Sullivan out of the picture, there was no one on the inside of the decision-making structure of the Coalition with experience in and connections with the steel industry. Without a Sullivan, virtually the entire function of oversight and evaluation of the consultants' work on the Campbell Works plan fell to Ed Stanton (supported to some extent by Bert Campbell, through his previous experience as a steelworker and business contacts at First Presbyterian Church). In raising questions about the planning work submitted by the consultants, Stanton became a lonely – and usually outvoted – voice of criticism. Meanwhile the "other Coalition" at the Federal Plaza campaign office identified Sullivan as an enemy of the Coalition effort.

For the Alperovitz group, the Youngstown contract represented a new opportunity. Before Youngstown, Alperovitz had worked within the foundation-sponsored think tank, the Exploratory Project on Economic Alternatives. The HUD contract gave the group its first chance to put its ideas into effect. The National Center for Economic Alternatives was set up as the operational arm of the Exploratory Project. Youngstown was a new venture, one to which the Washington office applied itself with energy and enthusiasm. Alperovitz projected a sense of moral mission about the economic effort that melded easily with the moral concern of the Coalition.

Besides the federal dollars, Alperovitz brought to the Coalition effort considerable skills in public relations. Virtually every one on the Coalition Steering Committee insisted that the effort would never have gotten so far without Alperovitz's connections with the press and media. Even an Alperovitz critic, steelworker official Jim Smith, called Alperovitz the nation's preeminent "public relations economist." Alperovitz was able to interpret and to publicize events in Youngstown on a national scope, not only in such publications as *The Progressive* and *Mother Jones*, but on the op-ed page of the *New York Times*.

The NCEA Plan

Although Alperovitz made a major contribution to the campaign effort of the Coalition, the principal task of the NCEA was to perform a detailed economic feasibility study and put together a technical and financial plan for the reopening.

Alperovitz's work plan (sixty-one pages) shows that he was interested in developing a spectrum of general, background research that would be useful in arguing the case for the Campbell Works, but would also double as potentially publishable research papers in the larger national policy context of HUD's newly authorized program of Urban Development Action Grants.[3] The work plan does show an intent to operationalize this material and apply it to Youngstown, but the accent is not on the unique nuts-and-bolts problems of starting up the mills at Campbell. Youngstown is studied more as a type of problem than as a particular case.

Most of the research itself was contracted out to consultants outside the NCEA (at an average billed rate of $428 per day). The Alperovitz group was responsible for coordinating the research reports, doing a summary report, and taking care of the application to and implementation in Youngstown. The original deadline for the final report was June 30, 1978. This was stretched out to September. But an interim report was presented to the Coalition and the Mahoning Valley Economic Development Committee in April. The interim report provided a summary of preliminary findings that did not differ markedly from the final report. Consequently the broad outlines of the NCEA plan were known several months in advance of the release of the final report itself.

The $3\frac{1}{2}$-inch-thick final report includes different types of material, from letters to a 229-page research monograph. The bulk of the report consists of eight research reports, several brief reports and letters on steel technology and engineering, and the interim and final summary reports. The entire report was sent to HUD in early September 1978. It was the subject of the Coalition's meeting with federal officials on September 27 to determine whether the Coalition could proceed to file a formal application for federal grants and loans. (This meeting and other negotiations with government will be detailed in the following chapter.)

Unbeknownst to the Coalition, the federal government conducted an independent evaluation of the NCEA final report by sending it for analysis to Professor Richard S. Rosenbloom, associate dean of the Harvard Business School. The Rosenbloom analysis did not become public until February 1979. The report may have been leaked by the government at that point as a warning to the Ecumenical Coalition not to expect approval of their proposal. The Coalition replied that Rosenbloom's critique was eight or nine months out of date and was no longer relevant to the grant proposal being submitted in March 1979. That was indeed true. But the Rosenbloom report remains the most extensive written analysis of the NCEA report. It is important for understanding the questions raised by federal officials about the NCEA plan.

Cost–Benefit and Public Policy

Two papers in the final report address the general situation of the Campbell Works closing. Christine Franz-Goldman's (1978) research, cited earlier in this study, addresses the question of pinpointing the real costs of the shutdown that were "externalized," that is, paid by the government and the community rather than Lykes–Sheet and Tube. As a thorough case study of such costs, the Franz-Goldman research provides the kind of information critical for evaluating public policy options. In addition to the direct and indirect costs to the economy as a whole, it is important to know the costs of the shutdown to government itself. Between September 1977 and December 1980, as much as $32 million in taxes was lost, while at the same time government had to spend an extra $34–38 million on welfare and unemployment benefits. Combined losses from unpaid taxes and extra program expenses would total in the area of $66–70 million.[4] The largest part of those losses could never be recouped, since a reopening would not take effect until well over a year after the shutdown. Franz-Goldman estimated, however, that a Campbell Works reopening in January 1979 could reduce the losses in the 39-month period alone by $13.9–19.5 million (ibid.: 9–10).

A paper by David Smith (1978) explores the public policy implications of such a cost–benefit analysis. He argues that an adequate policy response must accomplish three things:

1. It must ensure that future closings and decisions to shift production are made in a fashion that takes into account these costs which are now so easily externalized.
2. It must emphasize the social and economic importance of stable communities and must provide a capacity for residents of local jurisdictions to build their lives and communities with some confidence that stability will be maintained.
3. The public sector must develop the capacity to act as an investor on its own behalf and in support of the first two objectives. (Ibid.: 2)

Smith calls for a strategy of public intervention, in which the public sector clearly takes responsibility for managing community resources on a long-term basis. First, such a public policy stance demands information about the prospects for a community's economic base; Smith opts for a voluntary strategy in assembling such information making use of data and techniques available to private sector investors (e.g., Dun and Bradstreet information, investment rating techniques). Second, such a policy needs incentives to be employed by the public sector manager. Smith calls for an "employment maintenance strategy," saying that supply-side investment incentives (such as tax rebates to new business investment) "are likely to be ineffective in the absence of a strong and growing market for the product and will oftentimes be unnecessary if such a market exists" (ibid.: 10).

In the case of plant closings, Smith argued that "market forces do not explain all plant closings, and that a closing decision does not necessarily mean a non-viable firm." According to Smith, the directly calculable costs of a plant closing may warrant government reinvestment guided by a calculation of the "public balance sheet." Smith's calculation of the public balance sheet for Youngstown (using Franz-Goldman's numbers) indicated a public financial return from a reopened Campbell Works of approximately $6.75 million annually in increased tax revenues. "Therefore, using a public return of $6.75 million and an expected rate of return of 9%, we could justify a public equity investment in a plant reopening of $75 million" (ibid.: 29A).

While clearly calling for more aggressive government action for the economic redevelopment of local communities, the Smith paper manages a kind of moderate liberal economic stance. On the one hand, there is a clear call for government intervention in the local economy. On the other, this is proposed as an alternative to existing interventions, and in a style and approach that emphasizes a "business-like" approach to public management. And for Smith, the market is an ultimate limiting factor: "Determining the size and future of possible markets is crucial. If the market has been lost, there is relatively little that public policy can do to reverse that situation (short of guaranteed public purchasing contracts)" (ibid.: 25).

The Franz-Goldmann and Smith papers function on the whole as background information and general groundwork for the Campbell Works reopening plan.

Productivity

A major point in the original NCEA plan is the principle that "worker-owned companies are capable of higher productivity than similarly situated conventionally owned companies" (Frieden 1978: 12). The plan calls for an annual productivity gain of 2% for the first three years, 1.5% for the next two years, and 1% for the next four years. This assumption of higher productivity is based on a survey of the published literature and research findings on companies in which workers participated in ownership and/or decision making. The report concludes that workers' participation in a steel mill could have significant effects on productivity through "higher morale and greater motivation; more attention addressed to quality; improved coordination; reductions in waste and delays; preventive maintenance; less absenteeism and turnover; better utilization of energy resources; and improvements in job design" (ibid.).

NCEA and Coalition planners conducted discussions with about eighty Campbell steelworkers at the union local hall in June 1978 about the prospects for increasing productivity in the Campbell Works. There was a firm conviction among the workers that productivity could be drastically improved. Morale under Lykes management was clearly bad; workers took pride in their jobs, but were frustrated by Lykes's failure to modernize and even provide spare parts. They felt that they could turn in significant productivity gains provided that (a) management was willing to listen and (b) they were given financial incentives to participate in the production process.

Two questions were raised about the productivity point in the NCEA planning. First, the success stories of worker ownership came from smaller plants or work units, for example, plywood mills in Oregon and scavenger companies in California. The Campbell Works plan, employing 3,500 workers in a reopened mill, would have tested worker-participation procedures on a radically new scale, both in terms of the number of employees and in the level of capital investment per worker. Second, Rosenbloom (1979) pointed out that a successful productivity increase might bring with it a new problem. Because the productivity increase was projected to exceed the increase in plant volume,

an increment in productivity beyond this level means a reduction in employment at Campbell, unless it is matched by increasing market share. Given the projected volume of shipments, and the assumed rate of increase in output per worker, 6% of the initial jobs will be redundant after three years, and 14% within a decade. The possibility that this effect might be perceived by the workforce and consequently affect their attitudes toward further improvements is not discussed.

These questions, however, should not detract from the strong current of feeling among Campbell steelworkers that they could do a much better job working for themselves than for Lykes. The productivity discussions revealed a well of energy that workers were willing to place on the line. The author knows of at least one experienced mill operator who had elected to take early retirement after the shutdown but who offered to come back and work for a year without pay to teach his replacement how to handle the machinery.

Corporate Structure

The other report that integrated feedback from the local community was the report recommending a corporate structure (Dewan and Frieden, 1978). Five different corporate models were considered. The model recommended was a "for-profit" operating corporation, the board of directors of which would be selected by three different groups: (a) individual common stock shareholders, (b) a community corporation, and (c) an Employee Stock Ownership Plan (ESOP) representing current employees of the new corporation.

The corporation would issue two types of stock. Voting common stock would be limited and could be held only by local residents, the community corporation, or workers through the ESOP. The report recommended that voting common stock be restricted to local residents but admitted that these restrictions might not in practice be workable. In any case, the community corporation and ESOP together would inevitably hold a majority of votes on the board of directors, ensuring the principle of local control. A second class of nonvoting preferred stock would be issued that could be sold to outside investors such as religious institutions and labor unions.

The recommendations were discussed in Youngstown at two community meetings at First Presbyterian Church on July 26 and 27, 1978, with a total of 150 persons participating. These meetings selected as the most important criteria for evaluating the corporate structure model "(1) maintaining local control; (2) obtaining maximum financing; (3) maintaining the role of the labor union and encouraging workers' participation; (4) attracting qualified management" (National Center for Economic Alternatives 1978: 45). The two meetings accepted the recommended model, but introduced three qualifications: (a) The role of the community corporation on the board of directors should be limited to less than one-third representation. As a result of this recommendation, board membership was structured as follows:

Common stock shareholders	6
Employee Stock Ownership Plan	6
Community corporation	3

(b) The selection of directors representing the community corporation should not be left to politicians. (c) The role of individual investors in the operating company should be increased, while still safeguarding local control with stock restrictions and voting requirements.

Discussion with the United Steelworkers union introduced two points. First, the union would retain its role as representative of and bargaining agent for production workers. Second, the workers' pension plan would be kept separate from the ESOP. The steelworkers union was critical of the South Bend Lathe worker ownership scheme on both these points. The new management attempted to get rid of the union as a bargaining agent and tried to invest the workers' pension benefits in the company – leaving them with unfunded pension rights should the company fail.

Steel Technology

It was clear from the outset that the old open hearth furnaces in the Campbell Works would have to be replaced. The financial model used by NCEA predicted that, with open hearth technology, the mill would never be profitable. The question then became whether to go to oxygen or electric furnaces.

The Beetle report suggested strongly that a reopening strategy for the Campbell Works might include a change to electric furnaces. Since the electric furnaces would be charged with scrap, this would eliminate the need for other primary plant replacements: relining the blast furnaces, rebuilding the coke plant and sinter plant. (These facilities would be needed only if the Campbell Works were to continue producing hot metal from iron ore.) The disadvantages of such a change would be dependence on scrap in an area where it historically had been in short supply, possibly requiring that scrap be shipped in from Chicago or other scrap markets.

One alternative under consideration for a time was the "Super BOF," an improved form of oxygen furnace invented by Youngstown-area resident Albert Calderon and proposed by him personally. (Calderon also deposited $50,000 in a Save Our Valley account.) The super BOF technology was evaluated by two independent engineering consultants, both of whom advised that this new technology would probably take up to five years for debugging and was therefore inadvisable for installation at Campbell.

In the end, it was decided that the combination of lowest capital investment and best cost savings per ton of steel could be achieved with electric furnaces. (Republic Steel, in its $250 million capital improvement program being planned at the same time as the Campbell Works project, opted for installing electric furnaces at its mill in Warren.)

Federal-Government-Directed Procurement

In the latter 1970s, a regional economic competition between the Frostbelt and Sunbelt became increasingly apparent. One point in that debate was a pattern of federal spending that returned comparatively more federal moneys to areas already experiencing the greatest economic growth. As one way of promoting business in economically depressed areas, it was being suggested that the federal government direct its purchases to areas of high unemployment. The NCEA asked researchers at the Northeast–Midwest Institute to explore the legal framework for directing federal steel procurement to reopened Campbell Works. The report on procurement provided by the Northeast–Midwest Institute attempted to provide the justification for such a procurement policy. President Carter did eventually institute a policy of directed procurement. But the research report on procurement in the NCEA plan had two serious weaknesses.

The first was the legal grounds for such a policy. The researchers found that, under Title II of the first War Powers Act, a president in a national emergency could direct any federal department to enter into contracts without regard to other provisions of law, when he deemed that such action would facilitate the national defense. The researchers also found that President Truman had declared a state of emergency during the Korean War in 1950, which had never legally been rescinded. They proposed that President Carter use this legal basis for directing steel purchases toward a reopened Campbell Works. The White House could hardly take seriously the proposal that the president use a Korean War emergency declaration as the legal basis for such a directed procurement policy. The result was that this procurement section of the NCEA report damaged the credibility of the entire project at the White House.

Second, the Northeast–Midwest report curiously ignored the fact that the U.S. government does not purchase raw steel, but products made from steel, such as tanks, automobiles, typewriters, and filing cabinets. The NCEA team addressed the question in its final report summary. Discussions with the Office of Federal Procurement Policy suggested two approaches: designating steel as a "government-furnished equipment" item or directing purchases related to grants-in-aid (National Center for Economic Alternatives 1978: 39).

The final report summary (issued in June 1978) noted that "though not easy, targeted procurement *can be used* to aid the project" (ibid.). And in the marketing and financial plans that were part of the NCEA report submitted to the federal government in September 1978, federally directed purchases of up to three hundred thousand tons of steel per year would be necessary for the mill to be profitable. In later versions of the plan, the federal procurement idea disappeared.

Commercial Sales Forecast

The marketing and financial studies were done for the NCEA by Paul Marshall, cofounder of the Boston consulting firm of Putnam, Hayes, and Bartlett. Marshall, previously a faculty member at Harvard, had done consulting work for the American Iron and Steel Institute.

The "Commercial Sales Forecast" submitted by Marshall comprises a very thin report of only six pages. In many ways it is the most problematic piece in the entire NCEA final report. Marshall's methodology, first of all, was problematic. He began by taking the figures on national steel consumption for the past twenty years and, using regression techniques, projected the consumption for the next twenty years into the future. Marshall assumed that "U.S. consumption would follow the historic trend in the future." The problem here is that a *projection* is not the same as a *forecast*. An assumption that steel consumption would simply continue to increase fails to take into account such factors as the downsizing of automobiles and the substitution of other materials (aluminum, plastics, ceramics) for steel. Marshall's estimate, then, that American steel consumption would continue to increase at a rate of 2.25% per year is somewhat questionable. (The American Iron and Steel Institute, in a report written a year later, projected growth in steel consumption at 1.5% annually.)

Second, hidden within Marshall's assumption of overall growth is the assumption that growth would take place at the same rate in the specific product lines on which the Campbell Works was most dependent. Historically, the shutdown portion of the Campbell Works did 76–78% of its business in hot- and cold-rolled sheets, much of this delivered to the automobile industry. But according to John Stone, Sheet and Tube vice-president for operations at the Campbell Works, the auto manufacturers had recently been demanding steel coils that were both wider and longer than the rolling mills at Campbell could produce. (Though more accurate controls for the gauge [thickness] of steel could be fitted to the Campbell rolling mills, little could be done about the problem of width.)

Third, Marshall assumed that the Campbell Works could immediately recapture 100% of its historic market share – certainly an optimistic, if not a heroic, assumption. Based on an average of 1973–6, Marshall estimated the base figure for Campbell Works sales at 1.1 million tons per year. This questionable figure Marshall took as the base for the financial model. To this initial 1.1 million tons, it was necessary to project additional sales of 300,000 tons (a combination of federal procurement and sales growth at 2.25% per year) to reach a minimal level of profitability.

The assumptions involved in forecasting sales of 1.4 million tons per year were nowhere further justified. Yet the NCEA final report summary reaffirmed the 1.4 million ton market share as the base for financial planning. Then it added still further assumptions:

The study team concluded on the basis of these preliminary efforts that with a creative marketing plan, an aggressive sales force, an improved product, plus retention of some "captive" Lykes Corporation markets currently served by the Campbell Works, the retention of a 1.4 million ton share commercial market was a reasonable assumption. (Ibid.: 38)

The only evidence of a "creative marketing plan" was the following sentence:

The unique character of the project, its self-help aspects, and its broad support within the national religious institutions, were deemed marketing advantages by specialists consulted; an approach to General Motors (the largest consumer of steel in the U.S.) by the religious leadership was planned with the aim of securing some sales to this company (and hopefully to others). (Ibid.: 37)

The study team seemed unaware of Campbell's technical problems in supplying the auto industry, identified by John Stone. Likewise, the "aggressive sales force" was simply taken for granted.

All of these assumptions made the 1.4 million ton market share figure more a wish than a serious market analysis. To make matters worse, the "captive market" (supplying steel to the Van Huffel Tube division of Sheet and Tube) had just disappeared in the merger between Lykes and LTV. (The story of this merger will be taken up shortly.)

Financial Analysis

Paul Marshall (1978) was also responsible for the financial analysis report: "The purpose of this analysis is to evaluate the economic feasibility of reopening the idled facilities at Youngstown Sheet and Tube's Campbell Works under various assumptions" (18). Three major assumptions entering into the financial analysis were (a) that the Campbell Works would be able to recapture a market share of 1.4 million tons, (b) that at least 100,000 tons of targeted sales would come from federal procurement, and (c) that the worker ownership arrangement would yield extra productivity of 14% over ten years. The shakiness of the first three assumptions has already been detailed. Further assumptions were that "no major recession would take place and that inflation would equal 6 percent per year for all costs and prices in the future" (ibid.: 2). The assumptions about general economic conditions were, of course, proved wrong by double-digit inflation and 20% interest rates. The point is not that the analyst's crystal ball was out of focus, but that these conditions had to be fulfilled for the model to work.

Marshall's computer model was used to test the profitability of several alternative technological modifications to the Campbell Works. A computer run retaining the open hearth technology showed that the mill would never return a profit under those conditions, reaffirming that the decision to close the mill (without modernization) had been correct. The model revealed that the installation of electric arc furnaces would provide the best return for the least capital investment.

In Marshall's report, the capital investment needed for the electric furnace option was estimated at $345 million. Another $120 million was needed as working capital. There is no evidence that this figure was based on anything more than "back of the envelope" estimates; the NCEA report provides no references to engineering work beyond the preliminary study done by Beetle. In the summary, the capital investment is given as $525 million – a figure that is not reconciled with Marshall's total of $465 million. The extra $60 million may represent an adjustment for inflation and/or a contingency factor (which does seem called for in dealing with relatively soft figures).

The sources for the $525 million in capital investment are specified in the summary report as shown in the following tabulation:

Equity	$ 50 million
Stock sale, Mahoning Valley	10
Religious organizations, foundations	20
Urban Development Action Grant(s)	20
Tax loss sale	50
Ohio state grants and loans	50
Debt (private)	75
U.S. guaranteed loans	300
Total	$525 million

Clearly the new firm would have a much higher debt-to-equity ratio than even the most highly leveraged American steel firms, in which debt had been generally limited to about 40%. There was some difference between Marshall and the summary report on the definition of equity. Marshall assumed that this package represented a 9:1 debt-to-equity ratio. The summary report describes it as 75% debt and 25% equity, a 3:1 ratio.

Although a question mark could be placed behind each of those figures, perhaps the most controversial of all was the $300 million in federal guaranteed loans. The study team examined investment packages in which the federal loan amount was held at $100 million (as specified in the steel loan program). The higher level was chosen because the financial experts "felt that the Federal guarantee had to go above the $100 million level in order to induce sufficient private money into the project" (National Center for Economic alternatives 1978: 32)

Marshall calculated the return on equity on the basis of the assumptions listed above. The baseline sales figure was the 1.1 million tons in 1979, increasing to 1.4 million tons. In addition, Marshall included alternatives to the baseline by adding the effect of (a) additional productivity achieved as a result of worker ownership and (b) government-targeted procurement of 100,000 and 300,000 tons per year. The results are given in Table 7.1. According to Marshall, economic feasibility is defined as producing a return equal to or greater than inflation (taken as 6%). Using 6% return on equity as a criterion of economic feasibility, only the three possibilities within the boxed area on Table 7.1 are economically feasible. In other words, increased levels of worker productivity and at least some government-targeted purchases

Table 7.1. *Annual return on equity: twenty-year planning horizon using electric furnaces*

	No additional productivity (%)	Additional productivity (%)
Base sales forecast	−10.7	−1.5
Base plus 100,000 tpy [a]	−0.6	+5.9
Base plus 300,000 tpy [a]	+9.1	+14.8

[a] Tons per year.
Source: Marshall (1978), 15.

would be required, over and above the assumption of a 100% recapture of the historic market.

In May, Marshall was able to declare the Campbell Works reopening economically feasible – just barely. In June, however, after the news that the Lykes–LTV merger would be finalized, Marshall quickly did a fresh computer run to check the effect of a loss of commercial sales:

In order to determine the sensitivity of financial results to a change in sales forecast, I tried a run with 10 percent reduction in the commercial sales. This sales level yielded very disappointing results even given the most optimistic assumptions about the productivity increases and government sales. Specifically, the result for the electric furnace option with increased productivity and moderate government procurement showed a negative 2.3 percent annual rate of return and had total financing needs of 742 million over the first ten years, during all of which a loss was sustained. (Letter of Paul Marshall to Robert Brandwein, June 23, 1978)

These new numbers were not reported in the NCEA's final report.

Conclusion

Before we turn to the Lykes–LTV merger and what it meant for Youngstown, a brief comment on the NCEA report as a whole is in order. In general, the background work was well done. The socioeconomic study and policy paper and the corporate structure and productivity reports are of high quality. It is at the point where general ideas are turned into the specifics of starting a business that the report runs into trouble.

The summary of the NCEA final report notes at the outset that the merger drastically altered things:

Because of the importance of the merger decision to the prospects for success, and because the merger approval took place at the end of our study, . . . a full understanding of the project requires that the question of feasibility be judged both before and after the Attorney General's act.

This is as close as the study team comes to an admission that the original project as presented in the report might no longer be economically feasible.

Lykes–LTV Merger

For the second time in a decade, the Youngstown steelscape was altered by a corporate merger. The partners this time were New Orleans–based Lykes Corporation (owner of Youngstown Sheet and Tube) and Dallas-based LTV (owner of Jones and Laughlin Steel). The merger between the conglomerates would also effect a merger between the two steel companies.

On the side of Lykes, the merger originated in the "stabilization plan" developed for the ailing corporation by the New York investment banking firm of Lehman Brothers Kuhn Loeb. Lehman Brothers was responsible for the proposal to shut down the unprofitable portions of the Campbell Works and pin the steel company's hopes on the newer facilities at Indiana Harbor. Although Indiana Harbor was, at that time, losing $4–5 million every month, the consultants felt that these problems were largely managerial and could be straightened out without the significant capital investment needed to turn the Campbell Works around.

On the LTV side, the merger originated in the desire to acquire Lykes's earnings, cash flow, and debt-heavy corporate structure. Lehman Brothers was the investment firm working with LTV also, retained by LTV to search for acquisition candidates. Lykes fit none of the original criteria for a merger partner, but LTV executives who had come up from J & L Steel quickly perceived a remarkable "fit" between the two steel companies. LTV could profit in four ways from a merger with Lykes-Sheet and Tube:

1. No longer would J & L have to purchase coal and iron ore on the open market. Lykes could divert its excess of these materials – which it had been trying to sell during 1977 – to J & L's plants.
2. J & L's anticipated excess coke capacity could be diverted to the

Indiana Harbor Works where inadequate coke was tied to losses at that steelmaking facility.

3. Combination of marketing and corporate staffs would reduce overhead.

4. Freight cost would go down because the companies would be supplying each other's facilities. (Greenman, December 10, 1979)[5]

On paper, the merger seemed to be a profitable proposition. The major hurdle was whether the merger would violate the antitrust laws. The combination of Sheet and Tube, then the country's eighth-largest steel firm, and J & L, then the seventh-largest, would catapult the new firm into the position of third-largest steelmaker (behind U.S. Steel and Bethlehem). This fact alone was certain to attract the attention of the Anti-Trust Division of the Justice Department. Furthermore, LTV – because of its acquisition of J & L in 1970 – was still under a consent decree with the Justice Department not to acquire any company worth more than $100 million without the approval of the attorney general.

The merger appeared, on its face, to restrict competition. But the companies decided that if Lykes could be portrayed as a "failing company," the merger might be approved, without running the risk of antitrust litigation. Both companies said they would abandon the merger rather than take it to court. At the Justice Department, the antitrust staff began an investigation of the merger petition, looking particularly into the "failing-company" argument.

Meanwhile, the news of the merger brought fears of still more job cutbacks. The mill to be affected this time was Sheet and Tube's other Youngstown facility, Brier Hill. In a merger, steel from a more modern J & L plant at Aliquippa, Pennsylvania, would be used to supply the still-operating seamless pipe mill at Campbell. A shutdown at Brier Hill would mean the loss of at least one thousand more jobs.

The merger also had drastic consequences for the Ecumenical Coalition's project of reopening the shutdown portions of the Campbell Works. First, it meant that the newly merged company would continue making steel in the Youngstown–western Pennsylvania area. The new company would pick up former Sheet and Tube customers who would have been left without a convenient supplier if Sheet and Tube were simply to close up in Youngstown and concentrate on its Indiana facility. Second, the new company would supply the 185,000–200,000 tons of steel shipped annually to a "captive market" at Sheet and Tube's wholly owned subsidiary, Van Huffel Tube, eliminating the hope that this business might go to the Coalition's project. Third, the merger also raised questions about which facilities in the shutdown Campbell Works might be for sale.

The initial instinct in Youngstown was simply to oppose the merger. The Mahoning Valley Economic Development Committee voted to take this stance until questions about the Campbell Works were settled. However, the failing-company argument began to have an effect on Youngstown-area steelworkers. The rumor was going around the steel mills that, if Sheet and Tube were to go bankrupt, thousands more jobs would be endangered, and the pension plan could be seriously affected. The union, saying it had no way to judge the failing-company argument without access to company documents, decided to support the merger. But in a brief filed with the Department of Justice, Jim Smith argued for the union that the present problems in Youngstown had resulted in large part from a Justice Department decision in 1969 to approve the Lykes–Sheet and Tube merger. The union would not oppose this merger (Lykes–LTV), but asked the attorney general to approve it only under four conditions:

1. The merged corporation should be required to reopen the Campbell Works or cooperate with other reopening efforts.
2. The Justice Department should retain power to investigate the refusal to cooperate with a prospective buyer of the Campbell Works.
3. The merged corporation should commit itself not to close existing production units (e.g., Brier Hill) without permission of the Justice Department.
4. Permission for such closure should demonstrate severe losses and the inability to obtain modernization funds.

The Ecumenical Coalition ultimately, at the request of the union, decided to take a similar stance. But the Coalition requested conditions of its own:

1. A guarantee from Lykes–LTV to purchase a substantial portion of the new firm's output until such time as it could acquire its own marketing capability
2. Raw materials to maintain operations at the acquired facilities
3. Sale of any or all of Lykes's Mahoning Valley facilities at a price compensating for the failure to modernize.

The Coalition suggested that the Justice Department delay approval of the merger until the Coalition and Lykes had concluded an option agreement, or at least insist that Lykes bargain in good faith.

The Anti-Trust staff at the Department of Justice, meanwhile, had decided that the "merger would result in concentration significantly above that allowed by the department's merger guidelines in 12 different steel product areas" (Greenman, December 11, 1979). And after a four-month investigation of Lykes's failing-company argument, the principal investigator, Eric Kaplan, and the Anti-Trust staff decided that Lykes was not about to fail. Thus the staff report recommended that the attorney general disallow the merger. Griffin Bell, however, was not sympathetic with the viewpoint of Kaplan and the investigation team. Bell said that "he didn't believe respectable businessmen would shade facts." He did, however, believe that "the anti-trust staff was composed of 'messianics' whose positions were not to be taken seriously" (Greenman, December 12, 1979). Bell admits that he did not read documentation that cast doubt on Lykes's intention to declare bankruptcy should the merger not be approved. But he did agree with Father William Hogan, the steel expert from Fordham University who was called as expert counsel on the case. Hogan recommended that the merger be approved, since he felt that Lykes was in real danger. One June 21, 1978, the attorney general approved the merger, rejecting the appeals of the United Steelworkers and the Ecumenical Coalition for attached conditions. (The report circulated that Father Hogan had himself written the Justice Department statement. The information was faulty; Eric Kaplan wrote the statement at the direction of Griffin Bell.)

One member of the Anti-Trust staff, angry about the decision, called a staff attorney for the Senate Subcommittee on Anti-Trust and Monopoly, of which Senator Ted Kennedy was chairman. Bishop Malone had testified before the Kennedy subcommittee several months before (on May 21, 1978), so the subcommittee was familiar with the Coalition's project. The question of an investigation by the Federal Trade Commission was developed at the staff level over the summer. Eventually, in November, Kennedy did write a letter to the FTC (published in the *Washington Post*) requesting that the commission look into the Lykes merger. The matter was ultimately dropped, partly because of time pressure (the shareholders' meeting was scheduled for December), partly because the Justice Department staff and the FTC decided that it was politically unwise to infringe on each other's turf, and partly because (in the words of one FTC staffer) "of the absence of any real clear distinction that . . . a clearly erroneous decision had been made" (Greenman, December 13, 1979).

Reappraisal and Review

Shortly after the attorney general's announcement on June 21 of approval of the merger, Paul Marshall went back to his computer. The numbers were not favorable:

As things now stand one of our critical assumptions, namely regaining historic market share – is no longer within the realm of possibility. Thus a major compensating change in some other area would be required to preserve any hope of an economically viable reopened Campbell Works.

I believe this information should be conveyed to the Ecumenical Coalition so that they can reassess their plan of action. (Paul Marshall to Robert Brandwein, June 23, 1978)

The merger clearly presented the Coalition with a new situation, though it is not clear to what extent the bad news from Marshall was immediately circulated among or grasped by the majority of the Steering Committee and campaign staff.

Back in February, along with its account of the opening of the Save Our Valley campaign, the Warren *Tribune Chronicle* had carried the reminder "However, staff director Rev. Edward Stanton has repeatedly expressed the possibility that the buy-out may not become a reality" (February 16, 1978). In June, after the enormous campaign and planning effort that had been mounted, that possibility was difficult to contemplate. Numbers from a computer simply were not as real as the action in the Federal Plaza Office and around the country. Save Our Valley accounts were peaking, with a million dollars coming in from the national church offices. The national campaign office in New York had just been opened, and plans were laid to open state campaign offices around Ohio. While all of this was happening, it was difficulty to absorb the possibility that, in spite of the best campaign efforts, the project might not be economically feasible.

In June, even before the merger announcement, Bishop Burt had thought about the need for the Coalition to obtain an independent assessment of the work done by the consultants. He wrote to Malone on June 16, 1978:

It occurred to me that after the Alperovitz Report is finished, the Coalition might wish to have some independent appraisal made of its competency from an economic and engineering standpoint.

While I remain enormously impressed and pleased with the work of the National Center for Economic Alternatives, I would have to confess that I am not equipped to judge whether its technical judgments are sound.

If an independent appraisal were to be made of the Report, who might do it?

Burt put this question to Theodore R. Colborn, an Episcopal layperson in Cleveland and attorney representing the steel industry. The answer, which he passed on to Malone, was "Clearly the best known and most qualified expert for this purpose is the Rev. William T. Hogan, S.J. of the Department of International Economics of Fordham University." Hogan's name had also been suggested earlier to Ed Stanton by the Youngstown businessman Forrest Beckett "as the one who has the prestige to gain . . . support from financial institutions and from the industry." Because of his acknowledged expertise on the steel industry and his identification with the religious community, Hogan was in an ideal position to serve as an independent analyst of the NCEA's economic work, and Stanton was, of course, on a first-name basis with Hogan through their connection at WREDA. But Hogan's association with Attorney General Griffin Bell in the Lykes–LTV merger case made him anathema to part of the Steering Committee. For political reasons internal to the Coalition, he could not be invited to review the NCEA report.[6]

No independent, outside review of the NCEA work on economic feasibility was ever conducted by the Coalition. And internal review remained only tentative and rather halting. It certainly did not occupy the principal focus of attention.

Local campaign director John Greenman, who had come to the Coalition from a failed business attempt of his own, was particularly alert to the signals that this enterprise, too, might not make it. Greenman got the okay from the Steering Committee at its meeting on July 19 to spend two days talking with the consultants and others about economic feasibility. On July 20, he spoke with Paul Marshall. Greenman reported to the Executive Committee: "In summary, Marshall remains supportive of many economic assumptions, but is uncertain about commercial sales, productivity, and government procurement. He recommends that the

Coalition seek funding for the quiet consideration of other alternatives." Other sources (not named in the memorandum) warned about other weaknesses in the feasibility study: that the assumptions were too optimistic, that the debt-to-equity contribution could not be raised from the sources indicated. Greenman spoke about all this with Alperovitz in Washington. Alperovitz remained confident. He told Greenman that he had largely misunderstood the nature of the Coalition's effort. According to Greenman, "He said the aim has not been to show that the Campbell Works can be reopened on a more-or-less business-like basis, . . . (but) to put steelworkers back to work no matter what is required to do." Alperovitz said that the commercial sales and procurement questions were being rethought. But these were not a problem because, once it became involved, the government would have to keep the plant going. Alperovitz stated further,

While it is the case that we will be asking the government to take the finance risk on the front end and to protect its risk on the back end through procurement, we should not fear the withdrawal of procurement because in doing so the government would expose its financing to too high of a risk.

A week later, in a memo to the Executive Committee written the day before Alperovitz was to brief the Coalition on the final report, Greenman stated:

It is clear that the terms of the project have changed. No longer is the project one of community self-help with a minimum of Federal involvement. You will *not* be asking the Federal government to assume a minor risk in granting loan guarantees to a new company which can stand on its own in the market. You *will* be asking the Federal government to assume a major risk in granting loan guarantees to a new company that *cannot* stand on its own, and you will be asking the Federal government to protect itself against this risk by procuring a substantial part of the new company's output.

Greenman was convinced that, on these terms, the new project had little chance of succeeding. When the opportunity for a more stable long-term job as a newspaper reporter presented itself, he turned in his resignation and went to work for the Warren paper.

At the Executive Committee meeting of August 17, discussion of the imminent review and release of the NCEA report elicited a tentative discussion of where the Coalition stood and what its strategy would be for the future. Staughton Lynd suggested that "we level with our constituency" and admit that the Coalition might fail. Rawlings suggested trying to reverse the attorney general's merger decision. Reverend Laurie suggested keeping abreast of other proposals and devising an alternative plan. It seemed that a set of questions had been opened that had to be addressed at greater depth. A task force was appointed to study and report on a comprehensive strategy.

A sixteen-page memo was actually prepared for discussion later in August. Because of other pressing business and calendar problems, the comprehensive strategy review was never really addressed at this point. It simply was not the time for the group to sit back and reflect on fundamental questions.

Two impressions of what was happening in the Coalition around the first of September present themselves. First, the questions about economic feasibility raised by Marshall and transmitted to the Steering Committee by Greenman simply were not a major issue. There was little sense in the group as a whole that commercial sales constituted a critical question. That was Paul Marshall's problem, which the economist would somehow fix. Nor is there any evidence that Alperovitz or the other study coordinators ever pressed the question of economic feasibility with the Coalition as a matter calling for a critical and deliberate decision. The long memo written to guide the discussion on comprehensive strategy did not ask the question "Go or no go?" Alternatives, rather, were structured around the "yes" or "no" of the federal government.

Second, the campaign by this point had generated a powerful momentum. Meetings of the Steering and Executive Committees had to deal with such questions as arranging a meeting with the U.S. vice-president, whether the Kennedy Senate Subcommittee on Anti-Trust would hold hearings in Youngstown, what to tell the president of J & L Steel about appraisal of the facilities, opening statewide campaign offices, arranging for a national conference, and so on. The campaign at this point was faced with the problem of success. From the movement perspective things were working so well that there was neither the time nor the inclination to readdress fundamental assumptions on which the whole movement was based.

The NCEA final report, then, was accepted without any serious challenge. The sixty-six-page summary (the only portion of the heavy compilation of documents actually circulated) continued to insist that the Youngstown project was viable as a special case:

By June, the National Center had modified some of the assumptions in the preliminary study, but had verified its general conclusion – that the reopening of the Campbell Works was technically and financially feasible, if a decision were made to undertake the effort. It also had reaffirmed its conclusions stated and emphasized in the preliminary report that the goals of the effort were likely to be achieved *"only if the Campbell Works is seen in the eyes of the Federal government, National Churches and other interested outsiders as a unique project of special relevance to other communities: hence worthy of a unique and special effort as a national showcase demonstration site."* (National Center for Economic Alternative 1978: 39; emphasis in original)

The summary did indicate clearly that the merger decision, announced only nine days before the official completion of the study, had drastic consequences for its conclusions. The basic position taken in the summary was that the economic viability of the project was not in question before the merger of Lykes and LTV. Meetings with federal officials through the spring were cited as evidence that "the possibility of reopening the mill began to take on more understanding and credibility in various parts of the Federal government" (ibid.: 53). Any problem concerning the economic viability of the project, it was asserted, was due to the action of the federal government itself:

The key to the situation is obviously the role of the Federal government. The actions of the government in the decision of the Attorney General have caused specific damage to the prospects for reopening the mill; the Ecumenical Coalition, local steelworkers, and political leadership of the Valley feel they have reason to ask that the Federal government undo this new damage. (Ibid.: 62)

The substantiating evidence for economic feasibility remained the original Paul Marshall reports on commercial sales and financial analysis. The summary more or less admitted that these were outdated, but suggested that a way for the government to "undo the damage" would be through higher levels of targeted procurement: "targeting of a relatively minor percentage of overall government-related procurement can offset even the maximum estimate of the market loss caused by the merger" (ibid.: 62).[7]

This, then, was the final report that was submitted to the federal government in September. Despite the report's impressive weight (a full ten pounds in its black loose-leaf binder), the question began to come back: Is this all there is? Jim Smith, at the United Steelworkers headquarters in Pittsburgh, wrote to Stanton inquiring if there had not been some mistake. Was he sure that the financial justification for the project had not somehow been omitted?

Interviews with the Steering Committee indicate that virtually all except Stanton were by and large satisfied with the economic position outlined by Alperovitz. It is possible that few members of the Steering and Executive Committees seriously studied the numbers on which the proposal to the government was based. There was certainly a general awareness that government officials might say no. But when the representatives of the Coalition went to Washington for their appointment at the White House on September 27, 1978, the majority felt assured that they had a good case.

Stanton was clearly uncomfortable. At one point earlier in the campaign, he had, in answer to a reporter's question, estimated the chances at "fifty–fifty." Stanton knew enough about economic development to realize that the NCEA had not provided the kind of information that was necessary to start a business. The odds were dropping. But he also felt that the case for reopening was strong enough in general terms that it might get past the first hurdle in Washington.

The Coalition hoped for a yes, half-feared a no. What they got instead was a maybe. The answer in Washington was delayed for three weeks. Finally, on October 18, 1978, a letter from Jack Watson, domestic affairs adviser to President Carter, informed the Coalition: "I must report that it is not possible for us to reach a decision at this time. The information on which such a decision must be based is not fully available to us." Watson pointed to the problem of the uncertain market for Campbell Works steel:

As you know, the Coalition's own consultant at one time expressed the opinion that, under certain assumptions, the commercial market for the project could be viable. He has recently provided a written opinion that those assumptions may not be reasonable in light of the proposed merger between Lykes and LTV.

Watson also referred to the dependence on federal procurement:

According to the Ecumenical Coalition's consultant's report, the viability of the proposed new corporation would be dependent to a substantial degree on the availability of directed Federal procurement. Several questions have been posed as to the legality and practicality of the government's directing a substantial amount of Federal procurement of products produced by the proposed new corporation. The Office of Legal Counsel in the Department of Justice is reviewing these matters . . .

The letter advised that the community-based steel corporation was still under consideration and that HUD would be supplying an additional grant to the consultant for further research. The grant was subsequently fixed at $93,000.

The uncertain disposition of the Coalition's proposal in Washington, along with the natural rhythm of the campaign, led to something of a new phase in the Coalition. Campaign activity could not be maintained at the same pitch. The Save Our Valley savings account campaign had accomplished all it could. There was a hint of an ending; John Greenman had departed, the Ohio state campaign offices would be closed, Bishop Malone was beginning to talk of the need for a change in leadership. The November election was over, with Congressman Carney defeated. Circumstances were more conducive to the review and reappraisal that never quite took place earlier in August and September.

Stanton, at the request of Malone and Sharick (chair and vice-chair of the Executive Committee), drew up a memo dated November 15 on "future directions for the Coalition." Stanton emphatically noted in both a cover letter and in the text of the memo that "the first and main track strategy of the Coalition is to reopen the closed portion of the Campbell Works as a community–worker owned integrated steel mill enabling the reemployment of as many workers as possible." He indicated that the new marketing study was under way, as was legal work on a structure for the new Coalition. But he went on to note, "Given the possibility of that goal being unattainable, a second track strategy should be developed." Many, including media "off the record," had been asking what the Coalition would do in the event of a negative response from Washington. Some steelworkers were wondering how to plan their future. Signals were coming from the business community (particularly at a luncheon meeting between Pastors Bay and Campbell and members of their congregation on October 31) that it might be ready to back alternative plans it considered more feasible. It was in this context of slightly shifting positions that attention once again was focused on the plan.

The Revised Plan

From January 1978 through the submission of the final report in September, the NCEA had been almost totally responsible for development of the plan. In the late fall, however, the initiative shifted back to Youngstown. Three steel industry professionals – a union executive and two former Sheet and Tube executives – became associated with the project. Their involvement brought to the Coalition's inner circle in Youngstown a new level of technical expertise.

Jim Smith, assistant to President Lloyd McBride at the United Steelworkers Pittsburgh headquarters, was getting more and more interested in the Youngstown project. He had discarded his earlier impression of the Coalition as a front for Staughton Lynd. Relationships between the Youngstown locals and Pittsburgh, strained since the Atlantic City convention, were patched up in early October. The Coalition had no objections to the union's position that (a) worker ownership must not eliminate the union role as bargaining agent and (b) the pension plan must be separate from the employee stock ownership arrangement (the union's principal objections to South Bend Lathe). Smith increasingly placed his own expertise, as well as the weight of the Pittsburgh office, on the side of the Coalition.

At the same time, two retired executives from Sheet and Tube came onto the scene. Frank McGough had been assistant to the district manager at the Sheet and Tube works at Indiana Harbor. After his retirement, McGough worked privately as an engineering consultant, first in Pittsburgh, then eventually moving to Charleston, South Carolina. His son, Maurice, a community organizer near Washington, alerted him to the Coalition effort in Youngstown during the summer of 1978. The elder McGough wrote a letter on July 6 to Reverend Kim Jefferson, at the national office of the United Presbyterian Church in New York, to volunteer his services:

I have extensive personal knowledge of the Youngstown area and its steel plants and operations. This plus my general background and experience, would be an asset to any staff organization you are considering to implement this program.

Retention of my services would be minimal, principally expenses and a nominal fee arrangement. Either a long or short term association would be considered.

Jefferson passed on the letter to John Collins, director of the Interfaith Center on Corporate Responsibility.

It was not until January 3, 1979, that Collins answered the letter, inviting McGough to get in touch with Chuck Rawlings in Youngstown. Rawlings, who received a carbon copy of Collins's letter, contacted McGough immediately to invite him to Youngstown.

In the meantime, Len Balluck, a steelworker from the Campbell open hearth shop and eventually cofounder of Steelworkers United for Employment, decided in the late summer that it was time to take a more active role. He got involved with the Coalition and eventually began meeting with the Steering Committee. Balluck was concerned about the lack of on-the-scene steel expertise in the Coalition project. When the White House ordered the plan sent back to the drawing table in September 1978, Balluck made a call to an old family friend, John Stone. After the merger with J & L, Stone had retired and was living in the nearby suburb of Poland. Balluck telephoned Stone and asked if they could get together for coffee. That meeting led to Stone's association with the Coalition, initially as an informal – and unpaid – consultant.

Together, Stone and McGough brought unique experience and credentials to the Coalition effort. Stone had been plant manager, and McGough his assistant, at the Sheet and Tube mill in Indiana Harbor. Stone had gone on to become vice-president for operations of Youngstown Sheet and Tube, based in Youngstown. Their experience in operations and engineering gave the Coalition its first "hands-on" expertise in running a steel mill. McGough was immediately enlisted for a "walk-through" of the Campbell Works, providing the Coalition with an expert opinion on the quality of the facilities they were attempting to purchase.

In addition, the association of the names of Stone, McGough, and Smith with the Coalition project began to give the effort a new level of credibility in industry circles.

Phased Reopening

Stone and McGough suggested that the Coalition plan was starting at the wrong end of the steelmaking process. The most mod-

Table 7.2. *Phased reopening plan*

Phase	Cost ($000,000)	Jobs
1. Reopening and improvement of rolling mills	165	1,600
2. Installation of electric arc furnaces for steelmaking	220	1,000
3. Building additional finishing capacity	50	500
	435	3,100

Source: Community Steel, Inc.

ern facilities in the shutdown portion of the Campbell Works were the finishing mills. Rebuilt in the 1960s at a cost of some $60 million, the rolling mills needed some modifications, but they were still good equipment. It was the iron and steelmaking facilities – the coke plant, blast furnaces, open hearths – that needed the largest capital improvements. Stone convinced the Coalition that the place to begin with a reopening was not at the primary end. The old open hearths had been sitting for too long unfired; it would be problematic to depend on them at all, even provisionally. And putting in new electric or oxygen furnaces would take years.

Stone suggested a phased reopening, beginning at the "back end," with the finishing mills. The necessary improvements could be made relatively quickly, and the mills could be put into operation in about six weeks' start-up time. The immediate capital needs would be far less. And the one-step-at-a-time procedure would give the new company a chance to get organized internally, as well as reestablish its presence in the steel market. A three-stage reopening plan was devised (Table 7.2).

Phase 1. The facilities required to begin finishing operations were available from the new corporate owner, J & L Steel, at a reasonable price. According to Frank McGough, these facilities were reasonably well moth-balled. Phase 1 would begin with the reopening of the cold-strip mill. This equipment was in workable condition and did not need extensive upgrading. While the cold-strip mill was starting up, automatic gauge control and other equipment would be purchased and installed on the hot-strip mill. At first, hot-rolled bands would have to be purchased as material for the cold strip; when the hot-strip mill went into operation, it would replace outside suppliers as the source of hot bands for the cold-strip mill:

Following this plan, operations will start at Campbell on a gradual basis in order to avoid cost commitments that could not be justified by initial potential sales, and in order to provide time for careful de-mothballing of the facilities and for the orderly completion of the quality control improvements in the hot strip mill. (Community Steel, Inc. 1979)

Phase 2. Phase 1 of the plan depended on a steady supply of hot-rolled steel bands and then steel slabs. In order to secure a dependable supply of unfinished steel at a reasonable price, the new company would, in phase 2, redevelop its own steelmaking capacity. In this phase, the open hearth furnaces would be dismantled and replaced with new electric arc furnaces. This meant that the new company would depend on scrap for its steelmaking capacity, a decision in part influenced by the fact that supplies of iron ore and coal owned by Sheet and Tube had now become the property of J & L and would be used to supply J & L facilities. A further improvement in this phase would involve installation of a continuous caster.

Phase 3. Depending on the nature of available markets and private sector financing, facilities for galvanizing and making welded steel tubing would be installed.

Linkage. The major problem with the phased reopening concerned the availability of steel slabs, precisely at the same time the new company would be restarting the finishing mills. On this point, the experts disagreed. William Hogan told Stanton that he felt that it would be risky to depend on an outside source of slabs. Jim Smith believed that such arrangements could be made – though perhaps with a foreign steelmaker.

One proposed solution involved linking Brier Hill, which was about to be shut down, into the Campbell Works project. The idea was that Brier Hill could be used for a time to manufacture slabs for Campbell. The period of use would be two years, since the Brier Hill blast furnace was nearing the end of its campaign life. And there was also some question whether the facilities at Brier Hill could produce slabs of the proper size.

The Coalition proposal saw Phase 1 and Phase 2 as necessarily part of an integral package. The Urban Development Action Grant (UDAG) proposal stated, "The Coalition at this point believes that a plan of operations limited to the Phase 1 reopening of the rolling mills without a following Phase 2 would not be a responsible plan." On this point, too, Jim Smith was more optimistic. He thought that "each phase of the plan must be viable for the total plan to be viable." Phase 1 should pay for itself. If that were the case, it could be continued indefinitely. He felt, too, that the operation should remain at Phase 1 until a more thorough examination could be made of the choice between electric or oxygen furnaces for the steelmaking capacity in Phase 2.

Labor and Productivity

One problem with the earlier plan had been the need to factor into the financial model a 14% productivity increase over ten years, based on the estimated productivity associated with worker participation and ownership incentives. Although some productivity increase certainly appeared reasonable, how this was to be accomplished was not specified.

The revised proposal abandoned the concept of an accelerated rate of productivity increase, substituting a 20% reduction in historical labor cost projected for the first quarter of 1979. (This eliminated Rosenbloom's objection about workers working themselves out of a job.) The 20% reduction in labor costs could be achieved largely because J & L Steel had assumed the pension and seniority liabilities from Sheet and Tube, meaning that the new operator at the Campbell Works would be free to hire experienced workers without liability for their past service. This meant that the new company would be paying pension fund costs at 42 cents per hour, instead of the industry average of $1.15. The cost for vacation benefits would be zero in the first year, 22 cents in the second and third years, and rising to an average of 32.5 cents for the first ten years. These two items alone would account for an 8.5% reduction in labor costs. Impacts on other benefits could raise this figure to 10%.

At the same time, Smith estimated from his experience in labor negotiations that the Campbell Works was probably 5–10% overmanned. A one-time realignment of the manning tables at the outset of the new enterprise could effect as much as a 10% labor cost saving.

The union was not willing to consider any departure from the wage scale in the national contract. Such labor cost cutting would, the union feared, undermine the whole wage structure in steel. But a 20% labor cost saving could be achieved without cutting wages. And it would be met by a joint labor–management agreement at the outset rather than by a hypothetical gradual increase in productivity based on "ever higher levels of motivation through the mystique of worker ownership" (James Smith 1979, 20). Any further productivity increase associated with worker incentives would be in addition to the first-time 20% gain.

One particularly promising aspect of agreements between the Coalition and the union was a potential breakthrough in the prevailing pattern of labor relations in the steel industry – the adversary system. Smith argued that "the adversary structure of labor relations has evolved in steel, and U.S. industry generally, because it is an appropriate response to the underlying ethics and economics of profit-maximizing firms" (ibid.: 23). Such a system, he admitted, would not be suitable for a community redevelopment enterprise such as the Coalition's project. Smith committed the union to developing a new structure of labor relations tailored to the new situation at Campbell Works:

If the new company's workers select our union as their collective bargaining representative, and if they are willing to do so, the United Steelworkers would be willing to help design and implement a non-adversary labor relations system and structure, provided that the industry-wide wage levels and benefit standards are adhered to. (Ibid.: 24)

Smith concluded, "If such a system is established and operated, Campbell Works will have a competitive advantage in the steel industry" (ibid.: 27).

Personnel Recruitment

In addition to his work on the operational plans, Frank McGough began quietly making contacts among steelmen to put together a management team. One scenario had Stone and

McGough becoming chief executive and chief operating officers for the new company. When this possibility began to circulate, McGough received both printed resumes from steel executives and hand-lettered job reviews from experienced steelworkers. Some were in early retirement in Youngstown; others had gone to Florida or Houston. Within weeks, McGough had put together a list of general supervisors and turn foremen.

Market and Financial Analysis Reconsidered

While Stanton and the pro bono consultants in Youngstown were working out a new production plan and laying the foundation for a labor agreement, Paul Marshall in Boston was taking a new look at the steel market. The new marketing study eliminated any dependence on federally targeted procurement. And, of course, it had to take into consideration the loss of the "captive market."

Marshall focused on the market area within 200 miles of the Campbell Works. He estimated the market for hot- and cold-rolled sheet steel at between 16 million and 21 million tons for 1979. If the Campbell Works were to achieve its average historic market share, it could count on 0.7–1.0 million tons. In terms of 1974 market share (the Campbell Works' last good year), the range could be 0.8–1.2 million tons.

Marshall used a telephone survey to investigate the interest of potential steel purchasers other than the auto industry in buying from the Campbell Works. He found that "nearly two thirds of mill direct buyers indicated that, given comparable quality, price, and service, Campbell could become as large a supplier to them as their present largest supplier" (Marshall and Breitenberg 1978: 11). In addition, a steelbroker in New England estimated potential Campbell Works sales in that area as 100,000 tons. Marshall, then, estimated 0.8 million tons as a reliable market.

Using a sales figure of 0.8 million tons, Marshall estimated that annual revenues would be $312 million, yielding $82.5 million income before capital charges. Net annual income after taxes for the twenty-year horizon would be in the range $15–20 million. The company would not make a great deal of money. And it would have little cushion to pad any cyclical downturns. The analysis was not rosy but, unlike the earlier figures submitted, offered some realistic basis for thinking the company might make it.

Financing the three-phase program would require an investment of $335 million. As part of the UDAG proposal the Wall Street investment firm of Warburg Paribas Becker presented the opinion that "there is a strong likelihood that a feasible financing plan for the project can be developed and executed in full." In the proposal requesting a UDAG for $17 million to purchase the Campbell Works property and hire a management team, the sources of investment were projected as shown in the following tabulation:

Urban Development Action Grant	$ 17 million
Common stock purchases – ESOP funded by EDA grant	10
State of Ohio	10
Common stock purchases	3
Working capital financing secured by accounts receivable and inventory	50
Long-term debt, 90% financed by U.S. government through EDA	245
Total	$335 million

The acceptability of this financing package depended a great deal on the definition of "equity." The Coalition wanted to include the UDAG, EDA, and Ohio state grants as equity, totaling $40 million. Only if this definition were accepted would the new firm have as much as a 9:1 debt-to-equity ratio. The other problem was the $245 million needed in federal loan guarantees through the EDA's steel loan program. (This is a topic in itself, which will be treated in the following chapter.)

The financial analysis was not optimistic. But it was far more realistic than the plan presented in September. The proposal – and the company – were a long shot. But there was at least some basis for thinking, that a reopened Campbell Works might make it.

CHAPTER VIII

Negotiations

Moving the reopening plan from idea to reality called for the Coalition to conduct a complex series of negotiations in both the private sector and the public sector. On occasion, the site for these negotiations might be Lykes offices in Tampa or the National Council of Churches office in New York. But the two principal places of action were Youngstown and Washington.

In Youngstown, not only did the Coalition have to develop public support through campaigns such as the Save Our Valley savings accounts. It was also necessary to piece together the support of a network of government agencies at the local level. This sometimes involved reconciling some intense territorial and political rivalries. In addition, the Coalition had to do some hard bargaining, first with Lykes and then with Jones and Laughlin over a purchase agreement for the shutdown portion of the Campbell Works. On the whole, negotiations at the Youngstown end emerged successfully. It was in Washington that negotiations failed.

Negotiating with the Steel Companies

In order to reopen the Campbell Works under a new ownership plan, one of the first items to be negotiated was the purchase of the mill property. An early meeting with local Sheet and Tube executives in January 1978 was held to explore the possible terms and conditions of a sale. According to Stanton, it was apparent at this point that the steel company was not taking the Coalition inquiry very seriously. When pressed for a ball-park purchase price for the shutdown facilities, the figure of $67 million was named, an amount the Coalition considered out of the question. According to Stanton, it was also clear that the question of the proposed merger between Lykes and LTV was a complicating factor.

On February 3, 1978, Stanton participated in a closed-door meeting in Youngstown at Mayor Richley's office with Paul Thayer, chairman of LTV; Thayer was informing the mayor of the potential effects of the merger on steel employment in Youngstown. The following week, Stanton met with Lykes officials in Tampa, Florida, who had just heard the newspaper report of the Youngstown meeting. Stanton said the meeting was useful as an ice breaker, but it was clear that Lykes executives were no longer in charge and that serious negotiations would have to be undertaken with LTV.

The initial position taken by the Coalition was to oppose the merger between Lykes and LTV. Robert Embry at HUD even wrote to the Justice Department asking that any approval of the merger be delayed until the matter of selling the Campbell Works could be negotiated. Coalition opposition to the merger, then, became something of a bargaining chip in forcing the corporate owner back to the negotiating table.

On April 14, 1978, a Coalition negotiating team headed by Bishop Burt and Stanton met with Paul Thayer and other LTV officials at the offices of the U.S. Catholic Conference in Washington. At this meeting, the Coalition presented a list of "principles" including an option for the purchase of Campbell Works facilities, an agreement to supply the reopened facilities with raw materials, and an agreement to buy from the reopened company a "substantial portion" of the steel it would make (to replace the former "captive market"). LTV said it was "not prepared to sign anything today," but indicated a desire to "begin immediately to bargain in good faith" and promised to reply to Coalition requests the following week at a meeting in Youngstown.

On April 21, the Coalition met with Thomas Graham, president of J & L Steel. The LTV representatives offered a "non-exclusive option" on the rolling mills but would not offer to sell the blast furnaces (which would leave the reopened rolling mills without a dependable supply of hot metal). They also offered to supply raw materials for three years. LTV refused to provide a market for steel from the Campbell rolling mills, saying that it would be of inferior quality and would likely cause a loss of jobs in J & L's own plants. A clear purpose of the LTV team was, at this point, to be on the record as negotiating in good faith. At the conclusion of the negotiating session, Graham asked if the Coalition would now drop its opposition to the merger.

No further negotiations were undertaken while the merger was in process. After Attorney General Bell's approval of the merger on June 21, another meeting was held in July, which again found the two parties far apart. Stanton's view was that LTV at this point was still refusing to negotiate.

In the fall, the organizational structure of the newly merged steel company was worked out. The Sheet and Tube name would be dropped, and the remaining facilities would be integrated into Jones and Laughlin. R. Gordon Allen was named president of J & L Steel's Western Division and given authority to negotiate with the Coalition. Stanton and Gordon Allen met privately over dinner one evening in a Youngstown restaurant. Stanton acquainted Allen with the local public relations problem that J & L was inheriting together with the Campbell Works. Allen realized that the Coalition was serious about buying the facilities and promised to move the negotiations ahead.

About this time, Senator Howard Metzenbaum, ranking member (and soon to be chair) of the Senate Anti-Trust Subcommittee, felt that LTV was still dragging its feet in the negotiations with the Coalition. Metzenbaum on November 8 wrote to Attorney General Bell, asking him to withdraw conditionally the government's approval of the Lykes–LTV merger, "subject to meaningful and fulfilled negotiations with the Ecumenical Coalition of the Mahoning Valley" (Youngstown *Vindicator*, November 8, 1978). Although Bishop Malone had spoken with Metzenbaum in August about the lack of progress in the negotiations, the senator was at this point acting on his own initiative. In fact, negotiations had already moved forward at a meeting during the first week of November, when J & L promised to provide the Coalition with a purchase price for the facilities within thirty days. On November 17, Allen wrote to Stanton offering a list of currently idled facilities at Campbell and Brier Hill for $17 million, plus a second list of facilities to be shut down in the future for another $7 million. Allen also offered to maintain the facilities until June 1979, providing the Coalition an option until that time. With this offer, negotiations were on track.

In order to respond to J & L's offer, the Coalition needed access to information about the book value of the facilities from J & L company files. Allen offered to supply this to Stanton personally on a confidential basis, with the assurance that the information would go no farther. However, Coalition lawyers felt that this arrangement was unacceptable and filed a formal request for the information, which delayed the process for several months.

By the time the Coalition was ready to submit the UDAG application at the end of January, there was good assurance that an acceptable purchase price could be negotiated. The amount requested in the grant, $17 million, would have been sufficient to purchase the facilities with enough left over to hire a management team on a three-year contract and begin start-up work.

Negotiating with Local and State Governments

The announcement of Black Monday had been widely perceived as a disaster. But as people in the area began looking around six months to a year later, the disaster seemed not really to have happened – at least not on the scale that had been feared. Or perhaps not yet.

Shortly after he took office in January 1978, Mayor Richley warned that Youngstown was the focal point of the national steel crisis, saying, "We will be hit harder than any other city in the nation" (Youngstown *Vindicator*, February 6, 1978). It was easy to find hard-luck stories; just about everybody had a family member or knew someone who had been laid off and was facing a hard time. But paradoxically the collective unemployment picture for the area actually began to improve. One month after the Sheet and Tube shutdown, GM recalled a work shift of 1,600 and hired 1,100 new workers. The expected bulge in unemployment did not show up in the figures. Total nonagricultural employment in the two-county Youngstown–Warren metropolitan area actually increased steadily from January 1978 (202,700 employed) through December 1978 (216,000 employed). The unemployment rate went to 9.0% in March, eventually dropping off to 5.9% in October and November 1978. At no time in the year after the shutdown did metropolitan-area unemployment reach the levels experienced in 1975 (13.5% in August, with an average for the year of 11.4%). The extensive Trade Readjustment Act benefits evidently contributed to sustaining the area's economy. Thomas Petzinger (1978), a reporter who went from the Youngstown *Vindicator* to the *Wall Street Journal*, reported that "A Year After Closing of Youngstown Steel Plant, Economy, Employment Are Surprisingly Bright". The Youngstown *Vindicator* reported: "Bank loans are up 11% over a year ago and deposits have increased by 8% in the period. Construction spending is ahead by 24% and, perhaps most encouraging of all, retail sales, as measured by local sales-tax receipts, are up by 5% over a year ago (October 29, 1978).

Anthony Stocks, an economist at Youngstown State University, found both good news and bad news in the economic picture. The good news was that expansion in transportation equipment (GM) occurred just as steel employment declined. Employment in fabricated metals also rose, producing a new increase in manufacturing jobs relative to the same months in the previous year. "As a result, employment in every month since the Campbell Works demise has been higher than its counterpart for the preceding year" (Stocks 1979: 24). The bad news was that, compared with trends for the state of Ohio, "1978 yields an estimated loss of 6,850 nonagricultural jobs in the two county SMSA" (ibid.: 23). The economist concluded that "it seems likely that the negative elements will outweigh the favorable and produce a modest decline in Youngstown–Warren area employment of perhaps one to two percent by the end of 1979" (ibid.: 26).

In negotiating support from local politicians and public agencies, the Coalition had to deal with the problem of relative success in the local economy. The Campbell Works reopening had been launched as a "quick fix" strategy. But in 1978, the problems the Campbell reopening was designed to remedy seemed elusive and chimerical. The problems that did exist were narrowly focused: in Campbell and Struthers rather than in the metropolitan area as a whole; in a particular segment of unemployed steelworkers rather than in the entire labor force.

A year after the shutdown was first announced, religious and political leaders offered divergent interpretations of what was happening in the local economy. Politicians, notably Mayor Richley, were impressed by the business upturn, based on the strong showing of such companies as Sharon Steel and Commercial Shearing. At Thanksgiving time, the mayor was sounding positively upbeat: "We in the Mahoning Valley have a lot for which we can be thankful. In spite of all those gloomsayers, including the national media, who a year ago foresaw the Valley on the brink of disaster, all our economic indicators look good. And even more is in sight" (Youngstown *Vindicator*, November 23, 1978). By the first of the year, he was insisting that the Valley had weathered its crisis:

"I am weary of the constant gloom and doom that the national news media has cast over the valley since the closing of the Youngstown Sheet and Tube Co. plant," he said, adding that the media may be using the story to "tug at the heartstrings of the people."

"The valley remains very strong and very much alive despite the closing." (Youngstown *Vindicator*, January 27, 1979)

The mayor was concerned that pessimistic views of the area disseminated nationally would hurt efforts to attract new business. The Mahoning Valley Economic Development Commission (of which he was chairman of the board) had finally hired a director and was planning more intense efforts to bring new business into the area. Richley felt that continual talk of the Valley's problems and bleak future would discourage new investment.

On the other side, religious leaders conceded that the first year after the shutdown had not been as bad as they feared. But they pointed out that many unemployed steelworkers were still drawing benefits, which would soon run out. The Brier Hill mill was almost certain to shut down, laying off another 1,100 workers. And the future of the two U.S. Steel plants was in doubt, affecting the future of another 3,600 steelworkers. (In the following year, shutdown dates were announced for Brier Hill and for the two U.S. Steel mills.) The Coalition kept pointing out that it would take a great many fifteen- and fifty-job factories to replace the economic contribution of the steel mills. Religious leaders argued that a Campbell reopening was important for retaining the steel industry in the valley and for maintaining a healthy economy generally.

By mid-October 1978 (a year after the shutdown), local politicians were backing off from support of the mill reopening. At that time, the White House informed Coalition leaders that they would be receiving only $93,000 for another study instead of $300 million in loan guarantees. The Coalition felt that government leaders were temporizing, refusing to look at the Valley's long-term future, and hoping that if they could delay any decision long enough, the "preachers" would lose interest and forget the whole thing.

In this context, the Coalition decided to use the coming November elections to force politicians to take a public stand on the mill-reopening plan. On October 19, 1978, they sent telegrams to ten political candidates and officeholders: the candidates for governor, for Congress, the two senators, and the mayors of Campbell, Struthers, and Lowellville, asking them to make known their position "for the record." At this point, one poll had found that the Ecumenical Coalition was more popular with Mahoning Valley voters than any single candidate. The politicians could hardly refuse. Back came the telegrams unanimously supporting the Coalition effort.

The campaign telegrams were a confrontation tactic designed to force a showdown, not necessarily to win friends. (One politician described the effect of the telegram as getting hit in the face with an apple pie wrapped in the American flag.) It was an attention getter that had to be followed up with a more conciliatory style of negotiation. The Coalition project had to move through several legal and political steps at the local level before it could ever get to Washington.

CASTLO

The mayors of Campbell, Struthers, and Lowellville were not willing to cede the role of steel crisis leadership to the mayor of Youngstown. While Richley was boasting of Youngstown's ability to survive, the CASTLO communities were hurting. Expenses were far outstripping revenues in their city budgets, and unemployment was running as high as 30%. The CASTLO mayors had finally secured seats on the Mahoning Valley Economic Development Committee. But they had no great confidence that this Youngstown-dominated agency would look out for the interests of the river suburbs. Consequently they were quite willing to accept the assistance of Republican Governor Rhodes in setting up an independent development group headed by George Wilson, the governor's former director of economic development. A partisan political incident in the fall of 1978 revived the Youngstown–CASTLO rivalry – with consequences for the Coalition's Campbell Works project. In September, plans were being made for the Coalition, accompanied by political leaders for the Valley, to meet with administration officials at the White House to make a presentation concerning the NCEA final report and the Coalition's request for steel loan guarantees. The meeting in Washington was arranged on short notice, unfortunately at a time when United Air Lines – the only commercial carrier out of Youngstown – was on strike. Since there was no time to drive everyone to Washington, Governor Rhodes offered the state plane to fly all of the Youngstown representatives (including CASTLO, MVEDC, and the Coalition) from Ohio to the meeting at the White House. Word was received from the White House, however, that George Wilson, a Republican representing Governor Rhodes, was not welcome at the meeting. As a result of this slight, Rhodes canceled the use of the state plane for the trip. And the CASTLO mayors boycotted the White House meeting.[1]

When presidential assistant Jack Watson announced that the Coalition's reopening proposal would continue to be studied and that $100 million in steel loan guarantees was being reserved for a Mahoning Valley project, CASTLO sent a telegram to the White House asking for a delay in the commitment of the funds. CASTLO director George Wilson feared that the Coalition might be awarded the loan money, eliminating the possibility of a CASTLO project eventually qualifying for the same program. CASTLO requested a meeting of its own with the White House, which was held on October 14, 1978.

The position taken by CASTLO made things more difficult for the Coalition. Money to buy the Campbell site would have to come from an Urban Development Action Grant. Under the application rules, only the city of Youngstown was eligible to apply for the grant (which was restricted to cities with a population of more than 50,000). The mill property, however, was in Campbell and Struthers, not in Youngstown. It would be necessary for the CASTLO mayors to authorize the mayor of Youngstown to make the application on their behalf. Without such authorization, the Coalition project would fall through.

Stanton ultimately was able to convince the CASTLO mayors that it would not be a good idea to block the Campbell Works project, as long as it had any chance of success. The mayors did provide the necessary authorization to Mayor Richley of Youngstown. At the same time, the Coalition was able to accede to a request from CASTLO. That agency was interested in developing the Struthers portion of the Sheet and Tube property on which the Coalition held an option with J & L. Malone and Stanton readily agreed to give up the Coalition option on this property, if CASTLO could do anything with it. Under CASTLO sponsorship, a long-unused portion of the Struthers mill for manufacturing railroad spikes was eventually modernized and brought back into production by private investors. After a short period of operation, it ran into financial difficulties and was again shut down.

Mahoning Valley Economic Development Commission

MVEDC, founded by Congressman Carney, had been a competitor with the Coalition for control of the HUD research grant. When the Coalition was designated lead agent for the Campbell Works reopening, Stanton made the deal with MVEDC that that agency would be responsible for implementing the plan, if it were approved by the federal government. Stanton was named a member of the Commission, among other reasons to provide liaison between MVEDC and the Coalition.

The initial economic development thrust of MVEDC was the diversification strategy favored by the Chamber of Commerce and Laird Eckmann. When MVEDC received the research report that it had commissioned from Battelle Institute in Columbus, the rather exclusive concern for bringing in new industry was somewhat modified. Charles Minshall, author of the study, noted that the Valley needed to diversify its economy into such growth industries as furniture, printing, and chemicals and into financial and other services. But he also insisted that MVEDC strategy should "do everything possible to retain as much of the steel industry as possible – it is still the area's primary resource" (Minshall and Moody 1978: 25). Retention of the steel industry began to acquire more attention from MVEDC.

MVEDC developed a steel proposal of its own. Mayor Richley proposed the idea of using some of the vacant Sheet and Tube facilities – the headquarters office building, an adjacent research building, and a pilot blast furnace in the Campbell Works – as the site for a national steel research center. Spending for research and development in the steel industry had been among the lowest for all major U.S. industries, declining from $16,250,000 in 1968–71 to $9,250,000 in 1972–5. Only 3% of that research was federally funded, compared with a national average of 23.8% for all industries, excluding aircraft and missiles. Annual research and development spending in steel as a percentage of sales ranged between 0.4 and 0.8%, compared with an all-industry range of 3.0 to 4.6% (MVEDC 1978: 2). A national research center, it was argued, would be a major stimulus to revitalizing the nation's steel industry. Youngstown offered advantages as the site for such a center: 90% of steel-supportive industries (e.g., blast furnace manufacturers) were within a seventy-mile radius of Youngstown. The recently vacated facilities of Sheet and Tube were immediately available. A national research center would not be an employer on the scale of the Campbell Works, but it would be able to employ some personnel from the layoffs.

Richley's proposal was widely interpreted as an alternative to the reopening of the Campbell Works for steel production. The text of the proposal itself indicates that Richley had little hope for the future of steel in the Mahoning Valley. He termed waiting for the mills to reopen as "sadly and unfortunately, a false and empty hope."

There will be no massive investment in the Mahoning Valley's steel firms because of the on-line obsolescence and due to the lack of water transportation. The Valley is landlocked with Lake Erie to the north and the Ohio River to the South. There is no canal to provide inexpensive water transportation for the industry.

The federal government will not infuse massive amounts of federal funds to the Valley because of industrial errors of the past. However, the viable alternative is the realistic move to create a research and development center where new technology can be molded and tried. (MVEDC 1978)

The steel research center was backed by MVEDC and the Center for Urban Studies at Youngstown State University as the "realistic" alternative to reopening the Campbell Works.

Stanton worked to reconcile the two projects, pointing out that a steel research center would have a different purpose and serve a different constituency, that is, the national steel industry as a whole. Though it might be worthwhile on its own merits, the research center would employ few of the workers laid off by the shutdown. In contrast, the Coalition's project had a specifically local focus – quickly restoring jobs for unemployed steelworkers in Youngstown. Furthermore, Stanton pointed out that the two projects could easily share the Sheet and Tube facilities. A blast furnace within the Campbell Works could be made available to the research center for experimental purposes.

Although MVEDC was never exactly enthusiastic about the Coalition's project, Stanton was influential in maintaining its support, as long as there was a chance the Campbell Works project might fly. In the final draft of the structure for the new community–worker-owned corporation, MVEDC was identified as the "community corporation" that would designate three members of the board of directors.

In the long run, the federal government's evaluation of the research center proposal ultimately found it no more "realistic" than reopening the Campbell Works. Lehigh University studied the proposal and found it "unworkable and infeasible." The report determined that the research center was not needed and not wanted by the steel industry and that the facilities available in Youngstown were not suited to such a purpose (Kraft and Beidleman 1979).

Youngstown City Council

With CASTLO and MVEDC in line, still another problem to be negotiated was the Youngstown City Council. The question here concerned the eligibility of the city of Youngstown to submit a UDAG proposal to HUD. One of the criteria for UDAG eligibility was achieving a certain performance level in the supply of low-income housing to municipal residents. Although low-income housing as such was not materially related to the question of the Campbell Works, the failure of the city of Youngstown to meet HUD criteria would mean that the Coalition would have no way to apply for the federal grant.

A developer was proposing to build a number of housing units in the Schenley Park area on Youngstown's west side, which would have brought the city into compliance with HUD requirements. The developer's proposal called for the city to make available property designated for a street. Although the street had not actually been put in, approval of the City Council was necessary to place the property at the disposal of the developer. This the City Council was reluctant to do, since the development proposed to integrate a previously all-white residential area.

Mayor Richley was able to finesse this question in the City

Council long enough for the Coalition's proposal to be submitted. (Later, after a referendum on the issue, the city of Youngstown did lose its eligibility for HUD grants, imperiling the chance to acquire an aircraft plant promising to bring 1,400 new jobs to the area.)

Eastgate Development and Transportation Agency

EDATA, as the Circular A-95 clearinghouse for federal grant proposals, also had to pass on the Coalition proposal. In this instance, Rawlings represented the Coalition rather than Stanton. There were still problems outstanding between EDATA and WREDA (a question of getting some office furniture back from WREDA was on the same agenda as the Coalition's proposal), and Stanton was still WREDA treasurer.

EDATA was forced to consider the measure in some haste, and even without the market study, which Marshall was still completing. The lack of the marketing report and assessment of environmental impact raised some questions about conditional approval. But the proposal was ultimately endorsed by a nearly unanimous vote. A letter from Mayor Richley was helpful in gaining a speedy disposition at EDATA.

State of Ohio

Early in the development of the reopening plan, the Coalition contacted Governor Rhodes to request financial support in the form of grants and loans from the state. The governor was not able to give any funds in response to the first request because the budget for such purposes had already been allocated. The governor did call Stanton just before the November elections and pledged that he would provide $10 million in the next fiscal year.

Moving the proposal for a $10 million grant through the state capital became a smoothly managed bipartisan effort. Chair of the Ohio Senate Finance Committee was Harry Meshel, of Youngstown. Meshel held hearings at which Malone, Burt, and other representatives of the Coalition testified, as did Jim Smith from the steelworkers union. The Finance Committee unanimously approved the bill to provide a $10 million grant, on condition that the Coalition receive the grants and loan guarantees it was requesting from the federal government. The Senate bill had not yet been brought up for a vote in the General Assembly when a decision was announced in Washington.

Competition and Cooperation

Outsiders reporting on Youngstown picked up the element of competition among agencies in the Youngstown area (see, e.g., Peterson 1978). Disagreement and a certain amount of rivalry were clearly present. But the last word from the Valley was not internecine warfare. By the time the Coalition's UDAG proposal finally went to Washington at the end of January 1979, just about everyone knew that it was a "long shot" – as Mayor Richley said on a television interview days later. But it was a chance to help the Valley. And after some complex negotiating, all of the required signatures were in place.

Negotiating with the Federal Government

After the preparatory negotiations between the Coalition and federal officials in late 1977, the dynamic of the federal government–Coalition interaction can be described as a process of building up steam on the local front and taking the case to Washington. The Youngstown-to-Washington pattern was repeated three times: first, when the Coalition asked for conditions on the Lykes–LTV merger in the spring of 1978; second, when it made the preliminary request for $300 million in loan guarantees in September 1978; and finally, when it submitted the UDAG proposal and argued the case in Washington in March 1979. Each time the answer was negative. What happened in Washington?

Policy and Program

Youngstown was, if not exactly a pawn, then certainly no more than a rook in a Washington bureaucratic chess game. That was the opinion of Anne Hallmark, the staff associate at the Economic Development Administration who was in charge of the Coalition file. (Hallmark was assistant to the deputy director of EDA, Harold Williams.)

Youngstown hit the national spotlight as the Carter administration was in the process of formulating an urban policy. An "urban policy research group" was set up with Patricia Harris, secretary of HUD, as chair. Officials at HUD, particularly Robert Embry, saw the general policy review as an opportunity for moving HUD from its rather exclusive concern with housing and increasing the department's involvement in urban economic development. The new Urban Development Action Grant program, authorized in 1977, gave the department a useful policy instrument for this purpose. The flexibility of the UDAG program allowed for a wide latitude in grant projects, including business and economic development aimed at urban revitalization.

Urban economic development had traditionally been the preserve of the EDA in the Department of Commerce. An agency founded in 1965 out of the old Area Redevelopment Agency, EDA had overcome its shaky program start in Oakland. Within the Carter administration, the EDA under Robert Hall, director, and particularly Harold Williams, his deputy director, had the reputation of running a technically proficient, business-like shop. When the proposal for a guaranteed loan program to aid the steel industry was developed as a recommendation of Anthony Solomon at the Treasury Department, Solomon recommended that administration of the program be lodged at EDA. It was the first time that the agency had been given authority over a development program oriented toward a specific industrial sector. In managing this new venture, EDA was moving with some caution.

The steel loan guarantee program was financed by a fund in the Treasury Department. Since 1965, repayments of EDA loans had gone into a fund at the U.S. Treasury that remained frozen until 1978. At the end of fiscal year 1978 (September 30, 1978), there was approximately $225 million in this fund. One hundred million dollars of it were set aside for the steel loan program. This money was not loaned directly, but used as a guarantee to leverage 90% guaranteed loans on the commercial money market. In this fashion, $100 million could be used to guarantee $500 million of 90% guaranteed loans. (Approximately $125 million, with the power to generate another $687.5 million in guaranteed loans, was left untouched in the Treasury.) The EDA decided in its request for authorization from congressional appropriations committees that it would limit the amount of any single loan guarantee to $100 million. This procedural rule had the political advantage of spreading the money around, as well as the investment advantage of limiting the risk associated with any single venture.

In the fall of 1977, Alperovitz approached both HUD and

EDA with the idea of developing an operational plan for Youngstown. Alperovitz was known as a respected liberal economist with a solid background in congressional staff work and as director of the well-funded NCEA think tank; he was being touted as a candidate for the president's Council on Economic Advisors. Alperovitz had good connections at HUD, and his ideas about revitalizing old industrial cities through community ownership of abandoned industrial plants fit into the department's new thrust. When Alperovitz spoke to Harold Williams at EDA, however, caution lights went on. (When Alperovitz first approached EDA, Williams was not aware of any connection with a religious coalition in Youngstown.) Anne Hallmark described her dignified boss as "freaked" by the Alperovitz proposal. The perception at EDA was that the agency had had a good, consistent record for some years of developing and funding programs to deal with the future of steel in Youngstown (most recently with WREDA's unit train and joint blast furnace proposals). EDA felt if had long been aware of Youngstown's problems with the steel industry and was doing something about those problems. The EDA was leery of any move by HUD that would have implications for the EDA-administered steel loan program.

If Alperovitz were funded by HUD, it would mean committing the federal government to a direction that would ultimately involve EDA funds. In an effort to cut off any such end run by HUD, EDA proposed that the two offices discuss the matter.

At Williams's initiative, a large meeting was held in the secretary of commerce's conference room on December 20, 1977. Attending the meeting were officials from EDA and HUD, Senator Metzenbaum and Congressman Carney, the NCEA consultants, the Ecumenical Coalition, and other representatives from Youngstown. Williams's intention was to develop a joint EDA–HUD strategy. EDA offered to chair an interagency task force on the matter.

At the first meeting of the interagency task force it was announced that HUD had funded the Alperovitz proposal. After that, the task force initiative lapsed.

HUD was excited about the prospect of doing something big in Youngstown. The secretary of HUD, Patricia Harris, in announcing the contract with Alperovitz, stressed the urban redevelopment aspect of the project: "This commendable community support is precisely the sort of local effort we are looking for in

developing new Federal strategies to support areas like Youngstown that are determined to help themselves when faced with
devastating plant closings" (*HUD News*, December 30, 1977).
Undersecretary Jay Janis said on ABC–TV:

Simply put, the thing we'd like to accomplish is that we'd like Youngstown to be a showcase. A showcase of self-help and a showcase of
community involvement that somehow can be an example for the rest of
the nation. . . . And the key is, how can the Federal government, using
what resources we have, help communities who are interested in self-
help and local community development do that job?

In the course of the spring, as the NCEA began its planning
work and the Coalition campaign was gearing up in Youngstown,
Robert Embry asked the White House to take a coordinating role
in the Youngstown project. At that point, it involved not only
HUD, but also EDA and (because of the Lykes–LTV merger) the
Justice Department. The Treasury Department (because of the
fund used to back the steel loan guarantees) was also involved.
Coordination for the Youngstown project thus became the task
of Jack Watson, domestic affairs adviser to President Carter.

In late May 1978, the NCEA consultants and Coalition representatives had a meeting with Harold Williams about EDA's role
in the project. At that point, the intention of the coalition was a
full-scale, all-at-once reopening of the Campbell Works, requiring at least $300 million in loan guarantees. Williams told the
group that the limit was $100 million, period. Going above that
limit would involve authorization from the congressional appro-
priations committees and, in Williams's view, would be financially
unwise. If the Youngstown effort should fail, it would wipe out
the entire steel loan program. Furthermore, Williams found the
business planning for the enterprise extremely weak. The NCEA
and Coalition did not really believe Williams's strictures were
final. They knew that more money was available in the frozen
Treasury fund and expected that a decision at the White House
level would change matters. They continued to make their plans
using the $300 million figure.

1978 Election Campaign

The latter part of the Coalition campaign coincided with the
campaign for the congressional and Ohio gubernatorial elections

in November 1978. The White House was well aware of Republican Governor Rhodes's "meddling" in the CASTLO communities and wanted to avoid any move that could strengthen Rhodes and hurt the chances of Democratic challenger Dick Celeste. At the same time, in the congressional election in the Ohio 19th District, Congressman Carney's race looked surprisingly close. Carney had barely won the Democratic primary in June against Campbell resident George Tablack. Carney suffered from Parkinson's disease and, though not ill, did not appear that year to be in the best of health. He was bothered by a minor scandal involving the failure to return a large number of books (estimated in the thousands) to the Library of Congress. And his personal popularity in the district was not helped by the steel crisis. The Republican National Committee decided that Carney was vulnerable and sent the young, but skilled campaign organizer John Dalton to Youngstown to help elect the Republican candidate Lyle Williams, formerly a barber and commissioner of Trumbull County.

The Democrats took the challenge seriously. Already in June, Washington had sent trade ambassador Robert Strauss to Youngstown four days before the primary election, both, the assumption was, on a fact-finding mission and to polish Carney's image as chair of the Congressional Steel Caucus. In September, Anthony Solomon, author of the Solomon report, made an unusual campaign trip, also to support the image of Carney as a steel crisis leader. The parade of politicians through Youngstown included literally everyone short of the president himself; the more notable were House majority leader Jim Wright, HUD Secretary Patricia Harris, Senator Ted Kennedy, and Vice-President Mondale.

This was the political setting for the trip to Washington by the Youngstown delegation on September 27, 1978.

The View from the White House

The meeting at the White House, chaired by Jack Watson, included twenty-two Mahoning Valley religious and political leaders and a like number of federal officials. Mayor Richley led the political contingent; Reverend John Sharick was the principal spokesman for the Coalition. A number of proposals affecting the Mahoning Valley were on the table: In addition to the Campbell works reopening, the meeting also touched on the plan for a national steel research center and the unit-train transportation idea. At the conclusion of the ninety-five-minute meeting, Watson announced that the government would reserve $100 million in loan guarantees for a project to revitalize the Mahoning Valley economy. He said that an announcement about the specific project would be made in three weeks.

Reporters' questions and a comparison of impressions after the meeting indicated that the steel research and unit-train proposals had fallen by the side, since they did not appear to meet the government's criteria for jobs and funding. Watson was asked whether the $100 million dollar limit on the steel loan guarantee program would eliminate the Coalition's proposal for the Campbell Works. Watson was understood by the Coalition, and by reporter Dale Peskin (outside the meeting), to have said that the $100 million limit was not a problem. On September 28 and 29, Peskin articles in the Youngstown *Vindicator* reported Watson as dismissing the limit.

He argued that the government has the resources, for example, to back the Coalition's $350 million effort to reopen the Campbell Works. (September 28, 1978)

The extent of the government's financial and commercial interest in a community–worker-owned steel plant looms as the most significant obstacle in the coalition proposal. The takeover requires guarantees of at least $300 million from commercial banks, three times the amount the government has committed to date.

Watson, however, seemed unconcerned about the disparity. The additional $200 million is within the capabilities of the government, he said. (September 29, 1978)

The unanimous view of the Coalition is that they were told not to worry about the $100 million limit, that their plan was within the ball park.

Harold Williams has suggested that Watson may have been misinterpreted, that he meant that the federal government would not reject automatically a plan that went a bit over (meaning a few percent). Exactly what Watson did or did not say cannot be verified. (The cassette tape on which Rabbi Berkowitz attempted to record the meeting turned out to be blank.) But both interview and documentary evidence indicates that, at the time it met with the Coalition and considered the NCEA final report, the White House took a skeptical view of the Campbell Works project.

Two documents obtained in a Freedom of Information suit

indicate what the EDA was telling the White House. (a) In a memo to Bruce Kirschenbaum, deputy assistant to the president for intergovernmental affairs, concerning the clergy demonstration in Columbus and their request for a meeting with the vice-president, Robert Hall (head of EDA) wrote on September 8, 1978, "The NCEA thing is so far out and unrealistic that I worry about involving the Vice President and giving further 'credibility' to their effort." (b) An undated EDA briefing paper, evidently written at the end of the summer, but before September 15, reviewed EDA's work on steel adjustment assistance in Youngstown and characterized the organizations active in the steel crisis:

NCEA is less important than the other organizations mentioned. It will recommend the infeasible solution of spending vast sums of Federal dollars to reopen a facility which will never again regain its market share let alone be self-sustaining. Moreover NCEA and its ideas are strongly opposed by the Steel Workers Union and by private industry.

(It should be noted that EDA had copies of Paul Marshall's correspondence indicating his view that, after the Lykes–LTV merger, the Campbell Works could not regain its historic market share.)

Interviews with the White House staff indicate that the White House believed what it was hearing from EDA. Bruce Kirschenbaum, assistant to Jack Watson, was not at all happy with HUD's role in the Youngstown affair. According to Kirschenbaum, the Campbell Works project was brought to the White House by Robert Embry, assistant secretary at HUD. No action was taken at the White House until the Alperovitz preliminary report came in. At that point, Kirschenbaum, who had done previous work on federal procurement, found the ideas being advanced by Alperovitz "crazy." The White House, which had simply relied on HUD staff work, began to take a stronger interest in the project. It soon appeared from the White House perspective that HUD was trying to put the squeeze on EDA, sponsoring a project that could be implemented only with the use of EDA funds. The White House became suspicious of HUD on this question and began referring the matter to the EDA, which, it felt, had a far better technical capability in economic development.

Kirschenbaum believed that the White House was not well served by HUD in regard to Youngstown. The entire project, he thought, should have been cut off at the point of the preliminary reports. By the time the NCEA final report was submitted in September, the White House was already too deeply involved. At that point, the Democratic administration simply could not afford to reject outright any proposal concerning the Youngstown economy in the midst of a hard-fought election. According to Kirschenbaum, "Very frankly, we put off the decision because of the gubernatorial election, . . . and because of Carney."

This, then, was the background for the letter from Jack Watson on October 18 saying that "we shall continue our consideration of this proposal, and will have a decision as soon as the necessary information is in hand." In effect, the Coalition was bought for five and a half months for the price tag of $93,000 paid to Alperovitz for further studies.

From the vantage point of the White House it was all bad politics. According to Kirschenbaum: "We got ourselves into a position where someone was promoting with federal funds an idea which we should have realized was impossible to begin with, and then we ended up in the position of saying 'no' after playing a part and getting everybody's hopes up. I think it was irresponsible on the part of a number of people." Ironically, the temporizing did not work. Both Democratic candidates lost anyway; Rhodes returned to the governor's office and Lyle Williams replaced Carney in Washington. The administration was left with political losses that, Kirschenbaum said, "could never be recouped."

The View from EDA

In the bureaucratic turf fight between HUD and EDA, the Youngstown round was won by EDA. HUD could continue to pay the bills for an updated market study. But the economic development shop run by Robert Hall and Hall Williams in the Commerce building would make the final decision. Kirschenbaum said, "Jack [Watson] and I never really read all those reports. We trusted what we heard from EDA." The procedure was that the Coalition would submit an application for a UDAG to HUD for $17 million. But the decision on the grant would be deferred to EDA, since the Youngstown project was unworkable without up to $300 million in steel loan guarantees. Having started as clients of HUD, Alperovitz and the Coalition now were forced to play a new game, in which the rules were different. Where HUD was essentially interested in urban renewal, EDA was looking for business viability. The two objectives were not in opposition. But the angle of approach was different.

From the time of the White House meeting in September 1978, communication between the federal government, the NCEA consultants, and the Coalition steadily worsened. The White House was clearly skeptical of the Campbell Works reopening project. However, the message communicated to the Coalition in Youngstown was, "You don't have it quite right yet, but keep trying." And the Coalition continued to proceed on the assumption that a project requiring $300 million in loan guarantees was "in the ball park." In point of fact, Watson's letter of October 18, 1978, outlining the White House position, though it stated four outstanding questions concerning the Campbell Works project, made no reference at all to the $100 million limit. The implication of Watson's letter was that, though there were other problems, exceeding $100 million in loan guarantees was not one of them.

At EDA, Hal Williams (deputy director) and Anne Hallmark (special assistant assigned as coordinator of the Youngstown project) found it "frustrating" to deal with Alperovitz and the Coalition. One problem was that the latter simply did not believe what EDA was saying about the $100 million limit on loan guarantees. Williams insisted, "At no point did anyone here ever, in any way, give them any indication that the $100 million could be changed." Williams felt that the Coalition had "some mystical feeling about their political power," that the people at EDA were only bureaucrats, and that the Coalition would settle the question over their heads at the White House.

The other problem voiced at the EDA was that "none of the paper work received from the NCEA and the Coalition ever made any real hard business sense" (Hallmark). The arithmetic did not add up, raising questions for the EDA staff about the validity of the numbers in general. The EDA people found the plans "soggy," with the only clear point being "we'll get the money from you guys." Anne Hallmark cornered Alperovitz at a Washington cocktail party and tried to arrange some kind of backstairs review process, whereby the Coalition could get feedback before the submission of official documents. She suggested floating a copy of the proposal ahead of time, giving EDA a chance to respond "off the record," or getting an outside recommendation from a recognized steel industry expert. But nothing came back. Hallmark's view was that the EDA could work with people who were willing to engage in dialogue: "We had other projects easily as wild-eyed at the beginning, but where there was dialogue, we were able to do something with it."

Washington's objections to the Coalition plan were not to community–worker ownership as such. EDA had already funded projects involving worker ownership. At no point in the Washington interviews was this ever mentioned as a problem. Williams did raise a question about the effect community ownership would have on the level of steel expertise in the board of directors, but this seemed a question that was negotiable. Williams was far more worried about the quality of the management team for the new enterprise. Nor did Washington seem especially concerned about steel industry objections. According to Kirschenbaum, the White House did not hear from the industry at all concerning Youngstown. U.S. Steel was opposing the steel loan program as a whole, but EDA seemed willing to deal with this as long as it could defend the business validity of its loans. Even in the last round, the message from the White House – according to Hallmark – was "come up with something viable and we'll back you."

Decision

The Coalition took its case to the White House for a final decision on the Campbell Works project on March 21, 1979, eighteen months after the initial shutdown announcement. The agenda for this meeting was an oral presentation by the Coalition on its project as a whole. Technically, the proposal on the table was the application for an UDAG, which had been submitted in January. In fact, the government would be deciding simultaneously on the UDAG and the request for steel loan guarantees (even though no formal application for the steel loan program had yet been submitted).

There was a flurry of activity shortly before the Washington trip. By March 15, Paul Marshall had still not submitted the final numbers on his latest market study; pressure was brought to get those to Washington. Arrangements were made for a press conference in the capital. Finally, Coalition representatives and consultants assembled once again at the White House for a meeting with Jack Watson and other federal officials. The Coalition's front line was different this time. Because of Stanton's questions about the economic feasibility of the project, it was decided that others with fewer doubts should confront the government. The presentation was made, and once again everyone went home to wait; a decision was expected before April 1.

The other shoe fell on Friday, March 30. Jack Watson called Bishop Burt in Cleveland to say that the proposal had been turned down. A letter from Robert Hall, dated March 29, would arrive shortly. The $100 million limit on steel loan guarantees was mentioned as the first reason for rejecting the proposal, but Hall's letter also raised questions about the economic viability of the project in general.

Charles Rawlings and Staughton Lynd later charged that the EDA failed to provide the same level of attention to the Coalition as to other steel loan applicants. In response, Hal Williams said that the agency's policy was to work closely with candidates *after* they had been invited by the agency to make a formal proposal. The Coalition project never got that far. Yet Williams was aware of, and approved, his assistant Anne Hallmark's efforts to stay in touch with Youngstown "through the back door." For their part, officials at the EDA were frustrated by what they saw as the Coalition's failure to communicate.

It was also charged by members of the Coalition that EDA never even looked at the final version of the Youngstown plan. The documentation cited above shows that EDA had always been skeptical about the NCEA consultants' work. On the final round, the agency still had not received the new market study and financial plan on March 15, even though the Coalition wanted an answer on their proposal by March 31. In fairness, it was hard for the agency to act on a proposal that was stuck in the consultant's computer. Furthermore, documents obtained by the Coalition in a Freedom of Information request show that the EDA *did* read the proposal carefully enough to raise a number of critical questions.

The EDA files document a long list of "substantive weaknesses" that EDA identified in the Coalition proposal. Some of the most pertinent questions were the following:

- The $4,000,000 plus referred to as *"commitments" for community investment* in the project are not in fact "commitments," but simply money deposited in savings accounts with no commitment whatsoever.
- To the extent that a $10 million loan to purchase stock for the ESOP

is critical to the project, there is a problem, since *EDA funds for this purpose were limited* in the current year.

– There is no *commitment for the supply* of steel slabs and hot bands, and no firm price estimate.

– The estimates of $30–40 million for new quality control equipment are *several years old and not adjusted for inflation.*

– If EDA guarantees $245 million, someone will have to come up with $24.5 million in guarantees other than EDA, since EDA only guarantees 90%. The *source of this additional guarantee is not identified*, nor is there any recognition in the proposal that this may be a problem.

– We are not talking about a market that is presently unserved, or a new product for which there may be a demand. We are talking about carving out a *share of an existing market* with a product which is no different from that of the competitors. . . It may, thus, take more years than anticipated to regain a market share.

– An *interest cost of 10% is assumed.* This is probably low at this time, and the increase will add to fixed costs.

– The Warburg Paribas Becker letter on financial feasibility is *carefully hedged.*

– The environmental assessment has not been completed (problematic regarding Brier Hill as source for slabs).

– *Sources of private funds are not identified.*

– *Management has not been identified.*

– *A contingency of only $1.5 million* for a $335 million project appears to be wildly over-optimistic, particularly in view of the fact that detailed cost estimates have not been made.

– The *financial study* of the project's viability is done on a straight-line basis over a 20-year period. No allowance has been made for intermediate fluctuations when the demand for steel is weak and the company will need financial resources to withstand operating losses at a greater level than indicated by the straight-line trend.

These were, on the whole, legitimate questions. Given time, communication, and competence on all sides, they might possibly have been worked out. But as it stood in late March, the business plan submitted by the Coalition still failed the bottom-line standards of the EDA.

In one sense, the EDA was the winner in the series of moves involving Youngstown in the Washington chess game. The HUD power play was temporarily checked. In a larger sense, though, there were no winners, only losers. Anne Hallmark put it very well: "The real bottom line is, we've all failed somehow. And we're all responsible."

CHAPTER IX

Ending, Learning, Beginning Anew

For the members of the Coalition, who had worked for eighteen months on the Campbell Works project, it was the final piece of bad news. There was some anger mixed with the disappointment, because they felt that, in this round, Washington had not played fair. Their disappointment, their anger, and their concern about yet another round in the Valley's ongoing steel crisis – all are reflected in their telegram of response to Jack Watson:

We believe that the March 29 letter reflects a collapse of the pre-1978 election assurances passed out by you on behalf of President Carter to the unemployed of the Mahoning Valley. We believe that your failure to act portends destructive consequences of a most serious nature for Youngstown, Ohio, where another steel mill closing this year will cost 1600 jobs and the imminent closing of U.S. Steel facilities can add 4600 more jobs lost. Mr. Hall's letter reflects a lack of both will and ability on the part of the responsible parties.

The enormous efforts by the religious denominations, including the U.S. Catholic Conference, the National Council of Churches, the Synagogue Council of America were undertaken in faithful reliance on the good will and concern of the federal government and, during the past six months, on your own assurances of last fall.

We believe now, in the light of the March 29 letter, that we were misdirected in our efforts and our reliance.

Robert Hall's letter rejecting the Coalition proposal for reopening the Campbell Works invited the Coalition to meet with federal officials once again, if they desired. A meeting was quickly scheduled for April 3.

Ending

To prepare for the Washington meeting, the Coalition met on April 2 at the Catholic diocesan offices next to St. Columba's Cathedral. Developing a policy statement for the Washington meeting led to questions about what the Coalition should do next. On this point, there was heated disagreement, with the meeting lasting a full day. The Presbyterians and Catholics took the position that the Washington decision was final and that the Coalition should simply wind up the steel-mill-reopening effort. Charles Rawlings and Staughton Lynd, on the other side, took the position that the struggle should be carried on. Rawlings felt that the Coalition should consider Youngstown as only the first battle in a larger struggle and expand the Coalition effort to a national scale. Staughton Lynd argued that, with the failure of negotiations, the Coalition should take the movement to the streets, in the tradition of the civil rights and antiwar movements of the 1960s. Bishop Malone demurred, saying that he was bishop of *all* the people of the Mahoning Valley and that he would not lead his constituency in such a conflict strategy. No agreement on the future course of the Coalition could be reached; the group decided to take up the matter later, after still another trip to Washington.

On April 3, members of the Coalition once again got on a plane for Washington for another meeting with Jack Watson at the White House. In Washington, members of the Coalition once again voiced their sense of betrayal by the government. The federal officials reiterated their insistence on the $100 million limit on federal loan guarantees and said they were still willing to work with proposals for the steel industry in the Mahoning Valley that stayed within that parameter. The meeting changed nothing. The federal officials went back to their desks, and the Coalition representatives came home.

On April 5, the Executive and Steering Committees of the Coalition assembled at First Presbyterian Church for what was to be the last meeting on the Campbell Works effort. The real question on the agenda was the future of the Coalition. The Presbyterians, led by Coalition vice-chair John Sharick, submitted a written motion to terminate efforts at reopening the steel mill; in any case, the Presbyterian contingent intended to withdraw from further participation in the Campbell Works effort. They argued that to continue the struggle over the Campbell Works would be inconsistent with the realities of the situation and would leave the Coalition open to the charge of engendering false hopes. Although Bishop Malone, as chair, made no formal statement, it was clear that the Catholics supported the Presbyterian position. Charles Rawlings introduced a statement identifying areas of concern beyond Youngstown that might form the base for a broader movement. Others pointed to the continuing steel crisis in Youngstown, as the Brier Hill Works shutdown and the closing of U.S. Steel's mills at Youngstown and McDonald were imminent.

In the end, the group decided to terminate pursuit of the National Center for Economic Alternatives' plan for reopening the Campbell Works and to close the campaign office on Federal Plaza. This decision was simply an acknowledgment of the circumstances: There was neither time before the Coalition's option on the closed portion of the Campbell Works ran out on June 1, nor money left, to develop still another plan. Nor did the funds exist to continue paying a campaign staff. Still, the Executive Committee opted not to dissolve the organization, but to leave the Coalition structure in place. This position was taken for two reasons: first, because the structure and the working relationships that had been built up over the previous months might once again prove useful in the continuing Youngstown-area steel crisis; and second, because the religious leaders did not wish to give steelworkers the impression that they were abandoning their concern for the unemployed.

Technically, it was not the last meeting of the Ecumenical Coalition. The organization did meet again – one time, in fact, at the request of and in the offices of Congressman Lyle Williams. But for all practical purposes, the story of the Ecumenical Coalition of the Mahoning Valley ends on Thursday, April 5, 1979 (the day before Good Friday).

On June 1, the Coalition's option with J & L Steel on the closed portions of the Campbell Works ran out. Within the week, J & L announced that it was hiring William Sullivan, president of the now largely defunct Western Reserve Economic Development Agency, to manage the sale of the Campbell Works properties to new industrial occupants.

Learning

In program development and policy analysis, evaluation is the mother of learning. In the real world, few programs are so perfectly conceived and impeccably implemented that they are 100% effective on the first try. Virtually every program experience can profit from examination and analysis, so that its lessons can be articulated. This is, of course, simply to say in program terms what has often been asserted about the value of history – that those who do not know history are doomed to repeat it.

To their credit, the people in the Coalition were concerned that their effort be open to study. Particularly as it became apparent that their efforts would not likely result in steel rolling down the mills of the Campbell Works, the members of the Coalition were concerned that others have a chance to profit from their experience. The hope remained that other communities, caught by a similar situation of sudden unemployment, might learn from the efforts in Youngstown.

The intent of this study, then, has been to try to understand the situation in which the Coalition emerged and to see from the inside how it developed. The important thing is to "pin down the learnings" – to use Bert Campbell's phrase – from this significant event in the chronicle of church social action in the United States.

Many of the "learnings" from the Coalition story have no doubt suggested themselves in the course of this narrative. At this point, though, it may be useful to reflect on the Coalition experience and identify several key elements in the process and outcome. The framework of policy analysis provides a useful guide for identifying important features.

Definition of the Problem

In the development of a policy or program of action, a critical first step is defining the problem that one is trying to remedy. The definition of the problem – what must be fixed – shapes the process of figuring out what is to be done. In Youngstown, the Ecumenical Coalition made three critical decisions in defining the problem created by the closing of the Campbell Works.

First – and most important – the Coalition asserted that the steel mill shutdown was a *moral*, and not just an economic, problem. This means that the Coalition saw the shutdown not as the unavoidable result of an untamable force, like a hurricane or tornado. If the shutdown was a disaster, it was a man-made one, the result of human choice and action. As a moral event, the shutdown could be talked about as something that should or should not have happened. It was an event that demanded an accounting, an acceptance of responsibility for the suffering that it caused.

The articulation of the coalition's position can be found in the pastoral letter. "Economic institutions, although they have their own purposes and methods, must serve the common good and are subject to moral judgment." In the letter, the Coalition named the Lykes Corporation in particular as responsible, not only for its "decision to close the mill, but also [for] the manner in which the decision was made, the way it is being implemented, and the pattern of neglect which led to it." Steelworkers union official Jim Smith, himself an economist, stated that the major contribution of the Coalition was that it changed the terms of the discussion about plant shutdowns. After Youngstown, he said, a shutdown would have to be seen as a moral event with economic consequences.

Second, the Coalition defined the problem as one of reemployment, rather than as one of providing human services. In this way, the Coalition departed from what might be considered the expected response from the religious sector. A normal response from the churches and synagogues would have been to provide encouragement, perhaps counseling, maybe the help of church volunteers. The Coalition, however, chose to define the problem as how to reemploy the workers that were laid off, in jobs that would utilize their talents and provide the same level of income they had received before the shutdown. At the heart of the matter was jobs. If the workers could be reemployed, the special human services would not be needed.

It is important to note that the Coalition's purpose was to provide reemployment directly for the workers who were laid off in the shutdown. They left to other agencies (MVEDC, CASTLO) more long term development strategies. In this respect, the Coalition took on a responsibility that no other group was willing to claim.

Third, the Coalition – following their consultants – tended to define the problem of reopening the Campbell Works as more a political than an economic problem. There is little or no evidence that Gar Alperovitz ever changed his initial premise that "all of the significant issues in Youngstown are moral and political, not economic." A significant portion of the Coalition, including a majority of the Steering Committee, agreed with Alperovitz. It was a definition of the problem that guided the actions of both the Coalition and the consultants.

The basic game plan was for the religious coalition to deal with the moral dimensions of the Youngstown shutdown and to provide the leadership for a political movement targeting government decision makers. It was the consultants' responsibility to deal with the economic issues. Yet the consultants' definition of the problem as essentially political ultimately determined the strategy and program.

Goals and Objectives

The steel crisis conference held shortly after the shutdown (in October 1977) identified four tasks for the emergent religious coalition:

1. Provide public education (identify moral issues, engender hope).
2. Develop a national steel policy to retain jobs in distressed communities.
3. Develop national projects involving churches, with links to Youngstown.
4. Restore jobs at Campbell Works, through reopening under community–worker ownership or conversion of property.

The Coalition moved very quickly on the first task of public education through its pastoral letter, which was publicized in the churches and in the secular media through newspaper ads. The other three tasks rather quickly coalesced into the Coalition's Campbell Works project. From the official announcement on December 12, 1977, of the intention to pursue the reopening of the steel mill, the Campbell Works project held the Coalition together and provided its sense of purpose.

The coalition of religious groups, however, included a coalition of different approaches to that goal. Among the Steering Committee, legal counsel, and eventually the consultants, there were different ideas about how to concretize the goal in a specific objective. From the time of the agreement with HUD and the National Center for Economic Alternatives at the end of Decem-

Table 9.1. *Strategic approaches within the Ecumenical Coalition*

Revolutionary approach $\longrightarrow$	Reform approach $\longleftarrow$	Restorative approach
Basic restructuring of American capitalism	Community–worker ownership	Restoration of jobs through capital reinvestment

ber 1977, the principal objective of the Coalition became identified as community–worker ownership of the Campbell Works.

This objective represented a compromise between two approaches to economic development, as illustrated in Table 9.1. A
number of the Youngstown clergy, at least initially, arrived at the
community–worker ownership plan out of necessity. Depending
on major corporations to reinvest in the local community had not
worked. Nor did capital reinvestment in the Campbell Works
seem likely to be forthcoming from any of the traditional sources.
Community–worker ownership became the objective because that
seemed the only hope of realizing the capital reinvestment necessary to restore jobs. Stanton represented this position in a saying
that was remembered (and often attributed to him) within the
Coalition: "If I heard that an Arab sheik with an oil-stained
gunny sack full of thousand dollar bills was on his way to Youngstown to buy a steel mill," he said, "I would be the first to learn
Arabic on the way to the airport." The principal focus was on
capital investment. Community–worker ownership was a means
to achieve it.

In contrast, Alperovitz and Lynd saw community–worker
ownership as a means to a basic restructuring of American capitalism. They stressed in *Strategy and Program* that "radicals must
participate openly in other organizations and maintain a self-
consciously independent stance" (Lynd and Alperovitz 1973: x).
In that book, community-controlled economic endeavors are seen
as "counter-institutions" playing "an important educative role
in a more complex long-term political dialectic" (ibid.: xiii). To
some extent, Charles Rawlings also represented this position. He
made a personal and institutional commitment to the Youngstown Coalition because he saw that it was a place to win a battle
in the long-range struggle for urban socioeconomic change.

In terms of the community–worker ownership objective, the Coalition represented an ideological compromise, one that began to show some strain in the last months. As Ed Weisheimer, Pastor of Central Christian Church, put it, when the ball was within the ten-yard line, the team was simply not together enough to push it across the goal. The division according to social philosophy made communication and cohesive action increasingly difficult.

This difference in social philosophy also coincided to some extent with a different sense of the relative importance of the national cause versus the local project of restoring jobs and employment. Stanton, for example, was interested in a national project if it got jobs for Youngstown. The consultants (and to some extent Charles Rawlings) were interested in Youngstown as a means for generating a national cause.

Strategy

The Ecumenical Coalition has been described as an attempt at launching a social movement. The strategy the Coalition utilized became essentially that of a reform movement.

In a classic article entitled "Social Movements," Herbert Blumer (1951) outlined a typology of "revolutionary" and "reform" movements, postulating a consistent set of characteristics with each type. A third type of movement is also possible, in which the agenda is not social change, but the restoration of a status quo. This threefold typology (Table 9.2) may help to illuminate the strategy of the Coalition.

In terms of this typology, the Coalition was essentially a reform movement. Reversing the shutdown by purchasing the steel mill under a community–worker ownership plan was a specific change in the local economy (though as a "demonstration experiment" it was intended to have a national impact). The Coalition appealed explicitly to the Judeo-Christian biblical and ethical tradition in criticizing the manner of the shutdown. In calling for more participatory and fair economic structures, the Coalition attempted to reform the prevailing political–economic system rather than attack it head-on. The Coalition clearly made use of existing institutions, first by transferring the respectability of its church leaders to the movement itself and then seeking to con-

Table 9.2. *Typology of social movements*

Characteristic	Revolutionary	Reform	Restorative
Objective	General, broad-scale charge	Specific change	Restore previous situation
Ideology	Attack on prevailing ethics	Based on prevailing ethics	Traditional ethics
Relation to existing institutions	Independent of existing institutions	Seek respectability from existing institutions	Based on existing institutions
Target group	Distressed or underprivileged group	Middle class	Managerial elite
Procedure	Make converts to cause	Develop favorable public opinion	Negotiate with power structure
Leadership	From distressed group	From middle class	From managerial elite

Source: Based in part on Blumer (1951), 21–2.

firm the legitimacy of the organization and its objective with the assistance of local, state, and federal government agencies. The target group of the Coalition's Save Our Valley campaign became essentially the middle class, both in Youngstown and across the nation. Through influencing a broad spectrum of middle-class voters, the Coalition hoped to put pressure on Washington politicians. The Coalition made extensive and skillful use of publicity, both in the press and on television and radio, to develop favorable public opinion. The leadership of the Coalition finally came not from the distressed group, but from essentially middle-class clergy.

Toward the end of the campaign, the "two Coalitions" tended to pull apart. Lynd, and to some extent Rawlings, moved in the direction of a "revolutionary" strategy; Stanton, however, realized more and more that the success of the Coalition enterprise would depend on convincing highly placed decision makers in government and the financial world.

Table 9.3. *Operational dynamics of the Ecumenical Coalition*

Characteristics	Economic development	Political movement
Definition of objectives	Flexible, subject to redefinition	Inflexible, unwavering
Definition of issues	Complex	Simple
Decision-making style	Bureaucratic, based on expertise	Consensual, based on representation
Communications style		
Internal	Confidential	Open
External	Avoid publicity	Seek publicity
Support system	Elite: labor, government, business	Mass

Operational Dynamics

The Coalition in operation was two things at once: a political campaign and an economic development agency. The two operations were largely handled by separate personnel working out of separate offices. The work of organizing an economic development effort was very different from that of managing a political campaign (Table 9.3).

Definition of objective. The objective of the Coalition was defined as reopening the Campbell Works under community–worker ownership. For a successful campaign, commitment to this goal had to be firmly fixed. To ask people to buy into the campaign, Coalition representatives had to project confidence that their objective was attainable. The very success of the campaign itself made it more and more difficult to redefine or renegotiate the objective, even as circumstances changed drastically. From a business perspective, the Lykes–LTV merger seriously altered the chances for a successful reopening. In the face of such adversity, however, the political movement needed to demonstrate unwavering commitment.

As an economic development effort, the Coalition required some flexibility. On the first of January 1978, as the Alperovitz group set to work on developing a plan, the economic viability of the community–worker ownership approach was still an open question. But community–worker ownership was treated more as an absolute, fixed principle. For the economic side of the Coalition's effort, the assumption about community–worker ownership of a reopened steel mill tended to foreclose the creative consideration of alternative options. One consequence of this lack of flexibility is that the Coalition was left with no fallback position from which to salvage something of its effort.

Definition of issues. For the campaign, it was essential that issues be simplified. The complex variables of steel technology, industrial finance, market analysis, and even political accountability had to be reduced to simple terms, yielding unqualified answers. For campaign purposes, it was even useful to think of federal officials at the EDA as the enemy, whereas the reality was far more complex.

In contrast, the economic development effort required continually questioning assumptions, being suspicious of what was left out of the equation, dubious about what could go wrong. Thin margins had to be recognized for what they were, as cause for doubts and questions that had to be faced squarely. For the economic development effort, things were always more complicated than they seemed to people caught up in the campaign.

Decision-making style. The decision-making style of the Steering and Executive Committees was consensual, based on the political principle of representing in the decision a range of religious groups. Such a style was essential for the basically political nature of the campaign. Those involved in the economic development effort, however, needed to make decisions on the best expert knowledge, regardless of what the majority thought.

Communications style. The communications style appropriate to the campaign effort was an open style, in which the campaign staff could share successes and failures, using every effort to acquire publicity for the cause. The economic development effort, on the contrary, often had to be confidential, both within the circle and to the world at large. An important negotiation could be ruined by inappropriate publicity.

Clearly some kind of off-the-record communication with Washington was badly needed. But that was difficult to manage if there was a good chance that a phone call or conversation would be reported the next day on the front page of the paper.

Support system. Finally, the support systems for the campaign and economic development efforts differed. The campaign had to attract broad mass support. In the economic development effort, media attention and mass enthusiasm were meaningless unless they could be converted into dollar commitments on paper, through work with people who had the power to effect funding.

The differences between the economic development and political movement agendas of the Coalition clearly led to some tension, particularly at the Steering Committee level. A major part of the difficulty was the weakness of the financial and marketing plan. Given a more credible business proposition for the Campbell Works, the "two Coalitions" might have complemented one another far more effectively.

Economic Expertise

It is easy to understand why the religious leaders were impressed by Gar Alperovitz. As a speaker and writer, he was particularly skilled at interpreting the "big picture," at revealing the underlying themes of economic life, making them available for moral analysis. He could articulate for the noneconomist a convincing vision of a different kind of economy. Alperovitz's vision seemed to put into economic terms what the religious traditions were calling for in their social teaching. Furthermore, as a practical consideration, Alperovitz had access to government funding at a time when the Ecumenical Coalition was a fledgling organization seeking its first resources.

Alperovitz clearly did some excellent work for the Coalition. He spent time in Youngstown, staying at St. Patrick's rectory with Father Stanton. His ideas served as the framework for the Coalition effort. He provided connections with other consultants – experts on economic analysis, worker ownership, corporate structure, and so on. He had access to communications media – the *New York Times*, network television. His name and reputation gave the effort a kind of cachet, a sense of importance.

Alperovitz also brought some weaknesses. The National Center for Economic Alternatives itself had no experience with the steel industry. One consultant, Paul Marshall, had done economic research for the American Iron and Steel Institute. But none of the consultants had been involved in the steel business or had any firsthand knowledge of the steel-production facilities at the Campbell Works. As a result, the initial business plan proposed by the consultants was based more on national steel industry averages than on production and market figures derived from experience with the Campbell mills.

The research Alperovitz commissioned provided excellent monographs on topics relevant to the Youngstown problem. But the detailed work needed to start a business was missing. Only when former steel executives on the Youngstown scene, working with Jim Smith from the steelworkers union, brought a fundamental revision of the business strategy did the plan begin to have any credibility. If the kind of plan that finally emerged at the end of the Coalition effort had been devised a year earlier, the story might have had a different ending.

In devising the plan, the Alperovitz group also misread the political landscape in Washington. A major contention between the federal government and the Coalition throughout the life of the project was the $100 million limit on steel loan guarantees. Everyone knew that there was more money available in the special Treasury fund to back a larger steel loan guarantee program. Alperovitz's strategy was to insist that government guarantees much higher than the $100 million level were necessary. Alperovitz evidently did not communicate seriously with the EDA on this point. His assumption seems to have been that HUD and the political movement coming out of Youngstown would put so much pressure on the White House that the president would have EDA and the congressional committees change the steel loan program. This strategy misfired, first of all, because the business plan was simply not convincing enough to force serious consideration of this option. Alperovitz evidently thought that he could use HUD to manipulate the EDA. As it turned out, the White House listened not to HUD, but to the business people at the Commerce Department. It was a fatal political miscalculation.

In the end, the NCEA not only failed to provide its clients with the business plan that had been their original mandate. It also – paradoxically for economists – tried to use political means to deal with an economic problem. Even Gerald Dickey, the Youngstown steelworker who was the first to propose worker ownership, conceded that "we were trying to impose a political solution on an economic problem" ("Youngstown Sheet and Tube" 1979: 34). The net result was frustration for everyone, even the federal officials in Washington who wanted to help.

In hindsight, it is apparent that the terms of the contractual relationship left the Coalition in an ambiguous position for controlling the consultants' work. Since the contract was signed directly between HUD and NCEA, the consultants ultimately were working for HUD, and only indirectly for the Coalition. The Coalition – even had it wanted to – was not in a position to insist that the consultants focus on developing the *economic* strategy that was their primary mandate.

Clergy and Laity

Still another dimension to the Coalition story is the clergy–lay dynamic. Bishop Malone himself identified the issue in an interview conducted after the Campbell Works project had ended. "The problem," he said, "is that we had it all to do ourselves." Bishop Malone returned to this theme in his address entitled "Implementing Social Justice Ministry":

The ideal would have been that the coalition or some similar movement would have had a strong lay leadership and presence. In fact, the coalition was a clergy coalition with some lay involvement. . . . The coalition was perceived by many to be a clerical club – this may well have been one key to our lack of broad-based support. (Malone 1981: 376)[1]

As a matter of fact, there was some difference within the Coalition on this point. At First Presbyterian Church, the program of renewal launched by Pastor Bay and Pastor Campbell produced a different climate for clergy–lay interaction. Campbell was able to meet with prominent business people who were members of his church (e.g., at a luncheon on May 2, 1978) to develop an understanding of the Coalition's effort. One church member, Arthur Young, president of Mahoning Bank, helped to develop the Save Our Valley accounts and other programs.

Catholics, on the whole, were far less prepared to enter into this kind of cooperative relationship. In this respect, the Catholic Church in Youngstown showed its more traditional face to the world. In the immigrant church of the turn of the century, clergy led and people followed. Likewise, in the immigrant church at the turn of the century, Catholics were not involved (either priests or parishioners) in industrial management decisions. In the old days, Catholics were workers, not "iron barons."

By the 1970s, however, some Youngstown Catholics had made it to Ohio State or Notre Dame and had moved up from the mill floor to the management suite. With the new situation created by the Campbell Works shutdown and by the leadership of clerics like Malone and Stanton, Catholic lay people found themselves being expected to assume a new kind of responsibility, precisely as people of the church. Three factors made it difficult for them to do so.

First, there were career considerations. Lay people who had the kind of steel expertise the Coalition needed typically still had jobs in the industry that precluded their participation in the planning of a potentially competitive enterprise.

Second, the organizational structure of the Coalition, representing the denominations at both Executive and Steering Committee levels, did not provide any clear opportunity for lay people to become involved. Later on, their advice on the corporate structure model was sought. But there clearly was no role for them at the leadership level.

Third, lay people – and many clergy as well – were not theologically prepared for such a venture. The full meaning of the theological shifts in the Catholic Church marked by the Vatican II document "The Church in the Modern World" (1965) and the Bishops Synods of 1971 and 1975 had barely begun to penetrate the Catholic consciousness. Even in the theologically progressive Catholic diocese of Youngstown, a great deal of tradition had to be overcome for lay people to feel comfortable collaborating with clergy and their bishop about opening a steel mill.

The net result is that the Ecumenical Coalition ended up with a structural model that proved inadequate to the task, either organizationally or theologically. It has already been pointed out that, in organizational terms, the decision-making structure of the Coalition should have included some persons with technical and financial expertise in steelmaking. The failure to do so left the Coalition excessively dependent on their consultants.

In theological terms, the Coalition was left with a model for clergy–lay cooperation that was borrowed from Europe. On the Continent, the typical pattern for Catholic social action – whether through political parties, labor unions, trade associations, or other organizations – gives the clergy the role of enunciating moral theory and lay people the role of putting it into practice. In the Ecumenical Coalition in Youngstown, the clergy – at both the Executive and Steering Committee levels – took the role of making the moral case. It was the role of the lay consultants to develop the practical implementation.

The problem with this model theologically has been pointed out by Bishop Rembert Weakland (1986), chair of the Catholic Bishops Committee on the Economic Pastoral:

> Among the many practical concrete options open politically and socially at any given moment of history, it cannot be assumed that the choice of the morally most acceptable solution will be easy and self-evident, even if the theory is clear. In other words, the debate cannot cease at the transition point from theory to praxis. Such a neat deductive kind of moral process is idealistic and does not correspond to life's experiences. (205)

Weakland goes on to point out that "hidden within this model is not only a concept of the church but also a concept of the methodology for moral decision-making, a methodology that is foreign to the American inductive cultural and educational process" (ibid.). Weakland's concern is to open the field for and articulate an alternative model of clergy–lay cooperation that he sees developing in the United States. One of the keys to that model is a unity of the clergy and laity, dealing together with the interactive process in which moral theory asks questions of practice, and praxis in turn asks questions of moral theory.

The great contribution of the Youngstown clergy is that they dared – when no one else spoke up – to ask the moral questions. The great failure of the Coalition was that the questions from the practical side were not developed with equal seriousness and equal depth.

Post Mortem

This study has been intended to be more than a post mortem, an autopsy to determine the cause of death. Nevertheless, the question may still remain, Why did the Ecumenical Coalition fail to reopen the Campbell Works?

Part of the answer is the general situation of crisis for American steel that was sketched earlier. The American industry in 1979 was facing uncertainty over future markets, increasing competition from abroad, the need to open new sources of raw materials, and a shortage of capital investment for implementing new steel-making technology (Hogan 1983). The Campbell Works reopening project had to cope with these problems, just like other steel manufacturers.

In addition to the general situation of the industry, my view is that at least seven factors played a critical role in the failure of the Youngstown project.

Feasibility. Three of the factors are related to the feasibility of the project.

1. The merger between Lykes and LTV in 1978 made the reopening of the Campbell Works if not impossible, then at least a great deal more difficult. When the Coalition first announced their plan in December 1977, the feasibility of the reopening strategy depended on a comparatively quick reentry into production, so that the Campbell Works could continue to service its traditional market. In the spring and summer of 1978, the prospect of a merger between Lykes, the corporate owner of the Campbell Works, and LTV presented fundamental problems for the Coalition. First, it became clear that Lykes would not negotiate seriously about selling the Campbell Works while the merger was in process. And it was not clear what facilities the newly merged company would be willing to sell. Second, the merger eliminated the possibility of the Campbell Works continuing to sell three hundred thousand tons of steel annually to Van Huffel Tube, a subsidiary of Sheet and Tube that went to LTV. By September 1978, when the Coalition took their idea to the White House, the merger had fundamentally altered the business planning for a mill reopening. By that time it was clear that the mill could not enter into production within the twelve-month time frame originally projected by George Beetle. And it was also clear that new customers would have to be developed, a very difficult task given the intense competition in the American steel market.

2. The Coalition was not able to generate a sufficiently credible business plan. That project was made more difficult by the Lykes–LTV merger. Even the principal financial consultant, Paul Marshall, said after the merger that the Coalition should "reassess their plan of action" (see Chapter VII). Neither the Coalition nor the consultants could have foreseen the merger or its potential effects when they began their work in January 1978.

Nevertheless, the consultant group does bear responsibility for its failure to either (a) tell the Coalition that the plan was no longer feasible or (b) develop an alternative business strategy. The merger seems to have left the consultant group simply repeating the same theme, without any clear idea of how to justify it in financial terms.

The new approach of a three-phase reopening was developed not by the consultants, but by the steelmen John Stone and Frank McGough. If such a strategy had been advanced much earlier, the Coalition might have had time to refine the plan and resolve the problems that remained when it was submitted to the federal government in early 1979.

3. In addition to the difficulties with economic feasibility, the Coalition faced very considerable problems of political and administrative feasibility. The project was incredibly ambitious from the point of view of building consensus and achieving administrative implementation. The Coalition had to (a) persuade workers, community, and government officials that the churches had a legitimate role in trying to restore jobs; (b) develop a workable model for community–worker ownership in a major industry; (c) convince Youngstown that community–worker ownership was not Socialism (with a capital S); (d) persuade competing local governments in Mahoning County to cooperate on the project; (e) learn how to utilize two new federal government funding programs (the Urban Development Action Grant and steel loan program); (f) develop cooperation at the local, state, and federal levels across political party lines; (g) develop cooperation among federal agencies competing for control of urban policy. Any of those tasks was formidable on its own. The Coalition had to accomplish them all at the same time, and in a few short months.

Within each one of those tasks, the Coalition had to achieve agreement on multiple decisions. On this point, it is instructive to consider the Youngstown project in the light of an earlier EDA project in Oakland, California, in the 1960s. In their classic study *Implementation*, Pressman and Wildavsky (1979) show how the EDA's first major urban development project in Oakland foundered, in part because too many agreements had to be reached by too many people in too little time. And the Oakland project was less complex than the one in Youngstown.

The Coalition had to negotiate agreements at the local level (with such organizations as MVEDC and CASTLO, with municipal governments), the state level (across political parties), and the federal level (among competing bureaucracies), as well as with the steel companies. To its credit, the Coalition was able to negotiate most of the necessary agreements successfully. For example, an agreement with J & L Steel over the purchase price of the Campbell Works facilities was reached rather amicably. (In comparison, U.S. Steel later refused to talk with workers about purchasing the company's shut-down mills in Youngstown.) Given its negotiating agenda, it is hardly surprising that the Coalition fell short of 100% success.

Support. Three factors concern the lack of support for the project by critical groups.

4. The lack of support by the United Steelworkers officials at the outset of the reopening project severely hampered the Coalition. At least one local president was openly critical; the international president refused to talk about it. A direct mail approach to steelworker membership was canceled. The union eventually provided significant help in the person of James Smith. But more than a year was lost before the union began to assume any responsibility for helping the Coalition.

5. Lack of visible support by the unemployed steelworkers themselves hurt the credibility of the Coalition. Steelworker apathy remains one of the most disappointing chapters in the entire story. Only in Youngstown's so-called red local, led by Ed Mann, John Barbero, and Gerald Dickey, was there strong, united support for the Coalition. And this was the union that suffered the fewest jobs lost by the Campbell shutdown. In the locals more directly affected, some officials (notably Bill Sferra and Duane Irving) worked closely with the Coalition. But if only fifty workers (Stanton's estimate) out of the thousands laid off ever volunteered to help in the campaign, and if less than a hundred showed up at the downtown rally, the only conclusion to draw was that – whatever workers may have thought about the Coalition project in private – they did not put their bodies on the line in support of it.

Explanations for the general worker passivity are multiple (see Chapter VI). It may be that the Coalition should have been more skilled in drawing workers into the campaign, in soliciting and organizing volunteer efforts. The campaign may have been too much a white-collar affair. But the fact remains that workers did little on their own behalf. They had time to volunteer; they were collecting substantial benefits while not working. But for the first year, they "watched the grass grow," leaving the effort to others. Only a year after the shutdown, as the benefits began to run out, did the workers take responsibility as a group for their situation.

6. The lack of positive support from the civic and business community was felt by the Coalition. It can be argued that without a credible business plan, skepticism was an intelligent and defensible attitude. It is also true that the Coalition did not have an effective way of including business or steel expertise from the Youngstown community in the Campbell Works discussions. But the absence of the business community cannot be totally explained by any failures of the Coalition.

The reasons for business reticence are complex. At one level, the clergy-led project was an affront: Coalition leaders could get on the plane and go to meetings at the White House, something the Chamber of Commerce or similar groups could not do. At another level, business interests in a tough labor town saw a potential improvement in the business climate. Deference to the religious leaders for the most part prevented open confrontation. (The attacks by a vice-president of Republic Steel and the president of U.S. Steel were exceptions.) Generally business and civic leaders simply voiced their support for other initiatives: MVEDC or CASTLO or the steel research center. In the last analysis, the business community probably did not hurt the Coalition effort; but it did not help as much as it might have.

Federal government. The final factor is the role of the federal government.

7. The federal government ultimately played a divided and conflicted role in Youngstown. The Campbell Works shutdown figured significantly in the origin of the steel loan program. Early conversations with federal officials encouraged the Youngstown clergy to believe that their program was what Washington wanted. The Coalition's sense that they were working with Washington was certainly confirmed by the HUD planning grant in December 1977.

HUD officials, however, promised the Coalition more than they could deliver. Officials at EDA – for good reason – refused to be pressured by HUD. Communication within the government broke down. The White House temporized and bought off the Coalition to escape a decision at election time.

The failure of communication between Washington and the Coalition involves blame on both sides. Washington clearly did not speak with one voice; it is understandable that the Coalition wondered whom to believe. But at the same time, the Coalition – particularly through their consultants on the scene in Washington – should have cleared up any misconception about the loan limit before submitting their UDAG proposal.

EDA, the agency that turned down the Coalition proposal, became cast in the role of the "bad guys." Paradoxically, it was the federal agency that acted with the most integrity.

Unanswered questions. As the Coalition project came to an end in April 1979, two questions were left unanswered.

Would community–worker ownership have provided a workable corporate structure for a reopened Campbell Works? As a matter of fact, the community–worker ownership model devised by the Coalition and consultants was never tested. The proposal simply never got far enough for serious discussion on this point.

Could the Campbell Works have been reopened with a better plan? In hindsight, it is clear that the early planning started at the wrong end of the steel-production process. The "front end" – the blast furnaces and the open hearths – were the weakest links. Only as planning concentrated on the "back end" – the rolling mills – did the project begin to gain feasibility. But time ran out before a realistic and workable plan could be put in place.

Ed Stanton said once that he would go to his grave wondering what might have been accomplished with the right set of numbers. He did.

Beginning Anew

In one sense, it is clear that the Ecumenical Coalition of the Mahoning Valley was a failure. The Campbell Works never produced steel again. The old buildings continued to rust. People moved away in search of work. Finally it was suggested that the old mill and its smokestacks be torn down just to clear the sky, to empty the mute reminder on the horizon of a way of life that was gone.

The Youngstown Coalition experience, however, was a kind of

seminal event in the 1970s, which has sprouted new shoots in the 1980s:

- Bishop Malone became president of the National Conference of Catholic Bishops. During his administration the bishops have developed a path-breaking pastoral letter on the American economy, *Economic Justice for All* (1986).
- Charles Rawlings took the struggle for corporate responsibility and economic justice to the regional level, with his work in the Tri-State Conference on Steel. That organization developed a proposal for a Steel Valley Authority – a kind of TVA for steel – to save and revitalize the industry in the Pittsburgh area.
- Bishop John Burt helped sponsor the Great Lakes–Appalachian Conference on the Economic Crisis, which has developed state-level organizations dealing with unemployment throughout the Midwest.
- Staughton Lynd worked with steelworkers Ed Mann, Gerald Dickey, Duane Irving, and others on the next rounds of steel shutdowns in Youngstown. Following an opening statement by Ramsey Clark, he represented the steelworkers in a suit against U.S. Steel, asking that the corporation either be required to keep its Youngstown works open or be willing to sell the mill to the steelworkers (Lynd 1982).
- In the Chicago area, a Calumet Community Religious Conference emerged in response to the shutdown of the Wisconsin Steel mill and U.S. Steel's South Works, as well as the steel layoffs and job terminations in the Gary–Hammond area (Bensman and Lynch 1987).
- Gar Alperovitz has continued in his role as a preeminent "public relations economist," publishing with Jeff Faux the 1984 book *Rebuilding America: A Blueprint for the New Economy*. He continues to link economic criticism with religious values – for example, the piece in *Sojourners*, "Economics: Putting a Value on Values" (Alperovitz 1985).
- In Weirton, West Virginia, steelworkers bought the National Steel Corporation mill that provided the town's economic base, to become the largest company in the United States entirely owned by its employees. In spite of steel shutdowns elsewhere, Wierton has been successful. In March 1986, workers received their first profit-sharing checks, funneling $20,345,000 into the community. "Much of the thanks went to the employees themselves, who have played an increased role in the management of the plant" (*New York Times*, March 14, 1986).

A simple dismissal of the Coalition as a failed effort may focus too narrowly on one set of events and miss the big picture. A criterion for judging the Coalition was suggested at Notre Dame University in October 1978. Bill Sullivan, who continued – unofficially – to help his friend Ed Stanton with the Coalition effort, told the Catholic Committee on Urban Ministry:

Let me leave you with one thought. When you judge the importance of what went on in Youngstown, don't look to see if there are 5,000 people at the Campbell Works. If there are not, it doesn't mean we've failed. If other issues are being raised, if we are pursuing these other issues, if we are beginning to bring home the moral issues, if we are beginning to make government and corporations act responsibly, we haven't failed. And if we put them back to work, and it ends there, and we don't raise the other questions, I don't know that any of us could say that we've succeeded.

CHAPTER X

Epilogue

As this story comes to its end, post mortem accomplished, I am reminded once again why I undertook this study in the first place. I came not to bury the Coalition, but to praise it.

The Right Task...

The most fundamental judgment about the Coalition that emerges from this study is that the task the religious leaders set for themselves was the right thing to do. They identified and dealt with the problem as the revitalization of the steel industry in Youngstown, for the benefit of steelworkers and the community. That, to my mind, remains a correct definition of the problem. It presented a challenge no other group in Youngstown at the time was prepared to accept.

It is not certain — nor did the failure of the Coalition's effort prove — that the Campbell Works could ever have been successfully reopened.

In terms of the Coalition project itself, it is possible to argue that six specific and rather plausible changes in organizational and political behavior could have given the project a far better chance of success.

First, the Coalition itself might have done a better job in two areas. It might have recognized the need for better steel expertise in its decision-making structure and made a place for that function at the table much earlier in the process. Also, the Coalition might have done a better job of melding the social passion of Chuck Rawlings with the hardheaded pragmatism of Ed Stanton. Neither of these tasks could be called impossible.

Second, Gar Alperovitz and the National Center for Economic Alternatives could have done a better job on the economic side of the planning. In addition, they could have represented the Coalition more effectively with the federal agencies involved in the Youngstown project.

Third, the kind of expertise provided by Frank McGough and John Stone might have been utilized earlier in the project. McGough wrote the Interfaith Center for Corporate Responsibility in July 1978 to volunteer his services; his letter went unanswered for six months. In Youngstown, a better effort could have been made to include Bill Sullivan in the project and to solicit the help of retired or resigned steel executives such as John Stone and Tom Cleary.

Fourth, the Youngstown civic and business community might have seen the Coalition project as an integral part of a balanced economic development effort, instead of as a threat to their own position and competition for their own agendas. It is clear that Youngstown needed to diversify its economic base. It can also be argued that the diversification strategy would have been more successful if it could have been based on a vital – even if contracting – steel industry.

Fifth, the federal government might have acted more responsibly. The Carter administration could have done two things differently. It might have accepted the Solomon recommendation to provide $1 billion in steel loan guarantees, the money for which was actually available. By providing half that amount, the Carter administration ensured that not enough money was available to implement its policy of assistance to steel revitalization. Washington also might have done a better job of policy coordination; the lack of communication between HUD and the EDA served no one.

Sixth, Lloyd McBride and other officials of the United Steelworkers might have risen above union politics to put aside (or at least investigate) their suspicions of Staughton Lynd. McBride should have come to Youngstown within the week of the shutdown announcement. He should have pledged United Steelworker support for any effort at steel retention. He should have sent his assistant, Jim Smith, to coordinate strategy among the locals, the district, and international headquarters. And he should have pledged the organizing resources of the union to support the Coalition effort. Eventually, McBride did begin to make these efforts. Had they been initiated at the beginning of the Coalition project, they might have accomplished something.

In short, if some, or even all, of these six rather reasonable expectations had been realized, the Coalition story might well have ended differently.

. . . Ahead of Its Time

The Youngstown Coalition were pioneers in uncharted territory. Ten years after the Campbell Works shutdown, it is easy to forget how much the landscape of community economic and industrial development has been filled in with new pathways and new structures.

Local communities have learned – many the hard way – that their economic future cannot be taken for granted. In the face of the rapid shifts in the American economy in the 1970s and early 1980s, economic development organizations at the local level have sprouted faster than mushrooms. A 1981 study began with the following estimate: "There are about 15,000 organizations in the United States devoted to the promotion of local economic growth, and their number appears to be increasing rapidly" (Levy 1981: 1). By the mid-1980s, some of those organizations had developed experience. A three-day conference in 1986 entitled "Housing and Economic Development: State, Local and Grass-roots Initiatives" shared experiences and even some success stories from such new organizations as the Massachusetts Commission on Mature Industries and the Western New York Economic Development Corporation. (The plenary opening speech at the conference was given by Gar Alperovitz.)

The Ecumenical Coalition of the Mahoning Valley came too early in this development to profit from the accumulation of experience that is now available. The Coalition did register the point – in somewhat dramatic terms – that a local community such as Youngstown cannot afford to be passive about its economic future.

The role of the federal government with regard to disinvestment in manufacturing industries in 1977 was both uncertain and inchoative. Twelve years later, little has changed. Calls for a cohesive national industrial policy have become more frequent through the 1980s (e.g., Magaziner and Reich 1982; Johnson 1984). In the meantime, the United States has become the world's largest debtor, purchasing more and more of its steel, autos, and electronics from abroad.

To their credit, the Coalition and Gar Alperovitz succeeded at least in raising the issue with the federal government that investment in industrial revitalization was preferable to unemployment benefits. In the Campbell Works case, the government agreed with the Coalition on the principle, but not on the price tag. The one outstanding success story – the federal loan to prevent the collapse of the Chrysler Corporation – came later than the Campbell Works efforts.

In the late 1970s and early 1980s, it was fashionable to tout the secular shift from manufacturing to service industries as both inevitable and – in the long run – profitable for the country as a whole. The late 1980s are producing a second opinion. For example, the study *Manufacturing Matters* argues that the post-industrial economy is a myth (Cohen and Zysman 1987). The authors point out that high-tech services (such as engineering and design) are inextricably linked to the manufacturing process. To lose manufacturing will mean the loss of the most important and wealth-producing sectors of the service economy as well.

The Ecumenical Coalition was not in a position to articulate this type of macrolevel argument. But twelve years later, their intuition about what was good for the economy is beginning to look more respectable.

The Coalition project was also ahead of its time in claiming that an industry in which workers had a direct responsibility in operations would work more efficiently than an industry without worker involvement. Shortly after the failure of the Campbell Works project, it became apparent that American corporate management needed to go to school in Japan. The phenomena of American executives touring Japanese manufacturing plants and the import of the Japanese approach to worker involvement became a trend in the 1980s.

A new interest in various forms of worker participation in ownership also emerged in the 1980s – from stock option plans to outright ownership. With the end of the Coalition project, it remained for steelworkers in Weirton, West Virginia, to set up the largest company in the United States owned entirely by its employees. With the threatened shutdown of the National Steel Corporation mill that provided the town's economic base, workers and management implemented a successful buyout.

The Weirton Steel example marks the beginning of a trend toward employee-leveraged buyouts; the number of firms controlled by employee stock option plans tripled from 1980 to 1987. Worker-owned enterprises that can be counted as success stories include both service companies (such as Avis car rental) and industrial firms (such as Oregon Steel Mills Inc. and Cain Chemical). Oregon Steel Mills, acquired by workers in 1983, cut the labor input per ton of steel shipped from 9.3 man-hours to 3.4 man-hours and increased the market value of the company more than six times the 1983 level (Miller 1988).

Religion and the Economy

There is a proper role for religion in the management of an economy. As Youngstown illustrates, one entry point for religion is the question of norms: What is right or wrong? Are the economic decisions about who wins and who loses characterized by fairness? Are all parties to the decision recognized and accounted for equitably? What can be done to redress any wrong and prevent it from happening again?[1]

These fundamental ethical questions may or may not be addressed within the legal system and policy structures. In Youngstown, there was a strong sense that such channels had failed and that the religious sector – by default – was left the task not only of articulating the normative discussion but of taking the lead in any action. The task turned out to be far heavier and lasted much longer than the religious leaders first imagined.

The action by the religious coalition in Youngstown took place at three analytically different, and increasingly complex, levels.

1. The Coalition entered the public arena by declaring and naming the *wrong* that had been done to Youngstown workers and community. Their first word, in effect, was a "Thou shalt not . . ." directed to the people and the system that created the sudden shutdown. It was a stance consistent with, and to some extent modeled on, the prophetic tradition in the Bible. Regardless of the complex causes, they asserted, people should not be treated this way. Responsibility demanded that the injury to the community be publicly acknowledged.

2. The Coalition took a significant further step in declaring what was *right*, namely, the reemployment of the same workers laid off by the shutdown. Although in reality the Coalition stated this sentence almost in the same breath as the first, it is analytical-

ly a more complex proposition. It includes a range of circum-stances that call for discrimination and judgement. Should all the workers be rehired, or only those not covered by substantial benefits? Should they be rehired at the same steel jobs, or re-trained for other work? And so on. Each statement at this level raises a new set of questions, more and more intrinsically related to the parameters of concrete possibility.

3. The Coalition went still further in developing an *action program*, including the concrete objective of reopening the Campbell Works, with the strategies of worker–community own-ership and federal grants and loan guarantees. The choices and decisions at this level were more tentative still, based on the options that were understood to be available at the time.

The important contribution of the Coalition to the story of religion and economic affairs in the United States was its attempt to enter the arena of industrial production in order to provide jobs for unemployed workers and stability for an economically injured community. The Coalition went beyond sermons and pastoral letter and prayer services to negotiate with government and corporation on the workers' behalf. The Coalition did more than ask for social services for the laid-off workers. It dared to sponsor a specific business enterprise, targeted directly at the problems created by the plant closing. This was a new field of action for church-sponsored activity.

Religion and Public Affairs

In the Youngstown experiment, the Coalition found itself cop-ing with three problems endemic to public action by a religious group.

First was the problem of certitude. The religious leaders could feel quite confident about their statements at the first level – what *should not be*. But the confidence level and the ability to compel assent necessarily became more tentative as they moved on to fix a definite goal (reemployment), objective (mill reopening), and strategies. The Coalition did occasionally evidence some "creep-ing moral certitude," the tendency to talk with the same confi-dence at the third level as at the first. For instance, when the Coalition sounded as though it were staking a moral claim on $300 million in federal loan guarantees (instead of submitting a proposal), it may have succumbed to this temptation.

Second was the problem of communication, both internally and externally. The grammar and syntax of moral principle were a different language from the shoptalk of steelmaking and finance. The Coalition bumped into this obstacle in its own staff meetings, as well as in its dealing with government officials and others. Gar Alperovitz, perhaps more than any other, was able to speak the languages of economics and moral principle. In its more broad-brush public communications, the Coalition did a good job of communicating its message. It was at the planning and negotiating tables that communication sometimes faltered.

Third was the problem of power. The Coalition's purpose was to bring justice to people and a community that had been wronged. The religious leaders really had no political base other than the power of their appeal itself. They invited, but made no attempt to compel, support from their denominational membership. They were clearly aware that their program to reopen the Campbell Works, though founded on the highest moral motivation, nevertheless had to meet standards of business acumen and technical productivity.

The Coalition tried to maintain a style of action appropriate to its religious identity and to the tentative character of its program. On the one hand, it wanted to be aggressive enough to be a serious player in the worlds of politics and finance. On the other hand, the Coalition could not abuse its religious position by acting as just another power broker. The Coalition was not timid. It took control of the response to the shutdown, it challenged both government and corporate leaders, it took the case to the public, it even – one time – took to the streets. But the Coalition also demonstrated restraint and judiciousness. Its tone and rhetoric usually came back to a style of invitation and persuasion rather than force.

In its handling of the three problems of certitude, communication, and power, the Coalition wrote a valuable chapter for future efforts in religion and public affairs to study and to learn from.

Notes

Introduction

1 Youngstown Sheet and Tube Company owned two steel mills in the Youngstown area: the Campbell Works (actually located in the suburb of Campbell) and the Brier Hill Works (in Youngstown). One portion of the Campbell Works, the seamless tube mill manufacturing pipe for oil drilling, remained in operation.

2 In their study of signs of economic democracy and community power, Carnoy and Shearer (1980) interpreted the Coalition effort in Youngstown as one of the events in the 1970s "which gave at least some promise of progressive political change in the 1980s and 1990s" (358, 360–1).

Chapter I. Steeltown

1 Some of the old stone blast furnaces, dating as early as 1832, can still be found standing in the woods of western Pennsylvania. One of the best preserved, the Victory Furnace in Venango County (not far from Youngstown), is 23 feet across at the base and stands 35 feet high (Youngstown *Vindicator*, November 26, 1979).

2 The author was told this story by several long-time Youngstown residents. It appeared in print in an article by the veteran business editor of the Youngstown *Vindicator*, George Reiss.

3 The relationship between Sullivan and Stanton had an interesting origin. When Sullivan was running as the Republican candidate for mayor of Warren, he solicited Stanton's support. Over lunch, Stanton told Sullivan that, although he liked him personally, Stanton's support was already committed to the Democratic candidate. Moreover, Stanton told Sullivan he would lose the election, which indeed he did. Sullivan was impressed with Stanton's candor. He determined to involve Stanton in his efforts to shore up the Valley's economy, and the two men became close personal friends.

Chapter II. The Industry

1 The following sketch of the American steel industry in the late 1970s draws in particular on the following sources: Hogan (1971, 1972, 1977, 1983); Bari (1977); American Iron and Steel Institute (1980); Office of Technology Assessment, U.S. Congress (1980); Comptroller General of the United States (1981); Schorsch (1983); Scheuerman (1986); and Borrus (1983).

2 The timing of expansion in the steel industry was one factor; American steel capacity saw its significant expansion in the 1950s, whereas the Japanese and European expansion began in the 1960s. It has also been argued that more than an accident of historical timing was involved, that American steel management has been irresponsibly lethargic in investing in newer steel technology, preferring to use capital for corporate acquisitions outside the steel industry. For example, see Magaziner and Reich (1982) and Metzgar (1983).

3 The quotation is from the report of the Office of Technology Assessment (1980: 16). A survey by the Comptroller General (1981: ch. 2) of steel capacity forecasts found steel experts predicting a shortfall between 1985 and 1990.

4 A plan for building a "greenfield" plant on a "brownfield" site was developed for U.S. Steel's Youngstown Works by its superintendent Bill Kirwan, just before the decision by U.S. Steel to close the mill, announced on November 27, 1979. The plan was made public during the trial of a civil suit filed by United Steelworkers Local 1330 against U.S. Steel. Within company circles, Kirwan argued that modernization of the Youngstown Works could proceed without interrupting existing production lines and that it would be a more desirable alternative to simply closing the plant. Kirwan's plan was ultimately ignored (Lynd 1982: 169–72).

5 Based on a personal interview with John Stone, who was vice-president, Operations, of Youngstown Sheet and Tube Company at the time of the shutdown. Mr. Stone had been plant superintendent at Indiana Harbor. The interview was conducted on April 6, 1979, after his retirement from the company.

6 See also Kelly and Schutes (1978).

7 The quotation from Lambeth was reported in the Warren *Tribune Chronicle*, September 21, 1977. Company documents filed with the Department of Justice in 1978 in the petition for merger with LTV substantiate the statement.

Chapter III. Shutdown

1 Other studies documenting the relative lack of mobility of blue-collar workers, whether for economic or for psychological reasons, include the following: Mann (1973); Gordon and McCorry (1957); Smith and Fowler (1964); Whitman and Schmidt (1966).

2 In a study of the social response to natural disasters, Wenger (1978: 24) found that the "complex interplay between the measurement of this natural event and the measurement of its human consequences has always complicated estimates of the impact of disasters on communities. The physical side and the human side are two interlocking pieces of the larger puzzle."

Chapter IV. Coping with Crisis

1 The Sadlowski challenge in the context of rank-and-file protest has been studied by Nyden (1984).

2 The antipathy toward Staughton Lynd on the part of union officials was confirmed in the author's interview with James Smith, assistant to USWA President McBride, January 10, 1980.

3 This proposal had languished in EDA's Chicago office. Since it had not been acted upon before the shutdown occurred, the proposal was redrawn to set up a $1 million revolving loan fund to aid small businesses hurt in the economic crisis. This proposal was eventually funded and placed under WREDA administration.

4 An anecdote indicates that some officials in Youngstown continued to use Sullivan as a Washington link. In November, a Japanese manufacturing representative appeared in Youngstown, with the story that he had a contact in Japan interested in buying the Campbell Works. The publisher of the *Vindicator*, Mayor Jack Hunter, and other civic officials held a hasty Sunday meeting to decide who should constitute a mission to Japan. On Monday, Mayor Hunter asked Bill Sullivan, who was making a trip to Washington, to obtain passports for the Youngstown contingent. Sullivan in the meantime contacted Senator Glenn, who phoned Ambassador Mansfield to check on the supposed investor. The Japanese contact turned out to be a small appliance manufacturer worth only about $5 million. Plans for the trip were quickly canceled. The story released in Youngstown was that the trip had been canceled by the State Department.

5 Several months after writing the Coalition pastoral, Carr moved on to become national director of the White House Conference on the Family.

Chapter V. Religion and Urban Economic Crisis

1 Several themes from this document would be echoed in the pastoral letter of the Youngstown Coalition:

Opportunities to work must be provided for those who are able and willing to work. Every person has the right to useful employment, to just wages, and to adequate assistance in case of real need. (no. 5)

Economic development must not be left to the sole judgment of a few persons or groups possessing excessive economic power, or to the political community alone. On the contrary, at every level the largest possible number of people should have an active share in directing that development. (no. 5)

Government must play a role in the economic activity of its citizens. Indeed, it should promote in a suitable manner the production of a sufficient supply of material goods. Moreover, it should safeguard the rights of all citizens, and help them find opportunities for employment. (no. 5)

In our society, persons without a job lose a key measure of their place in society and a source of individual fulfillment; they often feel there is no productive role for them. . . . Unemployment frequently leads to higher rates of crime, drug addiction, and alcoholism. It is reflected in higher rates of mental illness as well as rising social tensions. (no. 11)

As a society, we cannot accept the notion that some will have jobs and others will be told to wait a few years and to subsist on welfare in the interim. For work is more than a way to earn a living. It represents a deep human need, desired not only for income but also for the sense of worth which it provides the individual. (no. 13)

2 The theory as well as the practical aspects of the program are reported by Bay and Campbell (1979). The account here draws both on the thesis and on interviews with Robert Campbell.

Chapter VI. Launching a Movement

1 Lynd had been working quietly for the last year in Youngstown with a local labor law firm. He was "discovered" in Youngstown partly as a result of a *New York Times* article that appeared in August 1977. His reputation as a "radical" (a strong word in Youngstown) was beginning to surface. The son of sociologists Robert and Helen Lynd, Staughton's academic training was in history. Lynd early became a socialist and lived for a time in a socialist community. He also became a social activist, serving as director of freedom schools in the Mississippi Summer Project of 1964 and as chair of the first march against the Vietnam War in Washington, D.C., in April 1965. With president of Students for a Democratic Society Tom Hayden, he visited Hanoi during the height of the war. Lynd left his history professor's post at Yale University to study law at the University of Chicago. While pursuing his law degree, he became active in community organizing in the Calumet area (the steel region along the Illinois–Indiana state line) and became an adviser and assistant to Ed Sadlowski's campaign against Lloyd McBride for the presidency of the United Steelworkers. Through that campaign, Lynd became acquainted with Ed Mann, president of the Brier Hill steelworkers local and a Sadlowski supporter; Mann subsequently invited Lynd to come to Youngstown as lawyer for his local union. While the Coalition effort was in progress, Lynd left the private law firm where he was associated to take a position with the Youngstown legal aid office.

2 For example, Thomas M. Gannon, S. J., chair of the Sociology Department at Loyola University of Chicago and president of the Association for the Sociology of Religion, wrote to President Carter on October 6, 1978:

I have been following with great interest the activities of the Youngstown Ecumenical Coalition to reopen the closed steelmill in that city. These activities are most important, in my judgment, because parliamentary democracies like our own will be able to survive only if their local parts – their more intimate circles – relate to and assume responsibility for the movements of the larger society.

I strongly urge you, therefore, to give your active support to the proposal of this Coalition. The Coalition's efforts so far have provided leadership in countering the threat of urban decay and the destruction of a long-standing and productive community. Their efforts also give inspiration to other citizens in the nation, encouraging them to responsible action.

His letter (and others like it) received a polite but noncommittal reply from Jack Watson, assistant to the president.

3 There were 3,484,991 shares voted in favor of the resolution and 2,707,836 voted against; 7.8 million shares were not voted (Youngstown *Vindicator*, December 6, 1978).

Chapter VII. The Plan

1 One such claim was made in October 1978. Bill Sferra, president of the Campbell steelworkers local, wrote to Stanton that two machinists had been called to work at 7:00 on a Saturday evening and given the job of removing a pedestal hoist from the no. 3 blast furnace so that it could be shipped to the Sheet and Tube plant at Indiana Harbor. Sferra wrote: "The #3 Blast Furnace cannot operate without a pedestal hoist, indicating that Lykes is definitely stripping the mill. Of the three Hot Strip cranes which have been in prior use, there is only one remaining. The other two cranes, as well as the conveyor line, have been removed."

2 Carney's judgment seems to have been based on Beetle's conclusions that a full-scale reopening would cost $535 million, close to a rough figure named by company president Jennings Lambeth. The report, however, provides far more useful information than simply a total cost figure. It remains the only piece of financial analysis actually making use of Sheet and Tube company records.

3 Several of the research papers commissioned for the Youngstown project were subsequently published.

4 "The federal costs will total between $45.6 and $51.1 million. State of Ohio costs will range between $6.9 and $9.7 million. The county and local governments will lose between $1.1 and $1.3 million, and $7.4 and $7.8 million, respectively" (Franz-Goldman 1978: 6).

5 After leaving the Coalition staff in August 1978, John Greenman became a reporter for the Warren *Tribune Chronicle*. He conducted an investigation into the Lykes–LTV merger and wrote a series of articles published December 9–14, 1978. This section draws on Greenman's reports.

6 Hogan had questions about the economic feasibility of reopening the Campbell Works, but as a courtesy to the efforts of fellow religious professionals, he refrained from any specific public comment on the Campbell Works project, saying simply that he had not had access to "the numbers." The American Iron and Steel Institute did ask Hogan to do an analysis of the NCEA report, an invitation that Hogan declined.

In March 1979, Hogan made some general remarks at a steel conference in Cleveland about the problem of outdated steel facilities. George Riess, the business editor of the Youngstown *Vindicator*, interpreted Hogan's remarks as an attack on the Youngstown Coalition. The headline for Reiss's article sharpened the note of attack: "'Steel Priest' Lambasts Efforts to Keep Obsolete Mills Alive" (Youngstown *Vindicator*, March 27, 1979). Hogan, speaking at a dinner near Youngstown the following evening, insisted that he had been misquoted and said so on a radio interview. But the newspaper report only strengthened already antagonistic feelings about Hogan. Responding to the report at a conference in Pittsburgh, Rawlings said that Hogan "seemed to speak from an incestuous relationship with the steel industry" (Youngstown *Vindicator*, March 28, 1979) and implied that the priest was linked with industry efforts to torpedo the Coalition's project. The unfortunate exchange in print is reported here not simply for its anecdotal value, but to underscore the suspicions of Hogan that existed within the "movement" side of the Coalition.

7 Although provisions for directed government purchases of steel from a reopened Campbell Works disappeared from final versions of the plan, the final report summary continued to insist on its role in the overall strategy. A footnote argues:

It is particularly important that a thorough review of the government's procurement strategies be immediately undertaken. The President's decision on March 27 to "target" procurement to distressed areas, together with the Executive Orders to this effect issued on August 16, form a general basis for one line of strategy. The use of procurement to help in the anti-inflation effort is a second basis. It is clear from staff discussions that a sophisticated use of procurement to achieve broad public policy goals has been gaining increasing force in Washington. (64)

Chapter VIII. Negotiations

1 Stanton was able to make arrangements for two private planes, one leaving from Cleveland, the other from Youngstown. The Youngstown plane was borrowed from Stanton's friend, Republican businessman William Lyden (actually without Lyden's knowledge – he was out of town on business). It was dubbed a "Democratic" plane in the press, a cause of some embarrassment to Lyden (who was happy to have the plane be used for this purpose).

Chapter IX. Ending, Learning, Beginning Anew

1 The occasion was a colloquy on the church's social mission sponsored by the U.S. Bishops Committee on Doctrine and the Joint Committee of Catholic Learned Societies and Scholars, held September 24–6, 1981, in Washington, D.C.

Chapter X. Epilogue

1 J. Bryan Hehir (1988) argues that the need for ethical debate about some policy issues emerges from their inherent moral complexity. Religion, as one source of moral wisdom in society, rightfully has a voice in public debate about what a society *should* do.

References

ABC-TV documentary. 1978. "The Fight Against Black Monday." Distributed by McGraw-Hill Films.

Abell, Aaron I. 1968. *American Catholic Thought on Social Questions*. Indianapolis, Ind.: Bobbs-Merrill.

Ahlstrom, Sidney. 1972. *A Religious History of the American People*. New Haven, Conn.: Yale University Press.

Aiken, Michael T., Louis A. Ferman, and Harold L. Sheppard. 1968. *Economic Failure, Alienation, and Extremism*. Ann Arbor: University of Michigan Press.

Aley, Howard C. 1975. *A Heritage to Share*. Youngstown, Ohio: Bicentennial Commission of Youngstown and Mahoning County.

Alperovitz, Gar. 1985. "Economics: Putting a Value on Values." *Sojourners* (November): 18–22.

  1974. "Notes toward a Pluralist Commonwealth." In *Exloring Contradictions: Political Economy in the Corporate State*, 205–32. Edited by Philip Brenner, Robert Borosage, and Bethany Weidner. New York: McKay.

Alperovitz, Gar, and Jeff Faux. 1984. *Rebuilding America: A Blueprint for the New Economy*. New York: Pantheon.

American Iron and Steel Institute. 1980. *Steel at the Crossroads: The American Steel Industry in the 1980s*. Washington, D.C.: American Iron and Steel Institute.

Bari, Richard S. 1977. *Steel: An Industry in Flux*. New York: Argus Research Corporation.

Barnet, Richard. 1974. *Global Reach*. New York: Simon & Schuster.

Barnett, Donald, and Louis M. Schorsch. 1983. *Steel: Upheaval in a Basic Industry*. Cambridge, Mass.: Ballinger.

Bay, Eugene C., and Robert J. Campbell. 1979. "The Revitalization of First Presbyterian Church, Youngstown, Ohio." Unpublished D. Min. thesis. McCormick Theological Seminary, Chicago.

Beecher, Henry Ward. 1869. "Sphere of the Christian Minister, 1869." In *The Church and the City: 1865–1910*, 154–81. Edited by Robert D. Cross. Indianapolis, Ind.: Bobbs-Merrill, 1967.

295

Beetle, George. 1978. "Preliminary Planning of a Unit Train Service Demonstration Project for Movement of Taconite Pellets from Lake Erie to the Mahoning Valley." Niles, Ohio: Western Reserve Economic Development Agency.

———. 1977. "New Steel at Campbell: A Study of the Feasibility of Reopening the Campbell Works." Niles, Ohio: Western Reserve Economic Development Agency; Youngstown, Ohio: Ecumenical Coalition of the Mahoning Valley.

Bensman, David, and Robert Lynch. 1987. *Rusted Dreams: Hard Times in a Steel Community*. New York: McGraw-Hill.

Berger, Peter, and Richard John Neuhaus. 1977. *To Empower People: The Role of Mediating Structures and Public Policy*. Washington, D.C.: American Enterprise Institute.

Bluestone, Barry, and Bennett Harrison. 1982. *The Deindustrialization of America: Plant Closings, Community Abandonment, and the Dismantling of Basic Industry*. New York: Basic Books.

Blumer, Herbert. (1951). "Social Movements." In *Studies in Social Movements*, 8–29. Edited by Barry McLaughlin. New York: Free Press, 1969.

Borrus, Michael. 1983. "The Politics of Competitive Erosion in the U.S. Steel Industry." In *American Industry in International Competition*, 60–105. Edited by John Zysman and Laura Tyson. Ithaca, N.Y.: Cornell University Press.

Brenner, Harvey. 1976. *Estimating the Social Costs of Economic Policy: Implications for Mental and Physical Health, and Criminal Aggression*. A Study Prepared for the Joint Economic Committee of Congress. Washington, D.C.: U.S. Government Printing Office.

Buss, Terry F., and F. Stevens Redburn. 1983. *Shutdown at Youngstown: Public Policy for Mass Unemployment*. Albany: State University of New York Press.

Carnoy, Martin, and Derek Shearer. 1980. *Economic Democracy: The Challenge of the 1980s*. White Plains, N.Y.: Sharpe.

Carter, Paul A. 1956. *The Decline and Revival of the Social Gospel, 1920–1940*. Ithaca N.Y.: Cornell University Press.

Catholic Bishops, National Conference of. 1986. *Economic Justice for All: Pastoral Letter on Catholic Social Teaching and the U.S. Economy*. Washington, D.C.: United States Catholic Conference.

Catholic Bishops' Synod. 1971. "Justice in the World." In *Justice in the Marketplace, Collected Statements of the Vatican and the U.S. Catholic Bishops on Economic Policy, 1891–1984*, 249–63. Edited by David M. Byers. Washington, D.C.: United States Catholic Conference, 1985.

Catholic Bishops of the United States. 1975. "The Economy: Human Dimension," a statement issued by the Catholic Bishops of the United States. In *Justice in the Marketplace, Collected Statements of the Vatican and the U.S. Catholic Bishops on Economic Policy, 1891–1984*, 469–75. Edited by David M. Byers. Washington, D.C.: United States Catholic Conference, 1985.

———. 1970. "Resolution on the Campaign for Human Development," a resolution adopted by the National Conference of Catholic Bishops. In *Justice in the Marketplace, Collected Statements of the Vatican and the U.S. Catholic*

Bishops on Economic Policy, 1891–1984, 467–8. Edited by David M. Byers. Washington, D.C.: United States Catholic Conference, 1985.

1933. "Present Crisis," issued with the authorization of the American Hierarchy. In *Justice in the Marketplace, Collected Statements of the Vatican and the U.S. Catholic Bishops on Economic Policy, 1891–1984*, 398–420. Edited by David M. Byers. Washington, D.C.: United States Catholic Conference, 1985.

1930. "Statement on Unemployment," issued by the Administrative Board of the National Catholic Welfare Conference. In *Justice in the Marketplace, Collected Statements of the Vatican and the U.S. Catholic Bishops on Economic Policy, 1891–1984*, 393–5. Edited by David M. Byers. Washington, D.C.: United States Catholic Conference, 1985.

1919. "Program of Social Reconstruction," issued by the Administrative Committee of the National Catholic War Council. In *Justice in the Marketplace, Collected Statements of the Vatican and the U.S. Catholic Bishops on Economic Policy, 1891–1984*, 367–83. Edited by David M. Byers. Washington, D.C.: United States Catholic Conference, 1985.

Cobb, Sidney, and Stanislav V. Kasl. 1977. *Termination: The Consequences of Job Loss*. Washington, D.C.: U.S. Department of Health, Education, and Welfare, National Institute for Occupational Safety and Health.

Cohen, Stephen S., and John Zysman. 1987. *Manufacturing Matters: The Myth of the Post-Industrial Economy*. New York: Basic Books.

Community Steel, Inc., City of Youngstown, Ohio. 1979. Application for Urban Development Action Grant. Youngstown, Ohio, January 29.

Comptroller General of the United States. 1981. *New Strategy Required for Aiding Distressed Steel Industry*. Washington, D.C.: U.S. Government Printing Office.

1979. *U.S. Administration of the Anti-Dumping Act of 1921*. Washington, D.C.: U.S. Government Printing Office.

Cross, Robert D. 1967. *The Church and the City: 1865–1910*. Indianapolis, Ind.: Bobbs-Merrill.

Dewan, Brad, and Karl Frieden. 1978. "Recommendations of Worker–Community Ownership Structure for Reopened Campbell Works." In *Youngstown Demonstration Planning Project Final Report*. Washington, D.C.: National Center for Economic Alternatives.

Douglass, Harlan Paul. 1927. *The Church in the Changing City*. New York: Doran.

DuBois, Tom. 1983. "The Myth of the $26-an-Hour Steelworker." *Labor Research Review* 1 (Winter): 52–3.

Dulles, Avery. 1975. Remarks at the conference "Liberty and Justice for All," National Conference of Catholic Bishops. Washington, D.C., February 3–5.

Dynes, Russell R. 1978. "Interorganizational Relations in Communities Under Stress." In *Disasters: Theory and Research*, 49–64. Edited by E. L. Quarantelli. Beverly Hills, Calif.: Sage.

Earle, John R., Dean D. Knudsen, and Donald W. Shriver, Jr. 1976. *Spindles and Spires*. Atlanta, Ga.: John Knox Press.

Ernst and Ernst Management Consulting Services. 1973. "Economic Impact of

Water Pollution Controls on the Mahoning River Valley." Niles, Ohio: Western Reserve Economic Development Agency.

Fainstein, Norman I., and Susan S. Fainstein. 1974. *Urban Political Movements: The Search for Power by Minority Groups in American Cities*. Englewood Cliffs, N.J.: Prentice-Hall.

Ferman, Louis A., and Michael T. Aiken. 1964. "The Adjustment of Older Workers to Job Displacement." In *Blue-Collar World: Studies of the American Worker*, 485–90. Edited by Arthur B. Shostack and William Gomberg. Englewood Cliffs, N.J.: Prentice-Hall.

Foltman, Felician M. 1968. *White and Blue Collars in a Mill Shutdown*. Ithaca N.Y.: Cornell University Press.

Forrest, Thomas E. 1978. "Group Emergence in Disasters." In *Disasters: Theory and Research*, 105–205. Edited by E. L. Quarantelli. Beverly Hills, Calif.: Sage.

Franz-Goldman, Christine. 1978. "Socioeconomic Costs and Benefits of the Community–Worker Plan to the Youngstown–Warren SMSA." In *Youngstown Demonstration Planning Project: Final Report*. Washington, D.C.: National Center for Economic Alternatives.

Frieden, Karl. 1978. "The Effect of Workers' Ownership and Workers' Participation on Productivity." In *Youngstown Demonstration Planning Project: Final Report*. Washington, D.C.: National Center for Economic Alternatives.

Friesema, H. Paul, and Robert Lineberry. 1979. *Aftermath: Communities After Natural Disasters*. Beverly Hills, Calif.: Sage.

Galida, Florence. 1976. *Fascinating History of the City of Campbell*. State College, Pa: Josten's American Yearbook.

Gannon, Thomas M. 1978. "Religious Tradition and Urban Community." *Sociological Analysis* 39 (Winter): 283–302.

Gordon, Margaret S., and Ann H. McCorry. 1957. "Plant Relocation and Job Security." *Industrial and Labor Relations Review* 2 (October): 13–16.

Greenman, John. 1979. "The Merger Puzzle." Warren (Ohio) *Tribune Chronicle*, December 9–15.

Hardin, Russell. 1982. *Collective Action*. Baltimore Md.: Johns Hopkins University Press.

Hehir, J. Bryan. 1988. "The Consistent Ethic: Public Policy Implications." In *Consistent Ethic of Life*. 218–36. Edited by Thomas G. Fuechtmann. Kansas City, Mo.: Sheed and Ward.

Hogan, William T. 1983. *World Steel in the 1980s: A Case of Survival*. Lexington, Mass.: Heath.

———. 1978. "The Feasibility of a Proposed Joint-Venture Iron-Making Facility in the Youngstown Area." New York: Industrial Economics Research Institute of Fordham University.

———. 1977. "Steel in Crisis." Niles, Ohio: Steel Communities Coalition.

———. 1972. *The 1970s: Critical Years for Steel*. Lexington, Mass.: Heath.

———. 1971. *The Economic History of the Iron and Steel Industry in the United States*, 5 vols. Lexington, Mass. Heath.

Ingham, John. 1978. *The Iron Barons; A Social Analysis of an American Elite, 1874–1965*. Westport, Conn.: Greenwood Press.

Johnson, Chalmers. 1984. *The Industrial Policy Debate*. San Francisco: Institute for Contemporary Studies.

Kelly, Edward. 1978. "Lykes and Its Bankers." Cleveland: Ohio Public Interest Campaign, April 13.

Kelly, Edward, and Mark Schutes. 1978. "Lykes' Responsibility for Closing the Youngstown Campbell Works." Cleveland: Ohio Public Interest Campaign.

Klauder, Louis T., and Associates. 1976. "Transportation and the Steel Industry in the Mahoning Valley." Niles, Ohio: Western Reserve Economic Development Agency.

Kraft, R. Wayne, and Carl R. Beidleman. 1979. "Report on Youngstown Feasibility Study." U.S. Department of Commerce, Project 99-26-09886. Bethlehem, Pa.: Lehigh University, Office of Research, March 30.

Lally, Charles. 1978. "Praise God and Pass the Federal Aid." *Beacon* (Sunday magazine of the Akron *Beacon Journal*), May 21.

Levy, John M. 1981. *Economic Development Programs for Cities, Counties, and Towns*. New York: Praeger.

Lynd, Staughton. 1982. *The Fight Against Shutdowns: Youngstown's Steel Mill Closings*. San Pedro, Calif.: Singlejack Books.

Lynd, Staughton, and Gar Alperovitz. 1973. *Strategy and Program: Two Essays Toward a New American Socialism*. Boston: Beacon Press.

Magaziner, Ira C., and Robert B. Reich. 1982. *Minding America's Business: The Decline and Rise of the American Economy*. New York: Harcourt Brace Jovanovich.

Mahoning Valley Economic Development Committee [MVEDC]. 1978. "A National Center for the Development and Demonstration of Steel Technology." Youngstown, Ohio: Mahoning Valley Economic Development Committee, Inc., August.

Malone, James. 1981. "Implementing Social Justice Ministry." *Origins: NC Documentary Service* 11, no. 24 (November 26): 283–302.

Mann, Michael. 1973. *Workers on the Move: The Sociology of Relocation*. Cambridge University Press.

Marshall, Paul. 1978. "Financial Analysis Model and Preliminary Results for the Youngstown Demonstration Planning Project." In *Youngstown Demonstration Planning Project: Final Report*. Washington, D.C.: National Center for Economic Alternatives.

Marshall, Paul, and Matthew Breitenberg. 1978. "Commercial Markets for the Youngstown Demonstration Project." In *Youngstown Demonstration Planning Project: Final Report*. Washington, D.C.: National Center for Economic Alternatives.

McShane, S. J., Joseph M. 1986. *"Sufficiently Radical": Catholicism, Progressivism, and the Bishops' Program of 1919*. Washington, D.C.: Catholic University of America Press.

Metzgar, Jack. 1983. "Would Wage Concessions Help the Steel Industry?" *Labor Research Review* 1 (Winter): 26–37.

———. 1980. "Plant Shutdowns and Worker Response: The Case of Johnstown, Pa." *Socialist Review* 53 (September–October): 9–49.

Meyer, Donald B. 1960. *The Protestant Search for Political Realism, 1919–1941*. Berkeley and Los Angeles: University of California Press.

Mick, Stephen S. 1975. "Social and Personal Costs of Plant Shutdowns." *Industrial Relations* 14 (May): 203–8.

Miller, James P. 1988. "Joining the Game: Some Workers Set Up LBOs of Their Own and Benefit Greatly." *Wall Street Journal*, December 12.

Minshall, Charles, and Cathy Moody. 1978. *The Mahoning Valley Economic Development Program: Suggested Program.* Columbus, Ohio: Battelle Laboratories.

National Center for Economic Alternatives. 1978. *Summary: Youngstown Demonstration Planning Project Final Report.* Washington, D.C.: National Center for Economic Alternatives.

Niebuhr, Reinhold. 1977. *Young Reinhold Niebuhr: His Early Writings, 1911–1931.* Edited by William G. Chrystal. New York: Pilgrim Press.

Niebuhr, Reinhold. 1932. *Moral Man and Immoral Society.* New York: Scribner.

Nyden, Philip W. 1984. *Steelworkers Rank-and-File: The Political Economy of a Reform Movement.* New York: Praeger.

Office of Technology Assessment, U.S. Congress. 1980. *Technology and Steel Industry Competitiveness.* Washington, D.C.: U.S. Government Printing Office.

Olson, Mancur. 1965. *The Logic of Collective Action.* Cambridge, Mass.: Harvard University Press.

Ong, Walter J. 1957. *Frontiers in American Catholicism.* New York: Macmillan.

Pellegrin, Roland J., and Charles H. Coates. (1956). "Absentee-Owned Corporations and Community Power Structure." In *Social Change and Urban Politics*, 65–73. Edited by David Gordon. Englewood Cliffs, N.J.: Prentice-Hall, 1973.

Peterson, Iver. 1978. "Public Money and Private Ambition Clash Over Future of Steel in Ohio's Mahoning Valley." *New York Times*, December 8.

Petzinger, Thomas. 1978. "A Year After Closing of Youngstown Steel Plant, Economy, Employment Are Surprisingly Bright." *Wall Street Journal*, October 18.

Pope, Liston. 1942. *Millhands and Preachers.* New Haven, Conn.: Yale University Press.

Powell, Milton. 1967. *The Voluntary Church.* New York: Macmillan.

Pressman, Jeffrey, and Aaron Wildavsky. 1979. *Implementation*, 2d ed. Berkeley and Los Angeles: University of California Press.

Redburn, F. Stevens, and Terry F. Buss. 1982. *Public Policies for Distressed Communities.* Lexington, Mass.: Lexington Books.

Rifkin, Jeremy, and Randy Barber. 1978. *The North Will Rise Again: Pensions, Politics, and Power in the 1980s.* Boston: Beacon Press.

Rosenbloom, Richard. 1979. "Analysis and Evaluation of Youngstown Report." Prepared for Robert C. Embry, Assistant Secretary for Community Planning and Development.

Ross, Wilbur T. 1976. "Work Without Want." New York: National Council of Churches, Division of Church and Society.

Rust, Edgar. 1975. *No Growth: Impacts on Metropolitan Areas.* Lexington, Mass.: Heath.

Scheuerman, William. 1986. *The Steel Crisis: The Economics and Politics of a Declining Industry.* New York: Praeger.

Schlozman, Kay, and Sidney Verba. 1979. *Injury to Insult: Unemployment, Class, and Political Response*. Cambridge, Mass.: Harvard University Press.

Schueller, George H. 1969. *Report on Merger Between Lykes Corporation and Youngstown Sheet and Tube Company*. Department of Justice File 60-138-137-5, April 30.

Shapiro, Helen, and Steven Volk. 1979. "Steelyard Blues: New Structures in Steel." *NACLA Report on the Americas* 12 (January–February): 2–40.

Slote, Alfred. 1969. *Termination: The Closing at Baker Plant*. Indianapolis, Ind.: Bobbs-Merrill.

Smith, David, with Patrick McGuigan. 1978. " 'Youngstown Is Not Unique . . .' The Public Policy Implications of Plant Closings and Runaways." In *Youngstown Demonstration Planning Project: Final Report*. Washington, D.C.: National Center for Economic Alternatives.

Smith, James W. 1979. Comments on the Rosenbloom Analysis of the Youngstown Report, and the Revised Application for Urban Development Action Grant, City of Youngstown, for the Ecumenical Coalition of the Mahoning Valley (Pittsburgh).

1978. Brief of United Steelworkers of America, AFL–CIO–CLC to the Department of Justice with Respect to the Proposed Merger of LTV Corporation and Lykes Corporation (Pittsburgh).

Smith, Luke M., and Irving A. Fowler. 1964. "Plant Relocation and Worker Migration." In *Blue Collar World: Studies of the American Worker*, 491–7. Edited by Arthur B. Shostack and William Gomberg. Englewood Cliffs, N.J.: Prentice Hall.

Smith, Wallace F. 1975. *Urban Development: The Process and Its Problems*. Berkeley and Los Angeles: University of California Press.

Solomon, Anthony M., Task Force Chairman. 1977. *Report to the President: A Comprehensive Program for the Steel Industry*. Washington. D.C.: Treasury Department.

Stelzle, Charles. 1907. *Christianity's Storm Centre: A Study of the Modern City*. New York: Revell.

Stern, Robert N., K. Haydn Wood, and Tove Helland Hammer. 1979. *Employee Ownership in Plant Shutdowns: Prospects for Employment Stability*. Kalamazoo, Mich.: Upjohn Institute for Employment Research.

Stocks, Anthony. 1979. "Employment Shifts in the Youngstown–Warren Metropolitan Area in the Year Following Black Monday." Unpublished manuscripts. Youngstown State University, Center for Urban Studies.

United Church of Christ, 11th General Synod. n.d. "Right to Earn a Living." New York: United Church of Christ, Office for Church in Society.

United Methodist Church, General Conference. 1976. "Unemployment: 1976 General Conference Statement." In *Journal of the 1976 General Conference of the United Methodist Church*, vol. 2. New York: United Methodist Church.

United Presbyterian Church USA, Task Force on the Impact of U.S. Economic Power. 1976. "Economic Justice within Environmental Limits: The Need for a New Economic Ethic," *Church and Society* (September–October):   –

United Steelworkers of America. n.d. "An Explanation of the Employment and

Income Security Program." Pittsburgh: United Steelworkers of America.

1977. "Report on International Election, April 28, 1977." Pittsburgh: United Steelworkers of America.

Walker, Charles R. 1950. *Steeltown: An Industrial Case History of the Conflict Between Progress and Security*. Yale Labor and Management Center Series. New York: Harper and Brothers.

Warren, Kenneth. 1973. *The American Steel Industry, 1850–1970: A Geographical Interpretation*. Oxford: Clarendon Press.

Weakland, Rembert G. 1986. "The Church in Worldly Affairs: Tensions Between Laity and Clergy." *America* 155, no. 10 (October 18): 201–5.

Wenger, Dennis E. 1978. "Community Responses to Disaster." In *Disasters: Theory and Research*, 17–47. Edited by E. L. Quarantelli. Beverly Hills, Calif.: Sage.

Whitman, Edmund S., and W. James Schmidt. 1966. *Plant Relocation: A Case History of a Move*. New York: American Management Association.

Wilcock, Richard, and Walter H. Franke. 1968. *Unwanted Workers: Permanent Layoffs and Long-Term Unemployment*. London: Free Press.

Winter, Gibson. 1961. *The Suburban Captivity of the Churches: An Analysis of Protestant Responsibility in the Expanding Metropolis*. Garden City, N.Y.: Doubleday.

Wogaman, J. Philip. 1980. "The Church as a Mediating Institution: Contemporary American Challenge." In *Democracy and Mediating Structures: A Theological Inquiry*, 85–96. Edited by Michael Novak. Washington, D.C.: American Enterprise Institute.

Wright, Joseph E. 1978. "Organizational Prestige and Task Saliency in Disaster." In *Disasters: Theory and Research*, 199–213. Edited by E. L. Quarantelli. Beverly Hills, Calif.: Sage.

"Youngstown Sheet and Tube – A Classic 'Takeover' Case." 1979. *Center Magazine* 12 (November–December): 33–40.

Index